The Diffusion of Ecclesiastical Authority

Princeton Theological Monograph Series

K. C. Hanson, Charles M. Collier, and
D. Christopher Spinks, Series Editors

Recent volumes in the series

Matthew J. Marohl
*Faithfulness and the Purpose of Hebrews:
A Social Identity Approach*

D. Seiple and Frederick W. Weidmann, editors
*Enigmas and Powers: Engaging the Work of Walter Wink
for Classroom, Church, and World*

Stanley D. Walters
Go Figure!: Figuration in Biblical Interpretation

Michael D. Morrison
*Who Needs a New Covenant?: Rhetorical Function of
the Covenant Motif in the Argument of Hebrews*

Lloyd Kim
*Polemic in the Book of Hebrews:
Anti-Judaism, Anti-Semitism, Supersessionism?*

David A. Ackerman
*Lo, I Tell You a Mystery: Cross, Resurrection, and
Paraenesis in the Rhetoric of 1 Corinthians*

The Diffusion of Ecclesiastical Authority
Sociological Dimensions of Leadership in the Book of Acts

DARIN H. LAND

☙PICKWICK *Publications* · Eugene, Oregon

THE DIFFUSION OF ECCLESIASTICAL AUTHORITY
Sociological Dimensions of Leadership in the Book of Acts

Princeton Theological Monograph Series 90

Copyright © 2008 Darin H. Land. All rights reserved. Except for brief quotations in critical articles or reviews, no part of this book may be reproduced in any manner without prior written permission from the publisher. Write: Permissions, Wipf and Stock Publishers, 199 W. 8th Ave., Suite 3, Eugene, OR 97401.

Pickwick Publications
A Division of Wipf and Stock Publishers
199 W. 8th Ave., Suite 3
Eugene, OR 97401

www.wipfandstock.com

ISBN 13 978-1-55635-575-2

Cataloging-in-Publication data:

Land, Darin H.

The diffusion of ecclesiastical authority : sociological dimensions of leadership in the book of Acts / Darin H. Land.

x + 246 p. ; 23 cm. Includes bibliographical references.

Princeton Theological Monograph Series 90

ISBN 13: 978-1-55635-575-2 (alk. paper)

1. Bible. N.T. Acts—Criticism, interpretation, etc. 2. Christian leadership—Biblical teaching. 3. Church—Authority—History. 4. Authority—Religious aspects—Christianity. I. Title. II. Series.

BS2625.2 L4 2008

Manufactured in the U.S.A.

Contents

List of Tables vi

Acknowledgments vii

Abbreviations viii

1. Introduction 1
2. Modeling Religious Leadership 18
3. Authority in Greco-Roman Religions 60
4. Authority in Second Temple Judaism 104
5. Authority in the Jerusalem Church 139
6. Authority in the Diaspora Church 181
7. The Diffusion of Authority in Acts 219

Bibliography 233

Tables

Table 2.1: Six Ways of Being Religious • 38
Table 2.2: Modeling Leadership in First-Century Circum-Mediterranean Culture • 57
Table 4.1: Roman Rulers of Judea, 6–66 CE • 113
Table 4.2: Jewish High Priests, 6–66 CE • 114
Table 4.3: Leaders in Synagogue Inscriptions • 122
Table 5.1: Typological Parallels between Jesus and Peter • 169–70
Table 5.2: Parallels between Iliad 24 and Acts 12:1–17 • 171
Table 6.1: Possible Authority Relationships Implied in Acts 20:17–38 • 198

Acknowledgments

THE DIFFUSION OF ECCLESIASTICAL AUTHORITY IS THE PRODUCT OF vital contributions from many people who inspired, shaped, and sustained me in a variety of ways. It is not too much to assert that without these key individuals, the book would not have come to fruition. I wish to acknowledge several of them by name.

The initial inspiration for the study sprang from the work of my parents, Warren and Della Land. As Free Methodist missionaries for more than thirty years, they participated in the extension of ecclesiastical authority through the empowerment of new leaders in Burundi and Haïti. Although my father passed away during the initial stage of my research, his life continues to be a source of inspiration to me.

Don Hagner read various versions of the manuscript. He affirmed the good in my work and pointed out those places where improvement was necessary. His words were often exactly what I needed to give me the fortitude to carry on with the project. David Scholer and Rick Beaton contributed to the study by opening my eyes to the richness of the Greco-Roman and Second Temple literature as sources for understanding the New Testament. S. Scott Bartchy generously agreed to meet with me regularly during his sabbatical term from UCLA. His investment in my development has been invaluable to me, and my understanding of first century cultures has been greatly enriched through our interaction. Chris Spinks provided expert assistance in preparing the manuscript for publication.

Most importantly, I owe an unrepayable debt of gratitude to my wife, Jill. Without her selfless support, this project would not have been possible. She proofread drafts of each chapter—often under time pressure at the end of her own ten-hour workday—and she has celebrated the completion of each phase with me. Her encouragement, expressed in a variety of subtle ways, inspired me to carry on with the work. Her self-sacrifice has been to me the embodiment of Christ's love.

Abbreviations

AB	Anchor Bible
ANF	*The Ante-Nicene Fathers*
BDAG	Bauer, Walter, Frederick W. Danker, William Arndt, and F. Wilbur Gingrich. *Greek-English Lexicon of the New Testament and Other Early Christian Literature*. 3rd ed. Chicago: University of Chicago Press, 2000
BDF	Blass, Friedrich, and Albert Debrunner. *A Greek Grammar of the New Testament and Other Early Christian Literature*. Translated by Robert Walter Funk. Trans. and rev. of the 9th–10th German ed. Chicago: University of Chicago Press, 1961
BETL	Bibliotheca ephermeridum theologicarum lovaniensium
BibInt	*Biblical Interpretation*
BJS	Brown Judaic Studies
BSac	*Bibliotheca sacra*
BTB	Biblical Theology Bulletin
BZNW	Beihefte zur Zeitschrift für die neutestamentliche Wissenschaft und die Kunde der älteren Kirche
CBQ	*Catholic Biblical Quarterly*
CIL	*Corpus Inscriptionum Latinarum*
Colloq	*Colloquium*
ConBNT	Coniectanea biblica: New Testament Series
CRINT	Compendia rerum iudaicarum ad Novum Testamentum
ETL	*Ephemerides theologicae lovanienses*
ICC	International Critical Commentary
IG	*Inscriptiones Graecae*
ILS	*Inscriptiones Latinae Selectae*
JES	*Journal of Ecumenical Studies*
JSNT	*Journal for the Study of the New Testament*
JSNTSup	Journal for the Study of the New Testament: Supplement Series
JSOTSup	Journal for the Study of the Old Testament: Supplement Series
JTS	*Journal of Theological Studies*
KEK	Kritisch-exegetischer Kommentar über das Neue Testament
LCL	Loeb Classical Library

LD	Lectio divina
LSCG	*Lois Sacrées des Cités Grecques: Supplément.* Edited by Franciszek Sokolowski. Paris: Boccard, 1962
LSJ	Liddell, H. G., R. Scott, H. S. Jones. *A Greek-English Lexicon.* 9th ed. with revised supplement. Oxford: Oxford University Press, 1996
NIB	*The New Interpreter's Bible*
NICNT	New International Commentary on the New Testament
NTM	New Testament Monographs
NTS	*New Testament Studies*
NTTS	New Testament Tools and Studies
PEQ	*Palestine Exploration Quarterly*
PRSt	*Perspectives in Religious Studies*
RB	*Revue Biblique*
SBLSP	*Society of Biblical Literature Seminar Papers*
SBSt	Sources for Biblical Study
SBT	Studies in Biblical Theology
SJT	*Scottish Journal of Theology*
SNTSMS	Society for New Testament Studies Monograph Series
SP	Sacra pagina
STAC	Studies and Texts in Antiquity and Christianity
SwJT	*Southwestern Journal of Theology*
TDNT	*Theological Dictionary of the New Testament.* Edited by Gerhard Kittel and Gerhard Friedrich. Translated by Geoffrey W. Bromiley. 10 vols. Grand Rapids: Eerdmans, 1964–1976
TDOT	*Theological Dictionary of the Old Testament.* Edited by G. Johannes Botterweck, Helmer Ringgren, and Heinz-Josef Fabry. Translated by J. T. Willis, G. W. Bromiley, and D. E. Green. 14 vols. Grand Rapids: Eerdmans, 1974–2004
TNTC	Tyndale New Testament Commentaries
TWOT	*Theological Wordbook of the Old Testament.* Edited by R. Laird Harris, Gleason Leonard Archer, and Bruce K. Waltke. 2 vols. Chicago: Moody Press, 1980
TynBul	*Tyndale Bulletin*
TZT	*Tübinger Zeitschrift für Theologie*
VCSup	Supplements to Vigiliae christianae
WUNT	Wissenschaftliche Untersuchungen zum Neuen Testament

1

Introduction

THE NEW TESTAMENT BOOK OF ACTS PROVIDES THE MOST COMPREhensive history of the early church that has come down to us from antiquity. As such, it is one of the most important documents available to scholars who would try to reconstruct the development of the church as it progressed from a marginal Jewish reform movement to a multi-ethnic, geographically expansive religion in its own right. Yet since the *Tendenzkritik* of F. C. Baur in the nineteenth century, scholars have recognized Acts as a theologically motivated document. What has not been as widely acknowledged, however, is that theological *Tendenz* and historical accuracy need not be mutually exclusive. This realization recovers Acts as a source for understanding and tracing the growth and development of the primitive Christian church.

Since Acts is an historical source, historical questions of Acts are legitimate. One such question revolves around the development of ecclesiastical authority as the church spread outward from its center in Jerusalem. The church in Acts, of course, is depicted as starting in Jerusalem with authority vested in the Twelve Apostles. Yet later in the account, the Twelve virtually disappear from the scene. Just as the church had grown throughout the Mediterranean region, so also leadership of the church had become more dispersed. A certain tension exists, however, between the depiction of autonomous local authorities and a strong, centralized authority in Jerusalem. For example, the church in Antioch commissioned Paul, yet he still seems to have submitted to James and the elders in Jerusalem. Thus the question that focuses the present investigation is, "What is the nature and extent of the dispersal and diffusion of authority in the primitive church during the time period depicted in the book of Acts?"

At this point, a word about "diffusion" is in order. For this study, diffusion will take on two distinct aspects. In the first place, diffusion will refer to a geographical process. More importantly, diffusion will also refer to the degree of centralization or decentralization of ecclesiastical authority. We will be interested, then, in the extent to which apparent diffusion of authority was actualized in practice. For example, it is possible that, despite mention in Acts of church leaders outside Jerusalem, in reality these leaders were devoid of real authority, or perhaps wielded only relative authority.

Importance of the Question

The question of the diffusion of ecclesiastical authority is an important one for a number of reasons, both with respect to New Testament (NT) studies and in regard to the church today. It is important for NT studies, first, because it will provide a deeper understanding of Acts. For example, the study will clarify the nature of ecclesiastical authority as understood by the author of Acts. Since the debate regarding the extent to which Acts is a tendentious writing involves issues of religious authority—for example, was the author trying to subvert or bolster ecclesiastical authority—a focus on ecclesiastical authority will provide insight into the discussion regarding the aims of Acts.

A second way that the topic contributes to NT studies is by casting new light on the long-standing debate over the polity of the primitive church. Contemporary proponents of particular ecclesiastical polities sometimes seek to validate their positions by producing evidence from scripture, which they view as normative. While our aim is not to argue for a particular political structure based on the NT, we will nevertheless be shedding some light on polity as it existed in the primitive church. This study brings two distinctive perspectives to the question. First, the study's cultural sensitivity suggests the possibility of diverse patterns of polity within the primitive church. It contributes to a growing awareness that polity can be locale-specific. Second, the study promotes a sensitivity to precedents for ecclesiastical authority. Borrowing an insight from the history of religions school, we assert that the polity of the primitive church was birthed out of and developed with reference to the authority structures of Jewish and Greco-Roman religions. Yet, as we shall see, ecclesiastical authority in the early church was implemented in ways that were more counter-cultural than is sometimes recognized.

Finally, the present study advances the field of NT research by exploring certain aspects of primitive church history. In particular, the study will clarify the relationship between the authority of Jerusalem and other centers of early Christianity. By focusing on the diffusion of authority, we will necessarily encounter mechanisms that drove that diffusion. These very mechanisms, in turn, illuminate the relationships in question.

Secondary Literature

By way of introduction to our topic, we will begin with a brief overview of related studies. For the sake of clarity, the secondary literature that will occupy our attention is divided into two sections. The first section deals with monographs on ecclesiastical office, ranging from J. B. Lightfoot's nineteenth century dissertation on Christian ministry to James Tunstead Burtchaell's treatment of the early relationship between synagogue and church ministries. The second section reviews a number of sociologically informed studies. Only one source, a doctoral dissertation by Randall Clark Webber, employs a thoroughgoing sociological methodology. The others demonstrate a sensitivity to sociological concerns by utilizing descriptive categories such as group identity and boundary markers.

The following pages make no pretense at being exhaustive. The sentiment that Eduard Schweizer expressed already in 1960 is apropos:

> A flood of literature has been published on our subject. It is no longer possible completely to master the whole of it, and I can only hope that I have not overlooked something that proves to be the most important of all.[1]

Therefore, we here aim only at sketching the contours of the discussion by offering a glimpse into some of the influential or distinctive contributions.

---

1. Schweizer, *Church Order in the New Testament*, 7.

Monographs on Ecclesiastical Authority

J. B. Lightfoot, *The Christian Ministry*

Lightfoot begins his discussion of the Christian ministry by affirming the priesthood of all believers. In a memorable turn of phrase he says, "This then is the Christian ideal; a holy season extending the whole year round—a temple confined only by the limits of the habitable world—a priesthood coextensive with the human race."[2] He goes on to argue that practical realities required certain believers to take on specialized functions. The three-tiered ministry developed from these functions. Originally, the Apostles governed the church. As the church grew, the Apostles necessarily designated certain of their duties, beginning with the least specialized. Thus the diaconate was the first ministry to be formed (as recorded in Acts 6), followed by the presbytery and then the episcopate. The lack of any historical record for the founding of the presbytery is expected because it was modeled on the leadership of the Jewish synagogue. The episcopate is the result of the specialization of the presbytery, which Lightfoot views as a progressive development. This development passed through specific stages but progressed more slowly in the Greco-Roman environment and more rapidly where Jewish influences were more strongly felt. Lightfoot concludes his study with an historical examination of the development of the sacerdotal conception of the episcopacy, which he insists is absent from the NT.

Adolf von Harnack, *The Constitution and Law of the Church in the First Two Centuries*

Harnack's investigation into church order opens with an examination of the evidence regarding the structure of the primitive Jerusalem community. In addition to the Twelve, leaders of the primitive community included apostles, teachers, and prophets. The Seven were a group of leaders opposed to the Twelve, and the emergence of James and the elders represents a constitutional change in the Jerusalem church. In the Gentile church, Christian communities were governed primarily by the membership as a whole under the limited influence of charismatic individuals. Yet a division existed between older church members, who held leadership positions, and younger members. The group of leaders

---

2. Lightfoot, *Christian Ministry*, 5.

quickly resolved into deacons, elders, and bishops. All presbyters were originally bishops, but as it became clear that the college of presbyters would need a president, there was a natural progression toward the monepiscopacy. The process was one of gradual development, a continuum from *primus inter pares* to monarchical bishop. By the end of the second century, a distinction between clergy and laity was being made, and by the third century all salient features of the Christian constitution were present except for the Christian emperor. For Harnack, the development of church structure was primarily the result of the actualization of its own inner genius, not conscious assimilation from Judaism or paganism.

Eduard Schweizer, *Church Order in the New Testament*

Schweizer's study of church order is divided into two parts, an examination of the primary sources and a systematic appraisal in terms of pre-determined categories. In the first part, Schweizer denies that Jesus intended the church, although the post-Easter community required adherence to the teaching of Jesus. Schweizer also doubts that the disciples actually became leaders in the church. Instead, the church lives under a new order led, not by the Twelve or the Seven (whom Schweizer insists were not deacons as Acts pictured them), but by individuals who exercised a self-justifying authority. In Matthew, the church is a *corpus mixtum,* an organization made up both of believers and unbelievers who will be distinguished only at the consummation; Matthew reflects no hierarchy in the primitive church. For Luke, the church is a *tertium genus,* a third way that is neither Jew nor Gentile, in which church order develops as the church matures. The Pastoral Epistles reveal a more settled church, where the authority of officers is based on effective modeling, and not on ordination alone. According to the Pauline conception, the church is Israel, and Jerusalem is still the most important center. Church order results only from the gifting of the Holy Spirit. In 1 Peter, Schweizer finds no dichotomy between the clergy and the laity, even though there is an increased recognition of the ordered ministry. In Hebrews, the church is anti-institutional. The Johannine corpus emphasizes individualism, and church order does not exist, despite the use of the term "elder." From this overview of the NT, Schweizer concludes that different churches had different self-conceptions, as well as different organizational structures. A similar result emerges from a study of early extra-biblical sources.

After having examined the literary evidence from the NT and other early Christian works, Schweizer offers a systematic reconstruction of church order in the early church. The NT conceptions occupy the middle ground between two extremes: a theologizing, utopian, ecstatic view and a historicizing, clerical view. Within this range, the choice of terminology in the NT for "service" indicates that Jesus is the only priest. The priesthood of all believers is meant in the sense that Jesus shares his priesthood with the church as a whole. There are differences of individual calling, but all giftedness is by grace. In the NT, all church activity is charism, whether charismatic or natural. Church order is a manifestation of the Spirit, who directed the church's movement away from the patterns of Jewish ministries. The NT exhibits a tension between all believers as empowered by the Spirit and ordination as special empowerment. Office, then, became increasingly emphasized, but there was still no apostolic succession in the NT.

Hans von Campenhausen, *Ecclesiastical Authority and Spiritual Power in the Church of the First Three Centuries*

For Campenhausen, authority in the early church starts with Jesus as revealed in his resurrection. Jesus' authority in the church was mediated first through apostles, whose authority was of a personal nature. The notion that the apostles were either petty office-holders or power-hungry stake-claimers is foreign to their time period. The apostle of whom we know the most is Paul. His authority derived directly from the fact that he was a personal, commissioned representative of Christ. While he was eager to gain the approval of the leaders in Jerusalem, the relationship was not one of ecclesiastical, hierarchical constraints but of fraternal deference. Paul's authority, then, derived from his personal relationship both with Christ and with his congregations, not from any office. In the Pauline congregations, prophecy and teaching were also important. Where apostles were itinerant, the prophets and teachers were attached to local congregations; neither comprised office-holders. There was no hierarchy, even though some received higher honor. Spiritual gifts brought order but not fixed offices. Yet this type of spiritual authority was unsustainable and soon gave way to official authority structures.

The book of 1 Peter, with its emphasis on elders, is based on a different understanding of authority. The elder system probably originated among Jewish Christians as a natural extension of the synagogue structure and spread quickly even into the Pauline churches. Bishops and deacons originated in Gentile-Christian circles. Paul and sources dependent on him know only bishops and deacons; Acts, 1 Peter, James, and Revelation know only elders. Luke deliberately tries to fuse the system of elders with that of bishops in Paul's farewell speech to the Ephesian elders.

In time, leaders became office-holders who guaranteed the tradition. The first writer to use official categories was Luke. He traces the origins of office back to apostolic times, stressing the role of the Spirit and public ordination. Around 180 CE, Hegesippus developed the concept into the apostolic succession of monarchical bishops. Also during the second century, the congregational leader would preside as judge. By the third century a more advanced concept of ecclesiastical office emerged. In Cyprian's formulation, for example, the separation between clergy and laity is absolute, with ordination the only bridge. The bishops are emblematic for the unity of the church, and they embody the freedom so prized in the Pauline churches but no longer practically available to the laity.

JAMES TUNSTEAD BURTCHAELL, *FROM SYNAGOGUE TO CHURCH*

From Synagogue to Church is an extended critique of what Burtchaell regards as a scholarly consensus concerning the development of ecclesiastical office, the general contours of which may be summarized as follows: Jesus initiated a thorough break with the Jewish religion of his day; the church that grew out of this impetus was initially led by charismatic individuals as opposed to hierarchical office-holders; ecclesiastical offices only developed late as an unfortunate fall from the initial genius of the movement; and the earlier, charismatic period is theologically normative. In contrast to this consensus (that institutionalized Christianity was a late development—associated with Protestant scholars) and its converse (that hierarchical structures were present from the earliest days and were innovations introduced by Jesus and his disciples—associated with Roman Catholic and Anglican scholars), Burtchaell espouses an alternative hypothesis, namely, that there was a continuity of authority structures between the church and its Jewish predecessors that enabled the navigation of such upheavals as did occur in the transformation into a new religion. In order to test this hypothesis, Burtchaell compares the organizational structures of the Jewish synagogue with those of the early church. Similarities include (1) a comparable range of community activities, such as meeting for prayer and providing alms; (2) a similarity of official structure and the authority accorded to officers; and (3) a parallel manner of coordinating their network of communities. While early Christianity did exhibit changes from its predecessor, the options for those changes were available within the previous system, and the types of changes were common to other sects of Judaism.

Sociologically Informed Studies

Raymond Brown and John Meier, *Antioch and Rome: New Testament Cradles of Catholic Christianity*

Antioch and Rome is a composite work in which John Meier studies the church in Antioch and Raymond Brown examines the church in Rome. Each author identifies one or more documents that relate to each of the first three generations in their respective churches. Meier describes the Jewish community of first-century Antioch as relatively stable, with close connections to Jerusalem and overseen by a single ruler and a council of elders. This model may have served as precedent for the Christian church in Antioch and its relationship with the Jerusalem church. Galatians 2 and Acts 11–15 narrate an incident in the Antioch church that was crucial for the first generation. Despite the gravity of the Antioch incident, there was no split in the Antioch church such as would give rise to two separate communities. Meier believes that Paul lost the argument and left on an independent mission; Peter remained in Antioch as a moderating influence. After Paul's departure, one or the other of the parties initiated a compromise proposal. The result was the table of kosher laws recorded in Acts 15:20, 29 and Acts 21:25. In the second generation, exemplified by the Gospel of Matthew, the church in Antioch was faced with a crisis of identity and unity in the face of both external and internal pressures. Matthew forged a synthesis that solidified the unity of the community and protected the interests of moderate conservatives. The synthesis was achieved by stressing a new vision of salvation history in which the church supplanted Israel while retaining its heritage, by emphasizing the confluence of Christology, ecclesiology, and moral authority, and by enshrining an organizational structure which embraces the importance of official leadership (especially as represented in the figure of Peter), of corporate responsibility, and of individual competency. The third generation, as represented by the letters of Ignatius, shows substantial development from the second generation: (1) an evolution from the loose ecclesiastical structure of prophets and teachers in Matthew into the strict, three-tiered monepiscopacy of Ignatius; (2) a shift to a different theological focus; and (3) the formation of a moderating stance between a left and right wing of the church.

Turning to Rome, Raymond Brown argues that missionaries with ties to Jerusalem founded the church no later than 49 CE. He supports this view by comparison with Rome's Jewish community, which also had a close connection with Jerusalem. Further support is gained by an examination of Paul's epistle to the Romans, which, according to Brown, exhibits a familiarity with the character of the church in Rome. Those parts of Romans that seem to demonstrate a Gentile, anti-circumcision stance actually reflect Paul's refutation of false testimony about his own position. Paul matured after the statements in Galatians, especially because he needed the acceptance of the Roman church in preparation for his defense in Jerusalem. Therefore, both Peter and Paul can be classified as moderate conservatives by the time they arrived in Rome. Peter would have remained more conservative than Paul, but both accepted circumcision for Jews without requiring it of Gentiles. Brown finds evidence for the second generation Roman church in 1 Peter and Hebrews, which he argues were written from and to Rome, respectively. In addition to a general Jewish-Christian outlook, 1 Peter exhibits continuity with three characteristics of Romans: a propensity toward the use of Jewish cultic language, a concern with submission to governing authorities, and an interest in church structure. Hebrews also exhibits a concern with the Jewish cult, but in this case from the perspective of a Hellenistic Christian trying to persuade Jewish Christians not to revert to Judaism. Brown sees this as evidence for Jewish Christians as a sizeable subset of the Roman church. First Clement represents the third generation in Rome. It also portrays cultic language (in this case exemplified by extensive use of the OT), concern for civil government, and substantiation of a particular church structure. First Clement moves beyond the view of the previous generation in its perspective on ecclesiastical structure. It is now validated more vigorously, and there is a closer association with the forms of the Roman Empire. Also, ecclesiastical office becomes not merely service to the community, but divine service. Meier and Brown conclude the study by noting the importance of Peter for both Antioch and Rome, They argue that, although Peter was bishop of neither Antioch nor Rome, he nevertheless had an enduring influence on the shape of Christianity in the centuries to follow.

Randall Clark Webber, "An Analysis of Power in the Jerusalem Church in Acts"

After defining power as "the ability to formulate and pursue objectives,"[3] Webber surveys a broad sweep of theorists who attempted to analyze and understand power. He asserts that these theorists fall into four historical and conceptual groupings: (1) those who associated power with individuals; (2) those who emphasized the constraints of socio-political structures in transmitting power; (3) those who noted the functions of structures and individuals; and (4) those who stressed the power inherent in symbols and values. From this background, Webber develops his own, eclectic model of power, consciously borrowing from each of the four. His model emphasizes three variables: (1) symbols and values, (2) structures, and (3) individuals.

Webber next examines power in the Jerusalem church in terms of these independent variables. Webber asserts that the symbols-and-values variable is most accessible via a study of language and ritual. Analysis of the language of the Jerusalem church in Acts shows that control of access to the cultus is an essential component of power. The Jerusalem believers laid claim to this control by insisting that they, not their opponents, were faithful heirs of Israelite history. An examination of the community's rituals reveals a high value placed on egalitarianism. Baptism, prayer, and glossolalia all conveyed this value because they afforded equality regarding entrance requirements and direct access to God. Furthermore, these rituals were flexible enough in their execution so as to require no hierarchical superstructure. That the Jerusalem church nevertheless granted members differing degrees

---

3. Webber, "Analysis of Power," 73.

of power indicates a certain tension between the community, with its egalitarian ideal, and the highly stratified society in which it existed.

According to Webber, the church's structures (the apostolate, the diaconate, and the council of elders) were established for the distribution of goods and for administration. In accomplishing these purposes, the church followed patterns familiar from the larger culture. The diaconate was a mechanism for ensuring indebtedness to the community rather than to individual patrons. Similarly, the apostolate performed common administrative functions and was organized along official lines. The elder council later took up the same functions. The church attempted to maintain its egalitarian ideal, but its structures contradicted that ideal. Pressure from the stratified culture produced dissonance between the ideal and actual, a dissonance only partially relieved by an appeal to pragmatism.

Individuals in the Jerusalem church exerted power through competitive honor/shame "games" consisting of violence (actual or potential), the use of the miraculous, and public speaking. Only God made effective use of violence in Acts; where others used violence, God intervened decisively to defend His honor. Games based on miracles were ultimately founded on God and His activity. While individuals might mediate divine activity, everything rested ultimately on God alone. Thus, God was the sole patron of the Jerusalem church. On the other hand, individuals with skill in public speaking gained honor over those who might challenge them. Therefore, the power of individuals in the Jerusalem church also reflected the tension between the egalitarian ideal and the concrete reality. Whereas violence and miracle reduced all members to a common plane of clientage to God, skilled speakers gained disproportionate power.

Harold E. Dollar, "A Biblical-Missiological Exploration of the Cross-Cultural Dimensions in Luke-Acts"

"A Biblical-Missiological Exploration" represents a sustained reading of Luke-Acts through the eyes of a missiologist. Examining the evidence of Luke 1 to Acts 5, Dollar argues that the author couches his narrative in the form of the dominant particularistic Jewish paradigm but increasingly fills the narrative with anomalous incidents. These anomalies serve to challenge Jewish particularism and lay the groundwork for the distinctive universalism of Acts 6–28, which Dollar examines for indications of Luke's sensitivity to and stance toward cross-cultural issues. He looks specifically at texts indicating rejection of the Jews because of their unbelief and texts related to the issue of Jew-Gentile table-fellowship. Dollar summarizes his findings by organizing them into four categories: cultic, geographical, ethnic, and relational. With respect to the cultic dimensions he asserts that the narrative of Acts points to radical changes in the cultic requirements. The Temple cult was no longer central to salvation. In geographical terms, the Luke-Acts narrative moves from Galilee and Judea to Samaria, Syria, Asia Minor and beyond. This movement, according to Dollar, does not necessarily imply cultural change within the church. Nevertheless, it does indicate an interest on the part of Luke to portray the Church as more than provincial.

Dollar has the most to say about the ethnic dimensions of his study. While stressing that Luke gives very little sociological data to support an ethnographic investigation, Dollar notes that by the end of Acts "the major cultural thresholds have be [sic] crossed."[4] He further emphasizes that the crossing of these boundaries was more difficult for Jewish believers than for Gentile converts. Yet a careful reading of the narrative reveals that the responsive Gentiles were usually those who were already Godfearers. Finally, with respect to relational issues, Dollar focuses on the issue of table-fellowship. He argues that, although Luke comes closest here to a description in cross-cultural terms, he is still most interested in the theological ramifications and soteriological attributes of table-fellowship. Dollar emphasizes the need Jews would have felt for maintaining boundary markers. Such restrictions had to be overcome in order to live out the universality of the gospel. The decree of Acts 15 provides a means of mitigating the discomfort Jews would have experienced over this open table-fellowship with Gentiles.

Craig C. Hill, *Hellenists and Hebrews: Reappraising Division Within the Earliest Church*

Hill begins his study by tracing the influence of F. C. Baur's perspective on Acts 6:1. Baur argued that the Hellenists and Hebrews represented two distinct groups with divergent ideological and theological outlooks. According to Hill, this view has gone largely unchallenged, even though

---

4. Dollar, "Biblical-Missiological Exploration," 298.

evidence of the intermixing of Jewish and Hellenistic elements during the first century suggests less of a dichotomy between Hellenists and Hebrews than Baur's view allows. To discredit the dominant interpretation, Hill notes that the term Ἑλληνιστής is used by Luke, not in a technical or theologically significant way in Acts, but merely as a shorthand expression for "Greek-speaking Jews from the Diaspora."[5] He goes on to argue that Luke's representation of the Seven as subordinate to the Twelve does not mask a rival authority structure within the early church. Furthermore, the death of Stephen was due to the mob action of Greek-speaking Jews, not to the legal action of the Jewish authorities as recorded in Acts. Any insight, therefore, that might have been gained from this narrative into the relationship between Hebrews and Hellenists is nullified. With these preliminary judgments in mind, Hill attacks one of the lynchpins of the dominant interpretation, namely, the supposed selective Jerusalem persecution recorded in Acts 8. Discussing the possible interpretations of Acts 8:1b, in each case Hill argues that a firm distinction between Hebrews and Hellenists is not required. He argues that, except for the Hellenist/Hebrew divide it supports, a minute literalism would not have been the preferred scholarly interpretation of this passage.

Hill's next target is the textual evidence regarding the Hellenist, Stephen. He asserts that the account of Stephen and his martyrdom cannot be used to discover any theological distinctives of the Hellenists. Stephen's speech does not provide the antinomian and anti-Temple propaganda normally attributed to it. Yet even if it did, according to Hill, the very nature of ancient historiography suggests that Luke composed the speech himself. He concludes that the Stephen material is based on sketchy traditions and cannot establish the presumed theological distinctions of the Hellenists.

Hill then examines the relationship between the churches of Antioch and Jerusalem. Because Acts 11:19–20 says that the church in Antioch was founded by believers who had left Jerusalem during the persecution, the affiliation of the two churches is often seen by scholars as emblematic of the relationship between Hellenists and Hebrews. Yet the founders of the Antioch church need not be identified with the Hellenists described in Acts 6. Such evidence as we do have regarding

---

5. Hill, *Hellenists and Hebrews*, 24.

the relations between Antioch and Jerusalem, notably the accounts of the Jerusalem council and the Antioch incident (Acts 15 and Gal 2), reveal a readiness to accommodate and compromise, not a tendency toward antagonism and calcification. The scholarly penchant for casting the two churches into opposing positions rests in part on viewing Paul as a prototypical representative of the Antioch perspective. Yet Paul may not accurately reflect the position of the Antioch church. Hill believes that the Antiochene believers accommodated themselves to the Jerusalem position, while Paul lost the argument recorded in Gal 2 and became estranged from both Jerusalem and Antioch.

Michelle Slee, *The Church in Antioch in the First Century CE: Communion and Conflict*

According to Slee, the history of the church in Antioch really begins in Jerusalem. The founders of the Antioch church perpetuated the same issues that they had encountered earlier in Jerusalem, namely, the problems reported in Acts 6. The central concern in Jerusalem was not simply that Hellenist widows were being overlooked, but that the Hellenists were participating in table-fellowship with Gentiles, rendering them unclean and unfit for association with Jews. In the ensuing persecution, Hellenists alone were expelled from Jerusalem. Some relocated to Antioch where they founded a church with the same openness to Jew-Gentile table-fellowship they had practiced in Jerusalem. There had already been Jewish precedent for the idea that Gentiles would be saved in the eschaton. Yet most Jews rejected the notion of eating with Gentiles because they thought it impossible for Gentiles to avoid contamination from idols. Still, the Antioch church persisted in Jew-Gentile table-fellowship without interference from Jerusalem until about 48–49 CE, when Roman pressure on the Jerusalem Jews inspired a Jewish centrist movement. This caused the Jerusalem church to insure its constituents were fully law-abiding. Thus, Jerusalem Christians in turn pressured Antioch believers to cease open table-fellowship and require Gentile Christians to be circumcised. The Antioch church responded by initiating the Jerusalem conference, where it was determined that Gentile Christians could remain uncircumcised. According to Slee, Acts 15 anachronistically includes the so-called Apostolic Decree, whereas Gal 2 correctly states that nothing more was required of Gentile believers. The Decree was promulgated from Antioch as a means of restoring table-fellowship between uncircumcised Gentile Christians and law-observant Jews by assuring that the Gentiles were untainted by idolatry. The Antioch church drafted the decree after Paul departed Antioch in defeat.

The Didache, which Slee argues was written from Antioch soon after the incident recorded in Gal 2, takes up and expands on the Apostolic Decree. The central concern of the Didachist is the unity of the Antioch church. Slee compares the Matthean community with that of the Didachist. She argues that the Matthean community had earlier shunned the Gentile mission but had recently undertaken such a mission in the aftermath of the destruction of Jerusalem. Part of the impetus for this mission was pressure from the Pharisaic party. Like the Didachist, the author of Matthew regarded Torah-observance as the consummate measure of perfection, but unlike the Didachist, required full observance now. Whereas the community of the Didachist made provision for table-fellowship between Jews and Gentiles by proscribing certain behavior, the Matthean community required no such concession. All members were already fully law-observant. Ultimately, however, the two communities were theologically close; both required Torah-observance for Jew and Gentile alike, differing only in the timing of implementation.

The historical, theological, and pragmatic differences between the two churches in Antioch resulted in different leadership structures implicit within the Didache and Matthew. Whereas the Didachist's community had always accepted Gentiles in a law-free state and now relied on Gentile patrons for their flourishing, the Matthean community had only recently accepted Gentiles into their midst. As a result, the Didachist's community valued the leadership of householder-patrons in addition to charismatic leaders who supported the Didachist's position on Jew-Gentile table-fellowship. The Matthean community, on the other hand, valued scribal-didactic leaders over charismatic leaders because the former provided a stable link to the Palestinian traditions and Jewish underpinnings of the Faith. In time, this state of affairs coalesced into the familiar three-tiered hierarchy.

Methodology

The methodology of the earlier writers on ecclesiastical authority was relatively simple. It might be described as a classical historical-critical method. The writers offered historical reconstructions of the development of the three-tiered hierarchy based on a close reading of the primary sources. Despite the differences in their conclusions, Lightfoot and Harnack share this common methodology. Campenhausen also follows a historical-critical method, even though he is able to offer more detail than the earlier writers by virtue of access to additional source material. In contrast, Schweizer and Burtchaell follow a different approach. Schweizer relates the NT documents to each other on the basis of their conceptions of ecclesiology. He groups the documents into four sections. Within each category he then traces how the ideas changed and developed. Finally, he draws conclusions about the time and place of developments in ecclesiology. In other words, Schweizer infers specifics on the basis of constructed generalizations. Burtchaell follows a superior methodology. He begins with the dominant interpretation regarding the evolution of ecclesiastical order, then suggests an alternative hypothesis, proceeds to test the hypothesis in the specific case in question, and finally draws conclusions.

The method of Meier and Brown can also be contrasted with that of Schweizer. Instead of grouping documents according to their conceptual relationships, they identify key documents on the basis of their provenance. Instead of ordering the documents according to their apparent conceptual development, they arrange them according to their date of origin, whether from the first, second, or third generations. From these organized documents, Meier and Brown derive the chief characteristics of the given locale and trace changes in the perspectives at each locale over time. Therefore, their methodology moves from the concrete to the abstract.

Of the authors employing sociological insights, Webber uses a methodology most closely wedded to sociology. He begins by exploring models and categories from the field of sociology. He then assesses the validity of these categories and adapts them as necessary for the NT. Finally, he interprets Acts at face value in terms of the sociological categories. The second step is a critical one, since it prevents gross eisegesis. Dollar's methodology is less sophisticated. He conducts a systematic reading of Luke-Acts with an eye toward cross-cultural issues. Then he organizes his observations and draws conclusions. The methodology of Hill bears some resemblance to that of Burtchaell in that he also begins with a dominant hypothesis that he wishes to challenge. Hill examines the evidence for the dominant interpretation and finds it wanting. Then he suggests an alternative hypothesis. Slee's method entails a sociologically sensitive historical reconstruction. She makes historical judgments regarding the events as stated in various primary sources, yet she sometimes seems to stand over texts or to employ a suspicious reading of the texts. Nevertheless she rightly recognizes that both theology and pragmatic concerns influenced the development of ecclesiastical order.

The methodology I propose for the present study draws on some of the strengths exhibited by the authors examined above. With Burtchaell I share the conviction that the most reasonable scenario is that the church adopted much of its structure from its religious environment. Moreover, as illustrated by several of our authors, the use of insights from sociology to inform a diachronic approach yields meaningful results. The essential foundation throughout remains exegesis of primary texts. The method I am proposing, therefore, may be described as a sociologically informed, historical-critical investigation of Acts. I will begin by developing models of authority relevant to the first century (chapter two). These models will then be used to examine the authority structures of Greco-Roman religions (chapter three) and Second Temple Judaism (chapter four). On the basis of the insights thus gained, I will offer a detailed exposition of those passages that relate to the question of the diffusion of ecclesiastical authority in Acts (chapters five and six).

2

Modeling Religious Leadership

THE LEADERSHIP STRUCTURES OF THE PRIMITIVE CHURCH HAVE BEEN the subject of scholarly investigation at least since the vested interests of the Protestant Reformation motivated the study. As might be expected, given the high stakes of the inquiry, scholars have sometimes been influenced more by their own perceptions of leadership than by the meaning of leadership within the first century. A fundamental presupposition of the present study is that an adequate understanding of the primitive ecclesiastical leadership structures must incorporate a robust analysis of religious leadership within the cultures of the first-century Mediterranean world. Such an analysis is greatly enhanced through attention to the central sociological features of ancient Mediterranean culture.

This chapter, therefore, will attempt to lay a foundation for the study of ecclesiastical authority in Acts by taking a sociological approach.[1] To that end, it will be necessary to proceed in three movements. First, we will explore definitions of leadership and related terms with the aid of sociological insights. Second, we will inquire into those features of first-century circum-Mediterranean culture that have particular bearing on the form and function of leadership.[2] Finally, we will develop heuristic

---

1. In general, this chapter will avoid drawing evidence directly from Luke-Acts. The purpose for this is to avoid a circularity of methodology. If Acts provided the source-material for describing first-century culture, then that description could not be used to illuminate Acts.

2. We will here use the notion that the whole region surrounding the Mediterranean Sea shared many common cultural characteristics to the extent that it could be considered a common cultural group. For a defense of this view, see Malina and Neyrey, "First-Century Personality," 69–72. Nevertheless, it is our contention that significant cultural differences remained, for example, between Jews and Greeks. Early Christian missionaries were probably cognizant of the ramifications of crossing cultures when

models of first-century leadership based on both sociological theories and first-century realities. These models will provide a basis for examining and explaining leadership in the early church. Throughout the remainder of the study, we will test the models by assessing their power to explain aspects of leadership as expressed in Acts.

This chapter, therefore, is an attempt to bring together a number of streams of research in order to form a foundation from which to investigate ecclesiastical authority in the book of Acts. The streams of research that will be of interest to us here are (1) the cultural attributes of the first-century world; (2) the methodological theory of anthropological sociology; (3) research regarding leadership, authority, and power; and (4) research into the nature of religious leadership. The chapter will be organized from general to specific. Therefore, we will begin with methodological theory; proceed to research regarding leadership, authority, and power; continue with research into the nature of religious leadership; and conclude with culture in the first century. From these four strands, we will attempt to formulate a model of religious authority in the first century that will allow us, in the next chapter, to investigate leadership in Greco-Roman religions and, in the fourth chapter, to explore religious leadership in Second Temple Judaism.

Sociology of Leadership

Theoretical Approaches to Sociology

When attempting to describe a foreign culture, it is desirable to explain the central features of the culture so that members of that culture could affirm the description. Anthropologists call such a depiction an emic description.[3] However, when the culture to be described is separated from the scholar's culture by great distances either in time, geography, or ideology, it may be necessary to describe that culture in terms familiar to the describer's own culture. A description from the perspective of the described culture may be so foreign as to be unintelligible. Such an etic description—one from the perspective of an outside observer—can be an indispensable bridge to a better understanding of the target culture.

---

they carried their message from Jews to Gentiles.

3. For a discussion of emic description and its converse, etic description, see Elliott, *What is Social-Scientific Criticism?* 38–40.

Early culture theorists employed an etic model to explain various cultures. They based their work on the evolutionary theory articulated by Charles Darwin. Thinkers such as Herbert Spencer and Lewis Henry Morgan postulated a series of discrete stages through which all cultures were said to pass.[4] Morgan's stages, for example, were savagery, barbarism, and civilization. Based on this and other evolutionary schemas, Western civilization was placed at the highest level of development, and other cultures were slotted along a scale of primitiveness.[5] From a twenty-first-century vantage point, it is easy to see the ethno-centrism of this construct.

The evolutionary model of cultural development was challenged by the work of Franz Boas and others early in the twentieth century. Boas's work among the Kwakiutl of the Northwest coast of North America demonstrated that the Kwakiutl were neither primitive nor as simplistic as the evolutionists hypothesized. Kwakiutl language, to take one example, had its own internal logic and sophistication.[6] Boas's studies set North American anthropologists on a course toward ethnographic analysis, which emphasized historical particularity. Each culture was to be viewed on its own terms, not in relation to a theoretical superstructure. As Boas himself said, "Civilisation is not something absolute but ... relative, and our ideas and conceptions are true only so far as our civilisation goes."[7]

Structural Functionalism

Meanwhile in England, Emile Durkheim launched the beginning of a distinctly different line of investigation. For Durkheim, culture could be an object of scientific study from which sociological laws could be derived. He viewed each society as possessed of a collective consciousness as part of an almost organic unity. Societies, then, could be classified into types, which were distinguished on the basis of characteristic features.[8] In time, this Durkheimian perspective led to both French structural-

---

4. On Herbert Spencer see Lewellen, *Political Anthropology*, 8. On Lewis Henry Morgan see Layton, *Introduction*, 8.
5. Rosman and Rubel, *Tapestry of Culture*, 18.
6. Rosman and Rubel, *Tapestry of Culture*, 48.
7. Layton, *Introduction*, 184.
8. Layton, *Introduction*, 18–24.

ism and British structural-functionalism.⁹ French structuralism may be understood as an attempt to map culture as the product of universal structures of the human mind. British structural-functionalism was likewise interested in universals, in this case the universal structures of human culture per se. Ted C. Lewellen astutely characterizes structural-functionalism thus: "If one were to reduce the structural-functionalist position to only four words or phrases, they might be *synchronic, teleological, Africa,* and *closed system.*"¹⁰ Structural-functionalism was synchronic because it attempted to understand cultures from a timeless perspective.¹¹ It was teleological in the sense that it viewed all cultural features as focused toward a single goal, namely the equilibrium of the system. Africa is a key word for structural-functionalism because most of the research was conducted in British colonial Africa. This narrow field of view sometimes yielded erroneous conclusions regarding the universality of findings. Finally, structural-functionalists perceived cultures as closed systems. Attention was paid to internal structures and their functions, but the relationships between cultures were largely disregarded. Structural-functionalists were more interested in supposedly untainted cultures than in the effects of contact between African and British cultures.

One theory that has its underpinnings in structural-functionalism is the group/grid model first articulated by sociologist Mary Douglas.¹²

9. Lewellen, *Political Anthropology*, 11.

10. Lewellen, *Political Anthropology*, 95, emphasis original.

11. The meaning of synchronic here is slightly different from the use in NT studies. Here synchronic is used to denote those features of culture which are universally true, regardless of a particular culture's location in time. In NT studies, on the other hand, the emphasis is on "thickened" descriptions within a narrow slice of time.

12. Douglas, *Natural Symbols*. Bruce J. Malina, whose explanation I follow here, reaffirmed the model for the field of New Testament Studies in *Christian Origins*. The enduring significance of Douglas's original work is amply testified by the appearance in 1996 of a new edition in the Routledge Classics series. In the preface to the 1996 edition, Douglas describes the purpose of her grid/group model as follows: "If we want to explain why some rituals are ecstatic and others not we need to go into comparisons of organizations and their objectives. This is what the grid-group analysis proposed in this book was intended to do" (Douglas, *Natural Symbols* 2nd ed., xvii). She further elaborates on the influence of the model in subsequent scholarship (xxvi–xxix). She acknowledges of the diagrams in the original work, "I hardly recognize them, but there is no point in my trying to correct the diagrams that are in this book to make them match something that is being done in the 1990s. There have been great developments" (xxix). It seems reasonable to assume, therefore, that Malina's appropriation of the

The group/grid social model is what might be called a theory of everything, since it attempts to explain central features of every human culture. It classifies cultures into one of four quadrants, which are delineated by placing group and grid onto two axes (see Figure 1, below). The group axis describes the extent to which individuals in a given culture find their identity within a group versus viewing the world through individualistic lenses (strong group and weak group, respectively). The grid axis, on the other hand, describes the degree of match between cultural values and individual achievement. In a high grid culture, cultural values are attainable by a high percentage of the population whereas in a low grid culture, individuals discover that cultural values are largely unattainable. For example, the dominant United States culture conveys that if one works hard, he or she will attain the "American Dream." This culture is usually considered high grid because individuals who work hard often do "get ahead." For certain sub-cultures, however, individuals are unable to attain the "American Dream" no matter how hard they work. There is a disjunction between the value of the dominant culture and the experience of the sub-culture. This sub-culture, then, is a low grid culture.[13]

---

model for New Testament Studies stands as a legitimate application of Douglas's work despite certain significant conceptual differences. Nevertheless, it must be cautioned that Douglas's original grid/group model rests on Durkheimian assertions that run counter to the truth-claims of the New Testament. For example, Douglas alludes to "the Durkheimian premise that society and God can be equated" and "the Durkheimian system in which God is Society and Society is God, where all moral failings are at once sins against religion and the community" (Douglas, *Natural Symbols* 2nd ed., 59 and 70, respectively).

13. The definitions Malina gives for grid and group are as follows: "By 'grid' [Douglas] means the degree of socially constrained adherence that persons in a given group usually give to the symbol system—the system of classifications, definitions, and evaluations—through which the society enables its members to bring order and intelligibility to their experiences.... 'Group' refers to the degree of social pressure exerted upon an individual or some subgroup to conform to the demands of the larger society, to stay within the 'we' lines marking off group boundaries" (Malina, *Christian Origins*, 13). Douglas's own definition of grid is as follows: "A classification system can be coherently organized for a small part of experience, and for the rest it can leave the discrete items jangling in disorder. Or it can be highly coherent in the ordering it offers for the whole of experience, but the individuals for whom it is available may enjoy access to another competing and different system, equally coherent in itself, from which they feel free to select segments here and there eclectically, not worrying about the overall lack of coherence. Then there will be conflicts, contradictions and uncoordinated areas of classification for those people. In effect, loss of coherence results in a narrowing

Figure 1: Group/Grid Model

Weak Group/ High Grid	Strong Group/ High Grid
Weak Group/ Low Grid	Strong Group/ Low Grid

According to Bruce J. Malina, cultures that share the same quadrant also exhibit a range of cultural similarities, while individuals from cultures in opposing quadrants find it difficult to understand one another.[14] "American" culture belongs in the weak group/high grid quadrant. As we shall see, the first-century culture within which the New Testament was written may be categorized as strong group/low grid.[15] Therefore, North American culture and the New Testament culture exist in opposite quadrants, and we should expect a high degree of unfamiliarity when trying to read the New Testament texts. It is precisely areas

---

of the total scope of the classification system. We can therefore take the scope and coherent articulation of a system of classification as one social dimension in which any individual must find himself. I shall call it grid." Douglas, *Natural Symbols* 2nd ed., 62.

14. Malina, *Christian Origins*, 28–29. He says, "If the cultural scripts belonging to respective grid and group quadrants are like the rules of team sports, then what happens when persons from weak group/high grid judge persons from strong group/low grid is much like what occurs when football players judge baseball players by football rules. More often than not, this is what U.S. Bible readers (presumably from weak group/high grid society) do when they read the New Testament (presumably from strong group/low grid society)." Douglas also was interested in developing an appropriate method for cross-cultural examination. She writes, "The book [*Natural Symbols*] was an attempt to develop Durkheim's programme for a comparative sociology of religion so that it could apply as well to Australian totemism as to modern industrial society" (Douglas, *Natural Symbols* 2nd ed., xxv).

15. Malina, *Christian Origins*, 37. Douglas classifies strong group/low grid as "small group." She describes small group cultures as follows: "Their culture promises them contradictory rewards and holds out impossible goals. They believe that it is good to be loyal and obedient and never to split a village into factions. They also believe that the proper ambition of every man is to become head of his own village—impossible without disloyalty and friction. They put immense pressure on one another and strive incessantly to define and close the circle of their friends. Accusations of witchcraft are the political idiom of out-casting and re-definition of social boundaries. The broad, normative concept of a human being for whom moral obligations are binding is contrasted with that of the man-eating witch. To convict a rival of witchcraft is to finish him politically" (Douglas, *Natural Symbols* 2nd ed., 67).

of cultural differences that call for special care when reading the New Testament, since our natural inclination is to misinterpret the cultural cues by virtue of their very foreignness.

Conflict Theories

Structural-functionalism fell into disfavor in the 1940s when researchers realized that societies were constantly changing and interacting in ways that did not contribute to the stability of the whole. From this realization arose a number of alternative meta-theories that collectively have been called conflict theories or process theories.[16] The central feature of these perspectives on culture is their emphasis on change and the processes that drive change. It should not be supposed, however, that structural-functionalism ignored change; rather, conflict and change were viewed as the efforts of cultures to re-establish equilibrium. It is no coincidence, as Lewellen has observed, that process theories began to appear at the same time that the British Empire was breaking apart.[17] The structural-functionalists had viewed societies as perduring entities, just as the Empire had seemed to be such. As the Empire dissolved, the underlying processes of change that had been masked by the fact of Empire came to the fore. These processes became the focus of the new theorists. Their work constituted a severe and sustained polemic against structural-functionalism. As a result, structural-functionalism fell into disfavor for a time, and some of the results of analysis from the structural-functionalist perspective were neglected.

As is the nature of the case when theories are defined in reaction against another theory instead of in positive terms, conflict theory has become a term that embraces a variety of perspectives. Properly speaking, conflict theory should probably be reserved for those ideas that developed in the immediate aftermath of the decline of structural-functionalism in the 1940s and 50s.[18] Nevertheless, a number of more

---

16. Lewellen, *Political Anthropology*, 17. He says, "The belated discovery that the world is in motion stimulated an enthusiastic disavowal of structural-functionalism, almost equal to that which had temporarily obliterated evolutionism at the turn of the century. *Structure* and *function* became unfashionable terms, to be replaced by *process, conflict, faction, struggle, manipulative strategy,* and the like."

17. Lewellen, *Political Anthropology*, 17–18.

18. Scott and Marshall, "Conflict Theory," 103.

recent theories have sometimes also been termed conflict theory.[19] These include neo-evolutionism, Marxist anthropology, and socioecology.

OTHER THEORIES

More recently, sociology has come under the ubiquitous influence of post-modernity. In this instance, the result is that scholars reject meta-theories as comprehensive explanations of reality, while at the same time accepting such theories piecemeal as partial explanations. The result is a pragmatic approach in which scholars are free to draw from parts of theories whenever convenient to explain a particular observation. I wish to take a slightly different approach. Although I will borrow from both structural-functionalist and conflict perspectives, I want to draw attention to a number of striking congruences related to these two meta-theories and their application to leadership in the first century. In the first case, structural-functionalism, as we have seen, is associated with the height of the British Empire. As such, the theory stressed continuity and changes that re-established equilibrium but was blind to forces operating in subversive or innovative ways. Leadership, therefore, was viewed as effective to the extent that leaders effected continuity and equilibrium. It is my contention that structural-functionalist conceptions of leadership reflected actual attitudes of members of British culture. In other words, bona fide members of the British Empire probably viewed leadership in the way structural-functionalists viewed leadership. I further contend that this view is predicated upon the fact of Empire; dominant cultures will tend to produce visions of leadership that emphasize maintenance of the status quo. The first century, of course, was dominated by its own Empire. One piece of the heuristic model to be developed in this chapter, therefore, is that the perspectives on leadership viewed from a structural-functionalist perspective will have a high degree of correspondence with the attitudes of leadership within the Roman Empire.

Secondly, conflict theory arose in the aftermath of the decline of the British Empire. Subversive activities, which had been masked to the structural-functionalists by the dominance of Empire, were now capable of study by the new sociologists. It should not be supposed, of course, that new forms of leadership emerged with the decline of the

---

19. Collins, "Conflict Theory," 414.

British Empire. Rather, researchers were newly aware of already existing patterns. Therefore, at least two kinds of leadership coexisted: (1) leadership associated with the dominant culture, which stressed continuity; and (2) leadership associated with the subordinate culture(s), which stressed innovation and substantive change. Turning again to the first century, it can be expected that patterns of leadership, authority, and power identified by conflict theorists will be visible in the attitudes of subordinated groups such as the Jews and Christians of first-century Palestine. Before we turn to a more thorough examination of first-century culture, however, we must first investigate another facet of sociological research.

Leadership, Authority, and Power in Sociological Research

Whereas in the previous section we discussed sociological theories, in this section we shall explore specific areas of sociological research, namely leadership, authority, and power. As we shall see, authority and power seem to have concerned individuals in the Greco-Roman world. Yet so far as we know, there is not even a word in Greek that can consistently be translated, "leader." In contrast, leadership has captivated the modern imagination, and innumerable volumes have been written on the subject.[20] The extent to which modern conceptions of leadership correspond to leadership in the first century is a topic that will continue to be a focus of our attention throughout the remainder of the study. In the same way, modern sociological research has explored the nature of authority and power, but it is not immediately obvious whether our understanding of these concepts corresponds to what a Greek meant when saying ἐξουσία or a Roman when saying *auctoritas*. We turn, therefore, to an examination of what sociologists today mean when using the terms leadership, authority, and power.

---

20. Even in the modern world, interest in leadership as such seems to be a culturally determined pursuit. The eminent British OT scholar, John Goldingay, has characterized the preoccupation with leadership as a distinctly American trait (Goldingay, "Leadership Theologically Considered").

Leadership

According to one recent book, leadership has been one of the most studied aspects within the field of sociological research.[21] Surprisingly, then, at least two dictionaries of sociology neglect to include any entry on leadership at all.[22] Another dictionary defines leadership as, "The ability to influence what goes on in a social system."[23] Yet the next sentence seems to place greater importance on authority and power than on leadership: "In most cases, leadership is based on some form of legitimate authority associated with a social status such as manager or president, but this is not necessarily the case."[24]

This apparent devaluation in the dictionaries seems to derive, not from a disinterest in the subject by sociologists, but from a lack of consensus on the definition of leadership. As John Antonakis, Anna T. Cianciolo, and Robert J. Sternberg astutely point out, "Leadership is easy to identify in situ; however, it is difficult to define precisely. Given the complex nature of leadership, a specific and widely accepted definition of leadership does not exist and might never be found."[25] Nevertheless, innumerable leadership definitions have been attempted.[26] Edwin A. Locke, for example, defines leadership as, "The process of inducing others to take action toward a common goal."[27] William J. Mea and Shawn M. Carraher prefer to operate by borrowing two definitions: "Leadership can be defined as the activity of influencing people to cooperate toward some goal"[28] and "Successful leadership results in the creation of transformation in others."[29] Despite their claim regarding the difficulty of

---

21. Antonakis, Cianciolo, and Sternberg, *Nature of Leadership*, 4.

22. Calhoun, ed., *Dictionary of Social Sciences*; and Scott and Marshall, eds., *A Dictionary of Sociology*.

23. Allan G. Johnson, *The Blackwell Dictionary of Sociology*, 173.

24. Ibid.

25. Antonakis, Cianciolo, and Sternberg, *Nature of Leadership*, 5.

26. Cf. Mea and Carraher, "Leaders Speak," 298: "Definitions of leadership are numerous and almost as varied and personal as the perspectives of the persons defining it."

27. Locke et al., *The Essence of Leadership*, 2.

28. Mea and Carraher, "Leaders Speak," 298. The quotation is from Tead, *The Art of Leadership*, 20.

29. Ibid. The quotation is from Bass, "Some Observations," 5. It should be noted that Bass distinguishes between attempted, successful, and effective leadership. Successful leadership results in changed group members, but effective leadership occurs when the changes are congruent with group goals.

defining leadership, Antonakis, Cianciolo, and Sternberg themselves offer a definition that they claim will satisfy most scholars "in principle."[30] They say,

> Leadership can be defined as the nature of the influencing process—and its resultant outcomes—that occurs between a leader and followers and how this influencing process is explained by the leader's dispositional characteristics and behaviors, follower perceptions and attributions of the leader, and the context in which the influencing process occurs. For us, a necessary condition for effective and authentic leadership is the creation of empowered followers in pursuit of a moral purpose, leading to moral outcomes that are guided by moral means.[31]

Whether this definition does indeed satisfy most scholars will probably continue to be debated. Despite the lack of consensus regarding a definition of leadership, however, there has been a significant amount of research on leadership in the last century. The bulk of the research is driven largely by an interest in improving leadership for business today rather than in understanding leadership as a phenomenon of human society and history. Despite the pragmatic focus of much leadership research, a great deal can be learned from that research to assist in understanding leadership in the first century, provided that one maintains sensitivity to the grids mentioned earlier.

According to Roya Ayman, the study of leadership until the eighteenth century dealt exclusively with rulers and monarchs, not other types of leaders.[32] At the beginning of the twentieth century, two models of leadership were created: the "great man" model and the "Zeitgeist" model. The former was the brainchild of Thomas Carlyle in England, and the latter of Karl Marx in Germany.[33] According to the "great man" model, leaders emerge because of the individual qualities of the leader. Certain personal attributes cause a person to excel in positions of leadership. Also coming from this perspective was a distinction between leader and manager. Leaders are viewed as change-makers; managers as sustainers of the status quo or implementers of a leader's vision. As Locke puts it, "The key function of a *leader* is to establish the basic

30. Antonakis, Cianciolo, and Sternberg, *Nature of Leadership*, 5.
31. Ibid.
32. Ayman, "Leadership," 1564.
33. Ibid.

vision (purpose, mission, overarching goal, or agenda) of the organization. The leader specifies the end as well as the over-arching strategy for reaching it."[34] The function of a manager, on the other hand, "is to implement the vision. The manager and subordinates act in ways to implement the vision. The manager and subordinates act in ways that constitute the means to achieving the stated end."[35]

The "Zeitgeist" model, in contrast to the "great man" model, proposes that circumstances create the leader. On this model, the necessities of the moment force individuals to take on leadership roles; particular situations provide the opportunity for the emergence of leaders. Put another way, leaders are created, not born. The qualities possessed by a leader are the result of unique experiences, not innate personal attributes. As a result, anyone can be an effective leader, provided the right experiences are encountered. Study, therefore, focuses on unique experiences common to the great leaders. Attention is paid to the question, What are the essential experiential factors that favor the emergence of greatness?

Subsequent investigation into leadership has tended to follow one of these two models. Studies that follow the "great man" model focus with ever more refinement on the qualities of effective leaders. As noted above, much of this research has a pragmatic bias, coming in service to potential employers who wish to hire individuals who possess those qualities that are most often associated with effective leaders. Batteries of tests are devised to assist hirers in identifying people with the greatest potential for leadership. Similarly, studies that follow the "Zeitgeist" model have also tended toward a pragmatic focus. In this case, attention is directed toward the kinds of experiences that are most likely to lead to the development of effective leaders. Instead of tests to identify potential leaders, leadership training is the focus. From a pragmatic standpoint, the two approaches need not be mutually exclusive. The argument can be made that potential leaders (identified via the "great man" model) benefit from leadership development (formulated with reference to the "Zeitgeist" model). The confluence of the two approaches has led the emergence of contingency models of leadership.[36]

---

34. Locke et al., *Essence of Leadership*, 4, emphasis original.
35. Ibid.
36. Ayman, "Leadership," 1565.

Including the contingency school, Antonakis, Cianciolo, and Sternberg identify eight schools of leadership theory: trait, behavior, contingency, contextual, relational, skeptics, information-processing, and new leadership.[37] The trait school was prevalent in the 1920s through the 1950s and again from the 1990s to the present. It focused on "stable leadership characteristics linked to leadership emergence."[38] Ayman designates this school, together with the next one, as having evolved out of the "great-man" theory of leadership.[39] The second school is the Behavior School, which gained ascendancy in the 1950s and 60s. The focus of this school was on successful styles of leadership, employee-oriented leadership, and production-oriented leadership. The contingency school, noted above as a confluence of the "great-man" and "Zeitgeist" models, was especially influential during the 1970s and 80s. The distinctive perspective of the contingency school was that leadership effectiveness depends on the quality of interpersonal relationships, the expectations regarding leadership, and the nature of the tasks at hand. Closely related to the contingency school and arising concurrently with it, the context school continues to be prevalent today. According to James G. Hunt, the contextual approach emphasizes four contexts for leadership: "stability, crisis, dynamic equilibrium, and the edge of chaos."[40] In other words, the contextual school evaluates the nature and quality of leadership when the studied group is (1) in a steady state; (2) faced with an extraordinary problem; (3) dealing with controlled change; and (4) encountering overwhelming flux.

The relational school was active during the 1980s and 90s. Based on what is called "vertical dyad linkage theory" and "leader-member exchange theory," the relational school hypothesizes that the success of leadership depends on the quality of the leader-follower relationship. During the 1970s and 80s, a number of scholars raised fundamental questions regarding leadership from a skeptical perspective. The skeptical school questioned the methodology for studying leadership and whether leadership even exists, suggesting that perceptions of leadership might simply be the result of organizational functioning, not of

---

37. Antonakis, Cianciolo, and Sternberg, *Nature of Leadership*, 6–8.
38. Ibid., 6.
39. Ayman, "Leadership," 1565.
40. Hunt, "What is Leadership?" 43.

fundamentally human relationships or functions. The seventh school, information-processing, takes a less cynical approach. Active in the 1990s until the present, the information-processing school notes that leaders are legitimized by the match between their personal attributes and the expectations of followers. Research from this perspective seeks to discover why leadership functions in this way. The final school, new leadership or neo-charismatic, transformational, or visionary leadership, has been prevalent since the 1980s. From this perspective, leaders inspire their followers to favor the common good over personal gain.

Recent research into leadership patterns has increasingly noted the interesting fact that different cultures value leadership in varying degrees. As William J. Mea and Shawn M. Carraher point out, "Differentiation of leaders from others in a society does not occupy the interest of all cultures."[41] In the New Testament, there does not seem to be much interest in leadership per se. This becomes apparent from the simple observation that the New American Standard Version uses "lead" or "leader" 98 times in the New Testament, but these occur-

---

41. Mea and Carraher, "Leaders Speak," 298. Mea and Carraher cite Stogdill in support of their assertion. They cite no page, but they may have in mind p. 7, where Stogdill says, "Words meaning 'chief' or 'king' are the only ones found in many languages to differentiate the ruler from other members of society. A preoccupation with leadership occurs predominantly in countries with an Anglo-Saxon heritage. The *Oxford English Dictionary* (1933) notes the appearance of the word 'leader' in the English language as early as the year 1300. However, the word 'leadership' did not appear until about 1800" (Stogdill, *Handbook of Leadership*, 7). Contrast the assertion of Antonakis, Cianciolo, and Sternberg, "Leadership is a universal activity evident in humankind and in animal species" (Antonakis, Cianciolo, and Sternberg, *Nature of Leadership*, 4–5). Ironically, Antonakis, Cianciolo, and Sternberg cite the third edition of Stogdill's work (Bernard M. Bass and Ralph M. Stogdill, *Bass & Stogdill's Handbook of Leadership*). Even as early as the second edition, Bass seems to have qualified Stogdill's earlier perspective. Rather than emphasizing the uniqueness of leadership language to the Anglo-Saxon, in the revised edition, Bass cites examples from Greek, Roman, and Egyptian primary sources to support the claim that "the study of leadership is an ancient art." He goes on to assert, "Leadership is a universal human phenomenon" (Ralph Melvin Stogdill and Bernard M. Bass, *Stogdill's Handbook of Leadership*, 5). The passage from the first edition, quoted above, has been modified as follows, "Words meaning head of state, military commander, princeps, proconsul, chief, or king are the only ones found in many languages to differentiate the ruler from other members of society. A preoccupation with leadership as opposed to headship based on inheritance, usurpation, or appointment occurs . . ." (Stogdill and Bass, *Stogdill's Handbook of Leadership*, 7). Of course, the two claims—that leadership is a universal phenomenon and that a preoccupation with leadership is culturally determined—are not mutually exclusive, since the activity can be present even when little attention is paid to its functioning.

rences translate 31 different Greek words.⁴² Moreover, these 31 words occur a total of 752 times in the Greek New Testament, meaning that they are translated as lead or leader only about four percent of the time. It should be clear from these statistics that the central meaning of these words is something other than what we mean when we use the words "lead" or "leader." This does not imply, of course, that the NASB translators necessarily mistranslated these words. On the contrary, it is likely that what we would call leadership occurred under a variety of different labels in the New Testament world. As we look back on that time period and try to make sense of what took place, it is sometimes necessary to explain circumstances using our own categories.

Two studies into leadership in non-Western cultures seem especially pertinent to understanding leadership in the first century. The first of these was conducted by Roya Ayman and Martin M. Chemers in Iran.⁴³ In this study, midlevel managers were asked to evaluate the leadership of their superiors. Whereas similar studies in the West had identified two distinct leadership styles, one that emphasized a task-oriented approach and one that stressed relational aspects, the leaders in Iran seemed to meld these two styles. The researches identified the preferred leadership style of Iran as "benevolent paternalism."⁴⁴ The ideal leadership pattern was described as "the warm but stern, benevolently paternalistic style of the Iranian father figure." ⁴⁵ In contrast, domineering behavior was associated with dehumanization and exploitation.

A different study in Japan produced a similar result. In this study, leaders were ranked on two scales: the P and the M. The P scale measured behavior associated with performance, or the achievement of specified goals; the M scale with group cohesiveness or self-preservation.⁴⁶ The

---

42. Accordance. The Greek words are ἄγω, αἰχμαλωτεύω, αἰχμαλωτίζω, ἀνάγω, ἀναφέρω, ἀπάγω, ἀποβαίνω, ἀποπλανάω, ἀποφέρω, ἀρχισυνάγωγος, ἄρχων, διάγω, εἰσφέρω, ἐκβάλλω, ἐξάγω, ἡγέομαι, ἡσυχάζω, θριαμβεύω, καθηγητής, περιπατέω, πλανάω, προάγω, προΐστημι, προκόπτω, πρῶτος, σκανδαλίζω, σπαταλάω, φέρω, φθείρω, χειραγωγέω, and χειραγωγός. "Leading" or "lead" also translates εἰς in the phrases πνεῦμα δουλείας πάλιν εἰς φόβον (Rom 8:15), μετάνοιαν εἰς ἐπίγνωσιν ἀληθείας (2 Tim 2:25), and σοφίσαι εἰς σωτηρίαν (2 Tim 3:15). Since these phrases clearly have little to do with leadership by individuals, εἰς is not included in the statistics.

43. Ayman and Chemers, "Relationship of Supervisory Behavior."

44. Ibid., 340.

45. Ibid.

46. Misumi, *The Behavioral Science of Leadership*, 9.

study identified four types of leader behavior, which were designated PM, Pm, pM, and pm, where the majuscule represents an above average rating for that scale and the minuscule indicates a below average rating.[47] It was determined that the most effective leaders exhibited the PM type. In other words, the ideal leader in Japan combined the attributes of performance focus and maintenance focus.[48]

Both Japanese and Iranian cultures share a dominant honor/shame system. As we shall see, honor/shame permeated first-century culture, as well. It should be no surprise, then, if leadership in the first century should be found to follow patterns similar to those found in Iran and Japan.

Authority

Concurrently with the development of early leadership models, Max Weber was studying, among other things, the nature of authority. According to Weber, access to authority is what distinguishes a person who is able to exert influence as a leader from one who must use some form of coercion or appeal to calculated benefit. He says, "Keine Herrschaft begnügt sich, nach aller Erfahrung, freiwillig mit den nur materiellen oder nur affektuellen oder nur wertrationalen Motiven als Chancen ihres Fortbestandes. Jede sucht vielmehr den Glauben an ihre »Legitimität« zu erwecken und zu pflegen."[49] Moreover, he asserts, "Eine durch monopolistiche Lage bedingte ökonomische »Macht« ... allein und für sich ebensowenig schon »Herrschaft« heißen, wie irgendein anderer: etwa durch erotische oder sportliche oder diskussionsmäßige oder andere Überlegenheit bedingter »Einfluß«."[50] A person with authority, therefore, is able to influence the behavior of others in his or her group because of a certain degree of compliance on the part

47. Ibid., 42.
48. Ibid., 12.
49. Max Weber, *Wirtschaft und Gesellschaft*, 157. ("It is an induction from experience that no system of authority voluntarily limits itself to the appeal to material or affectual or ideal motives as a basis for guaranteeing its continuance. In addition every such system attempts to establish and to cultivate the belief in its 'legitimacy'" [Weber, *Max Weber*, 325].)
50. Ibid., 158. ("[Economic 'power' based on monopolistic position] will not, taken by itself, be considered to constitute 'authority' any more than any other kind of 'influence' which is derived from some kind of superiority, as by virtue of erotic attractiveness, skill in sport or in discussion" [Weber, *Max Weber*, 326].)

of the influenced persons. The influenced person agrees to a greater or lesser extent that the person in authority has a right to dictate his or her behavior. Weber identified three kinds of authority: *legale Herrschaft*, *traditionale Herrschaft*, and *charismatische Herrschaft*.[51] For Weber, *legale Herrschaft* (legal authority) has a rational basis. It exists when an authoritative position has been formalized, usually by being written into some sort of code. Functionaries within a constitutional government hold this type of authority. Policemen in our culture, for example, hold authority not because of any personal qualities they might possess, nor—in most cases—because of the weapons they carry, but because the whole weight of the legal system stands behind the symbol of their uniform. *Traditionale Herrschaft* (traditional authority), on the other hand, is the deference or submission paid to an individual by virtue of that person's social location as the occupant of a leadership position. For example, in paternalistic societies, fathers have authority over their families for no other reason than that they occupy the role of father. Unlike the first two types of authority, *charismatische Herrschaft* (charismatic authority) depends on the personal qualities of the individual. The personal, intangible attributes of the leader draw people to him or her in such a way that followers willingly do the bidding of the leader. Weber hypothesized that an organization formed around a charismatic leader lasts only so long as that leader retains his charisma.[52] Should the leader die or be supplanted by someone with greater charisma, the organization will disband. Unless the organization undergoes a process of the "routinization of charisma,"[53] it cannot last beyond the founding leader's generation. People will follow a charismatic leader only so long as they perceive that the leader has the most desirable attributes available. For this reason, charismatic authority is unstable, since it is always possible for someone new to come along with more charisma.

More recently, researchers have identified a fourth type of authority, professional authority.[54] This type, like charismatic authority,

---

51. Weber, *Wirtschaft und Gesellschaft*, 159.

52. "The only basis of legitimacy for [charismatic authority] is personal charisma, so long as it is proved; that is, as long as it receives recognition and is able to satisfy the followers or disciples. But this lasts only so long as the belief in its charismatic inspiration remains" (Weber, *Theory*, 326).

53. Weber, *Wirtschaft und Gesellschaft*, 182.

54. Johnson, *The Blackwell Dictionary of Sociology*, 23.

depends on the authority-holder's personal attributes, or at least the perception of such. However, professional authority depends more on cognitive qualities, while charismatic authority depends on interpersonal qualities. The leader with professional authority is authoritative by virtue of his or her expertise in a certain field. For example, a doctor has professional authority regarding a patient's medical care because he or she has spent many years learning how the human body functions. Similarly, an auto mechanic has professional authority when it comes to the fixing of a car, because of special knowledge about cars. Professional authority, therefore, depends on what someone knows. The old adage, knowledge is power, seems to reflect this kind of authority.

As Weber pointed out with respect to his three types of authority, his types, together with professional authority, are all best described as ideal types. As ideal types, these constructs are not present unmixed in the real world. In other words, although these types can be separated for the purpose of analysis, any real leader's authority necessarily rests on some combination of the ideal types. For example, it is possible that a father's authority rests primarily on traditional authority, while at the same time being supported by formal authority by virtue of rights written into the law of the land. From a heuristic standpoint, therefore, it becomes important to explore other possible sources for a leader's authority, even after the most apparent source has been identified.

Leadership researcher, Ronald Heifetz, construes authority differently from Weber. On Heifetz's view, authority is something granted to leaders in a formal way. He says,

> I define authority as conferred power to perform a service. This definition will be useful to the practitioner of leadership as a reminder of two facts: First, authority is given and can be taken away. Second, authority is conferred as part of an exchange. Failure to meet the terms of exchange means the risk of losing one's authority: it can be taken back or given to another who promises to fulfill the bargain.[55]

For example, in the United States, politicians have authority by virtue of having been elected by a majority of the voters among a given constituency. Those who have formal leadership positions lead with authority, while those who somehow stand outside the system they are trying to

---

55. Heifetz, *Leadership Without Easy Answers*, 57.

influence lead without authority. It is therefore possible to lead with or without authority. As Heifetz demonstrates, each of these ways of leading has its own benefits and challenges.

Power

Power is closely associated with leadership and authority. Leadership functions on the basis of authority, which is a particular kind of power. Power, more broadly construed, has been defined as the ability of one person to exert his or her will over another, to get people to do one's bidding.[56] Power, therefore, can take a variety of forms ranging from physical force or coercion to moral authority and peer pressure. This definition has dominated thinking about power for the last century. It has been described as "power over."[57] Power over is characterized by the ability of one person or group to control the actions of another person or group. Thus, the entity with power has control over the powerless. Investigation into this type of power tends to focus on the sources of power and the means used to maintain power.

More recently, an alternative definition has been employed, arising out of feminist and other liberation perspectives. Instead of viewing power as "power over," it is viewed as "power to." Without denying the existence of "power over," researchers focusing on "power to" look for ways in which individuals gain power to effect their own future. To return to the earlier discussion regarding structural-functionalists' and conflict theorists' perspectives, it should be apparent that "power over" will be associated with the former by virtue of its affinities with Empire, while "power to" will be associated with conflict theory and subordinate cultures. In the first century, therefore, leaders operating under the auspices of the Roman Empire (whether Romans themselves or merely aligning themselves with the Romans as did certain members of the Jewish nobility) probably valued leadership qualities of "power over,"

---

56. The perspective on power described here is based on Weber's definition. He says, "*Macht* bedeutet jede Chance, innerhalb einer sozialen Beziehung den eigenen Willen auch gegen Widerstreben durchzusetzen, gleichviel worauf diese Chance beruht." Weber, *Wirtschaft und Gesellschaft*, 38. ("'Power' (*Macht*) is the probability [*Chance*] that one actor within a social relationship will be in a position to carry out his own will despite resistance, regardless of the basis on which this probability rests" [Weber, *Max Weber*, 152].)

57. Johnson, *The Blackwell Dictionary of Sociology*, 235.

while leaders operating from subordinate positions would have gravitated toward what is now being termed "power to." These observations will form part of the heuristic model developed in this chapter, which will be tested against the historical record in subsequent chapters.

A Typology of Religious Leadership

Before turning to models of religious leadership in the first century, it is necessary to consider a typology of religious leadership. The effort to develop such a typology bears strong affinities with the structural-functionalism discussed earlier. Any typology of religion must account for religious phenomena and attempt to explain the purposes of those phenomena. It may be inevitable that such typologies will be both idealistic and reductionistic. They will be idealistic because they deal in ideal types; reductionistic because they reduce the complexities of religious life to a few succinct categories. Nevertheless, a religious typology can be invaluable for examining the internal logic of religious systems, provided that the abstract constructions of the typology are constantly checked against the concrete facts of the religion under consideration.

Dale Cannon, philosopher of religion from Western Oregon State College, has developed an interesting heuristic tool for studying religions of various types. He posits six ways of being religious: ritual performance, reasoned inquiry, mystical quest, shamanic mediation, deeds of devotion, and social action.[58] Historian and NT scholar S. Scott Bartchy has extended this tool, arguing for a systemic approach which postulates a substantive connection between the way of being religious and the associated conception of ultimate reality, the problem addressed, and the type of leadership necessary to accomplish the resolution of the problem.[59] Thus, the problem addressed by ritual performance is chaos or the lack of order; ultimate reality is viewed as supreme order; and the necessary leader is a priest, who can perform the rituals in the correct, orderly manner. For reasoned inquiry, the problem is ignorance, ultimate reality is supreme mind or rationality, and the leader is a teacher. For mystical quest, the problem is suffering and the material world, ultimate reality is nothingness or monadic unity, and the leader is a guru who can direct the novice toward unity

---

58. Cannon, *Six Ways of Being Religious*.
59. Bartchy, "Cultural and Religious Environment of Early Christianity."

with the cosmos. For shamanic mediation, the problem is weakness, sickness, or material lack; ultimate reality is the source of all goodness; and the leader is one who can channel the goodness on behalf of the religious person. For deeds of devotion, the problem is meaninglessness and disconnectedness, ultimate reality is one's personal patron, and the leader is a preacher who can stir individuals to fervent service. Finally, for social action, the problem is injustice, ultimate reality is community-forming power, and the leader is a prophet who is able to identify and publicly decry injustice. These six ways of being religious may be summarized as in Table 2.1.

Table 2.1: Six Ways of Being Religious

	Ritual Performance	Reasoned Inquiry	Mystical Quest	Shamanic Mediation	Deeds of Devotion	Social Action
Ultimate Reality	Order	Mind/ Rationality	Cosmic Unity	Source of Goodness	Personal Patron	Community-Forming Power
Existential Problem	Chaos	Ignorance	Suffering	Material Lack/ Weakness	Meaninglessness	Injustice
Leader	Priest	Teacher	Guru	Shaman	Preacher	Prophet

Cannon has been criticized of over-simplification and of creating a procrustean bed.[60] While it is undoubtedly true that not every form of religious practice falls neatly into one of the categories, the paradigm is nevertheless useful in a number of ways. Provided that the six ways are viewed as ideal types, which in practice are found in complementary or even contradictory juxtaposition, they can be helpful for deciphering the internal logic of a particular religious tradition. Moreover, the paradigm can lead to an appreciation of traditions different from one's own, since fundamental problems addressed by each way are to greater or lesser extent universal in human experience. For our present purposes, the value of the model is that it offers an explanation of the function of religious leaders within the context of the larger religious system.

60. For an extended critique, see Foster, "Saying What We Mean."

I should like to hypothesize that the quintessential way of being religious for a group in power is ritual performance. So long as everything is done properly (or, as Bartchy is wont to say, "In the right place, at the right time, with the right stuff, in the right way, by the right people"), chaos will be staved and the worshippers will retain their place in the present order. Put another way, ritual performance creates regular times, places, and events, all of which function to maintain social equilibrium. Thus, ritual performance becomes a means of perpetuating the status quo. For these reasons, one should expect that the usual religious leader in the Roman Empire would have been a priest, i.e., someone who is competent to correctly perform the requisite rituals.

Similarly, I would postulate that the way of social action resides naturally within a context of subordination to an external power. When people experience powerlessness and oppression, the desire for justice comes to the fore, and the notion that an even greater power is on one's side would certainly be attractive. Since, for the way of social action, the conception of ultimate reality is a God who forms just communities and opposes the powers of injustice, justice will ultimately prevail, and activity toward that end will be rewarded.

Of course, the way of social action is not the only possible religious response to adverse circumstances. The way of sacred ritual will be attractive to those people who feel powerless in most areas of life but desire to maintain a certain sense of control through the regular, orderly performance of religious ceremonies. Alternatively, the way of the mystical quest may appeal to individuals who view the present situation as hopeless. The mystical quest, then, becomes a means of escape. Jewish apocalypticism appears to have affinities with this approach. The worldview apparent in apocalyptic literature is one of extreme pessimism regarding the possibility of improvement in the present order. Only with the in-breaking of God will the situation be rectified.

These three approaches to an oppressive situation seem to have been present in first-century Palestine.[61] As we have just argued, Jewish apocalyptic is a pessimistic religious response to the domination of Rome. In what may be regarded as a "realistic" religious response, the Temple hierarchy accommodated to Roman rule but maintained the Temple ritual as a means of perpetuating a semblance of control. In

---

61. Alongside these primary ways of being religious, it appears that in the first century all groups had interest in shamanic mediation.

contrast, the way of social justice may be regarded as an idealistic or optimistic religious response. As we shall see, the primitive church incorporated elements of social action into their conception of true religion. Thus, there was an array of religious options in the first century, but each seems to involve a response to the political realities of the day. We should expect, therefore, that the religious leaders of the first century would have incorporated a variety of the leadership roles associated with the ideal types. To the extent that sacred rite is present in a given religious group, we can expect to see priests maintaining the rites. Similarly, those groups that emphasize social action will have leaders who exhibit traits of a prophet, apocalyptic groups would have crystallized around leaders who were expert in receiving and interpreting apocalyptic visions, and so forth.

First Century Culture

Strong Group/Low Grid

Having explored current research regarding the sociology of leadership and the nature of religious leadership, we turn now to an examination of those cultural features of the first century that would have had the most bearing on leadership patterns in the early church. The first feature of first-century culture that we shall investigate is the strong group/low grid quality of much first-century experience introduced above. As already discussed, the group/grid model is based on a structural-functionalist understanding of culture. From this perspective, it is possible to make a number of useful observations about first-century culture.

According to Malina, one of the characteristic signs of a strong group/low grid society is the proliferation of groups.[62] Because of the group emphasis of this quadrant, groups tend to make exclusive claims upon members and to endure over long time periods. Yet because of the low grid condition, dissatisfaction with existing groups is not uncommon. Over time, therefore, new groups are formed while older groups remain in existence. The net result is that the number of groups steadily increases. In such a situation with a multiplicity of groups, competition between groups becomes inevitable. Therefore, groups tend to place great importance on boundaries. Carefully defined and diligently main-

---

62. Malina, *Christian Origins*, 38.

tained boundaries indicate who is in and who is out of the group. Rites often serve to maintain boundaries and to mark boundary crossings. Initiation rites, for example, highlight the movement of individuals from outsiders to insiders.

The proliferation of groups has another consequence: since groups compete for the same space, group identity is no longer associated with a particular locality. As a result, sacred space is reinterpreted in terms of the group, not of geography. Language then becomes the locus of the sacred. As Malina says, "Discourse within these groups, whether words of a portable Torah, the story of Jesus, or the exhortations of the philosopher-teacher, becomes the mobile, portable, exportable focus of sacred place, in fact more important than the fixed and eternal sacred place of strong group/high grid societies."[63]

Strong group/low grid societies also exhibit confusion about social roles. The low grid situation produces uncertainty regarding how one ought to act in order to achieve desired ends. Moreover, group proliferation may require that individuals play different roles in different contexts. No single role would accurately reflect the totality of a person's attributes. Since external actions are the result of role-playing and not personal choice, the internal state of a person would seem unknowable. Therefore, it would seem inappropriate to judge based on external actions.

Despite this role confusion, there is nevertheless a heightened concern for social structures. This concern persists even though the structures themselves are regarded as inadequate and temporary. As Malina says,

> Since strong group mainly points to emphasis on social structures (means) while grid points to social values (ends), strong group scripts are heavily concerned with social means, social structures, and social institutions. But the low grid situation makes the existing structures appear to be temporary, transient, and essentially unsuitable for the job of realizing the values that they should, that is, the values of the grid.[64]

Strong group/low grid situations also exhibit a tendency toward anthropomorphism and dualism. Persons influenced by a strong group

63. Ibid.
64. Ibid., 40.

perspective see order and personal causality in the universe. Yet the unfulfilled expectations inherent in a low grid environment lead to the postulation of a dualistic cosmology with a personal, evil entity who thwarts hopes. Any experience of good, therefore, is considered likely to be fleeting. Healing, for example, would be considered only temporary, with repeated healings necessary even though the initial healing was complete.

The strong group/low grid quadrant is distinguished by acquisition maintenance. Individuals in this quadrant are likely to accept their lot in life and look to an afterlife for an improved lot. Yet they are concerned to maintain their current situation without deterioration. Old age is valued for establishing group history, but the old may become scapegoats for the low grid circumstance. Efforts to improve the circumstance are aimed at moving up the grid, that is, toward aligning experience with the cultural values. However, such efforts may remain unsuccessful or unattempted, since cultures can remain in a low grid state indefinitely.

Limited Good

In the first-century circum-Mediterranean culture, as in many cultures today, all commodities, all attainable values, indeed, anything deemed good, were perceived to exist only in a fixed quantity. Therefore, valuables—both tangible and intangible—were moved from one recipient to another but never produced or increased in quantity. This was true of everything from money to honor. This contrasts sharply, of course, with the perception of individuals embedded in Western cultures. We believe that all good is unlimited, that hard work increases the quantity of any good. We even measure "Gross Domestic Product" as an indicator of the amount of good that a country has created in a given year. We rarely stop to consider whether this good was accumulated at the expense of some weaker entity. Yet first-century individuals regularly thought in these terms. If one party accumulated wealth or honor, it was assumed that this accumulation came at the expense of others, who were thereby robbed of what was rightfully theirs.

This perception of limited good had far-reaching and sometimes surprising ramifications. First, it produced a specific orientation toward honor. The honorable person was one who was able to maintain his—not her, since female honor was embedded within male honor—inherited position. As Malina says,

> The honorable man, the first-century male ideal, is one who knows how to live out and live up to his inherited obligations. He neither encroaches on others nor allows himself to be exploited or challenged by others. He works to feed and clothe his family. He fulfills his community and ceremonial obligations. He minds his own business in such a way as to be sure no one else infringes on him, while looking for possible advantages for himself. In sum, he does not seem to be outstanding, but he knows how to protect his entitlements bound up with his inherited status.[65]

Thus, there was no sense of "trying to get ahead" or defining success according to the accumulation of goods. Since any accumulation was perceived to have come at the expense of another, envy was the supreme evil. It entailed a grasping for good that was due others; it was robbery and it upset the social order. Traveling merchants and tax collectors were considered dishonorable because they accumulated wealth beyond their inherited station. While we might consider such individuals as industrious and resourceful, first-century individuals would likely have considered them untrustworthy and greedy.

The terms rich and poor were also differently understood. The two were not opposite ends on a scale of accumulated wealth. Rather, the rich were those individuals who had increased their wealth by defrauding others; the term did not refer to an absolute measure of wealth, but to wealth relative to an earlier time or to others of a comparable standing.[66] Poor, on the other hand, did not refer to individuals who had the least amount of wealth but to those who could not "maintain their inherited status due to circumstances that befell them and their families."[67] Thus, individuals whom we would consider destitute were not considered poor so long as they maintained their inherited standing.

Finally, first-century people viewed compliments as a positive challenge to one's honor (see pages 44–47). A compliment appeared as an assertion that the complimented person was progressing in the acquisition of good beyond the rate of his or her peers. The person who

65. Malina, *The New Testament World*, 91.
66. Esler, *Community and Gospel*, 197.
67. Malina, *New Testament World*, 100.

paid the compliment would have been saying, in effect, "You have gathered an excess of a certain value (at my expense)." The complimented person would therefore reply that the perception of an excessive accumulation was actually mistaken. Recipients, therefore, regularly denied compliments. Similarly, expressions of thanks were uncommon. To say, "Thank you," could be viewed as an admission that one had received undue good(s). Moreover, an expression of thanks would signal an end to an on-going relationship. Relationships were regularly maintained by the exchange of goods in a balanced fashion (for a relationship among equals) or in an unbalanced way (for a patron-client relation, see pages 47–49). An expression of thanks in such a situation was an indication of an inability to reciprocate; it was an admission that continued relations would result in a dishonorable accumulation of good in the absence of adequate means for repayment.

Honor/Shame

One of the pervasive characteristics of the first-century circum-Mediterranean culture was its placing high value on honor and its correlate, shame. Honor is the public esteem of an individual or group by the general population. Shame is not the exact opposite of honor. Shame actually has two distinct aspects, one related to the male in honor/shame societies and one related to the female. Male shame is considered a negative value and is usually used as a verb, "to be shamed." To be shamed is to have one's honor stripped away, as the result of failure to meet the expectations (moral or otherwise) of the society. Female shame, however, is a positive value. On occasion we still use this meaning in English when we ask, for example, "Have you no shame?" The sense here is that shame is a preventive motivator, one that keeps individuals from acting in culturally unacceptable ways.

Honor was valued in the first-century circum-Mediterranean culture as money is in ours. Yet honor is not identical to wealth. It resided in the family, and families could be honorable without great accumulation of financial wealth.[68] This explains a number of features in the New

---

68. Perhaps one fitting analogy is the distinction expressed in the term "new money" versus "old money." New money is something that comes upon an individual suddenly. He or she now has plenty of money but may lack the "culture" that comes from being raised in a family with a long history of affluence. Someone with "new money" may have more financial wealth than someone with "old money," but the person with "old

Testament which otherwise seem odd to our ears. For example, the parable of the unjust steward (Luke 16:1–9) demonstrates the expendability of mere money in order to gain honor. According to Malina,

> Any concern people show for the acquisition of goods derives from the purpose of gaining honor through generously disposing of what one has acquired among equals or socially useful lower-status clients. In other words, honor is acquired through beneficence, not through the fact of possession and/or the keeping of what one has acquired. Thus money, goods, and any sort of wealth are really a means to honor, and any other use of wealth is considered foolish. The acquisitive and grasping rich are greedy fools![69]

Like all other good, honor was considered to be limited. Honor/shame manifests itself largely in what have been called honor/shame games. In such games, male vies with male for increased honor at the expense of the other. In our culture, because we consider good to be unlimited, we can approach one another "in good faith." This approach expects that the other party is looking out for common interests rather than trying to gain advantage at the expense of the other. In honor/shame driven societies, however, such "good faith" is only expected from members of one's own kinship group. It is assumed, therefore, that any outsider is acting dishonorably until proven otherwise. This is akin to what we might call a presumption of guilt rather than of innocence. The only place where the male was free from the constant honor games was within his own household. Even within a small village, there was a constant competition for honor among villagers. In order to facilitate normal relations between these neighbors, a system of balanced reciprocity was practiced. In this system, exchanges between individuals were kept to a minimum and carefully balanced in such a way that one was always able to quickly repay any receipt. For example, individuals

---

money" may still look down on the one with "new money" because he or she does not belong to the same social class.

69. Malina, *New Testament World*, 37–38. Philip Francis Esler takes a slightly different perspective on the use of wealth in the first century. He says, "The whole point of acts of generosity in this culture was to establish reciprocal relations which could be cashed in at a later date. A classic example of this outlook is found in the policy of the dishonest steward in Lk 16.3–7. Of course, it only made sense to be generous to those who were in a position to do you a favour in return . . . ." (Esler, *Community and Gospel*, 194). Thus, he discusses wealth here without recourse to an honor component.

would be careful to invite to a banquet only those persons who would be able to return the generosity in kind, as some of Jesus' parables suggest.[70] Generalized reciprocity contrasts with this balanced reciprocity. Generalized reciprocity, which was practiced within kinship groups, consisted of liberal generosity with no expectation of repayment. Members worked for the common good without fear of honor games. But outside the kinship group, the need for balanced exchanges led to constant monitoring of relations and an incessant concern for honor as played out in the honor games.

An understanding of honor games may help to explain the sudden shifts in loyalty expressed in certain situations in Acts, such as the scene of Paul and Barnabas in Lystra (Acts 14:8–20). There, Paul and Barnabas would have initially been received with much distrust. Expressions of this distrust would have been perceived as challenges to Paul and Barnabas's honor. When they successfully met this challenge by healing the lame man, the priest of Zeus and the people of Lystra issued a positive challenge by claiming Paul and Barnabas were gods. When the two declined this honor, the citizens of Lystra would have perceived a reciprocal challenge to their own honor. The only honorable response would be to retaliate against Paul and Barnabas. Thus, the entire exchange was predicated upon challenge and response, not upon irrational attributions of divinity and emotional responses.

One of the more telling examples of honor-seeking in the first century is the building of public works as a means of garnering public praise and honor. The Greek word used to express the motivation for such philanthropy is φιλοτιμέομαι, literally "I love honor."[71] According to Moulton and Milligan, this word occurs frequently in inscriptions as part of the honor bestowed upon the donors who financed public works.[72] The word can be translated, "have as one's ambition."[73] This translation does capture some of the pervasive motivational aspects that drove the funding of public works. Yet it masks the nature of that motivation. In our culture, ambition is usually toward increased wealth

---

70. Jesus, of course, challenged this notion of balanced reciprocity by teaching that even the destitute should be invited to banquet (Luke 14:16–24). Cf. Esler, *Community and Gospel*, 194.

71. cf. Moxnes, "Patron-Client Relations," 250.

72. Moulton and Milligan, φιλοτιμέομαι, 672.

73. "φιλοτιμέομαι," BDAG, 1059. Cf. "φιλοτιμέομαι," LSJ, 865.

or power, not honor. When the word is translated using "ambition," the object of the verb becomes the motivation for the ambition. For example, if the phrase, φιλοτιμέομαι οἰκοδομεῖν, were translated, "I make it my ambition to build," the act of building is what is desired. A better translation would be, "I seek honor by building." In this case, honor is clearly the desired good, while building is merely the means for attaining that good. This translation, then, correctly emphasizes honor as a fundamental value in first-century circum-Mediterranean culture.[74]

Patron/Client Relations

Honor games could only be played among persons of equal social standing. Among individuals with dissimilar social positions, a different system operated in interpersonal interactions. Interactions between persons of unequal standing were usually characterized by patronage. Patronage is a system where a person higher on the social scale (the patron) serves as a benefactor for someone lower on the scale (the client) in exchange for certain things the client has to offer. We have already seen an example of how this happens when we were looking at honor, namely the pursuit of honor by financing public works. In this case, the patron donates financial resources in exchange for honor granted by the clients, the general public. Moxnes says of patronage,

> Patron-client relations are social relationships between individuals based on a strong element of inequality and difference in power. The basic structure of the relationship is an exchange of different and very unequal resources. A patron has social,

---

74. It should be emphasized that primitive Christianity stood in dialectical relationship with the dominant, circum-Mediterranean culture. Much of its value-system was taken over from the dominant culture, yet specific values could be re-interpreted, not merely accepted or rejected outright. For example, there is evidence to suggest that the primitive churches retained honor as a primary value but perceived the source of that honor as emanating from a different place. Gal 1:10 (Ἄρτι γὰρ ἀνθρώπους πείθω ἢ τὸν θεόν; ἢ ζητῶ ἀνθρώποις ἀρέσκειν; εἰ ἔτι ἀνθρώποις ἤρεσκον, Χριστοῦ δοῦλος οὐκ ἂν ἤμην.), for example, expresses a lack of concern for what other men might think. Romans 12:10b (τῇ τιμῇ ἀλλήλους προηγούμενοι) is variously understood but should probably be translated, "regarding the giving of honor, outdo each other." (Cf. προηγέομαι, BDAG, 869.) Likewise, 1 Thess 4:11 (καὶ φιλοτιμεῖσθαι ἡσυχάζειν καὶ πράσσειν τὰ ἴδια καὶ ἐργάζεσθαι ταῖς [ἰδίαις] χερσὶν ὑμῶν, καθὼς ὑμῖν παρηγγείλαμεν) speaks in terms of φιλοτιμία, but finds honor in "being quiet and doing your own things and working with your own hands," not in incessant competition with others or in paying others to complete impressive building projects.

economic, and political resources that are needed by a client. In return, a client can give expressions of loyalty and honor that are useful for the patron.[75]

The system of patronage is based on a paradox. On the one hand, patronage required and perpetuated a disparity between patron and client. Today we would call this an exploitive system. On the other hand, the system required a high degree of personal interaction. It relied on friendly relations and was entered into voluntarily, at least ostensibly. There was, in fact, an implied mutuality between the patron, who offered material benefit, and the client, who offered intangible, social benefit. Similarly, there was a tension within the system because potential patrons often competed with each other for public office. Such individuals had to meet definite expectations both in order to attain and retain public office. The system, therefore, was only possible in a context where individuals had a strong sense of their personal place in society and acceptance of that place. The first-century circum-Mediterranean culture, as a strong group/low grid society, afforded just such a context.

One form of patronage common in the first century was brokerage. In this form, clients did not have direct access to patrons but had to rely on a middleman, the broker. The broker functioned as a conduit connecting the central authority with the periphery via personal relations. Brokers acted as patrons to those under them but as clients to those over them. Thus, society became stratified. Individuals actively sought potential patrons and clients and regularly pursued better connections with well-placed brokers. Today we might call such activity, "networking."

Such was the ubiquitous patronage system of the first century. Moxnes rightly observes, however, that Luke favors a transformation of the patronage system.[76] Luke does not reject patronage outright but sees the system as modified in the church. For example, the apostles in Acts may be viewed as brokers within a patron-client relationship between God the Father (patron) and the church. The apostles, as patrons, shared Jesus' authority. Yet they were not to behave like the leaders of the surrounding culture. Luke, then, accepts the leadership structures of his day but transforms the role of those leaders. No longer were leaders

---

75. Moxnes, "Patron-Client Relations," 242.
76. Ibid., 267.

to act in their own interests or to receive honor for their benefaction; rather, they were to use their positions in service to others.

Dyadic Personality

Dyadic personality is perhaps the most difficult feature of circum-Mediterranean culture for the contemporary Western mind to grasp. Individuals raised in the United States, to cite an extreme example, are socialized into acute individualism. It is difficult for such individuals to believe the assertion that this type of individualism is unique among the world's cultures.[77] Instead, they are taught that the ideal person is one who stands alone, who knows who he is, who needs no one; anything else is viewed as immaturity. Yet most cultures, including the first-century circum-Mediterranean culture, value dyadic personality over individualism.

The dyadic person defines him- or herself only in relation to the other: "I am who you say I am."[78] This should not be confused with a lack of self-consciousness. A simple examination of volitional statements in the first-person singular should dispel such a misconception, since awareness of one's own desires surely constitutes at least an incipient self-consciousness.[79] Rather than a lack of self-consciousness, dyadic personality entails a devaluation of self-estimation in favor of other-estimation. In other words, though a dyadic person is aware of his or her own opinion of him- or herself, that opinion is valued less than the opinions of others. More than that, however, the opinion of others is allowed to affect one's self-image, so that the dyadic person's own opinions become inextricably entwined with the opinions of his or her significant dyadic partners. Therefore, people in the first century would have been constantly seeking the perspective of those around them to complement their self-understanding. As John J. Pilch points out, first-century individuals only knew they were ill when those around them said so.[80]

---

77. Malina and Neyrey, "First-Century Personality," 72.

78. This formulation brings to mind Buber's classical work, *I and Thou*. Buber distinguishes between subject-object and subject-subject relations. The latter may be compared with dyadic personalities.

79. θέλω, for example, occurs in the first person singular 43 times in the NT.

80. Pilch, "Sickness and Healing," 195.

Yet there is another component to the dyadic personality, related to what we earlier described as strong group. This factor is perhaps even more important for understanding the first-century culture. We have said that the first-century circum-Mediterranean culture emphasized the groups to which individuals belonged. In turn, these individuals found their identity in these groups. To say that an individual belongs to a particular group is to know that individual, since the group defines the individual. This is similar, of course, to what we today regard as stereotyping. Yet there is one crucial difference: to the extent that individuals regarded themselves as a members of the stereotyped group, they believed themselves to actually possess those qualities attributed to the group. They strived to live up to the expectations in every respect.

Thus, to know someone's group (or groups) was to know everything of relevance about that person. Questions regarding individual attitudes, thoughts, or motivations were simply viewed as irrelevant. According to Bruce J. Malina and Jerome H. Neyrey, "Modern questions of 'consciousness' (Did Jesus know he was God?) make no sense in terms of dyadic personalities, who depend on others to tell them who they are, what is expected of them, and where they fit."[81] An individual, then, would be personally aware of his or her own distinctive internal attributes, but these would have held little interest for others and would not have been allowed to supercede group consciousness. Evidence for this perspective is readily available by examining the type of material included in ancient biographies of prominent persons. Invariably there is no interest in the "psychological" make-up of these individuals.[82] Similarly, the saying, τίς γὰρ οἶδεν ἀνθρώπων τὰ τοῦ ἀνθρώπου εἰ μὴ τὸ πνεῦμα τοῦ ἀνθρώπου τὸ ἐν αὐτῷ; (1 Cor 2:11a) reflects the conception that a person's inner psychological workings are unimportant for understanding that person. Again, this does not reflect a lack of self-consciousness, but a heightened concern for group consciousness.

To summarize, the dominant characteristics of first-century culture relevant to the study of leadership are strong group/low grid, perception of limited good, honor/shame, patron/client relations, and dyadic personality. We shall discuss the relation between culture and

---

81. Malina and Neyrey, "First-Century Personality," 73.
82. Malina, *New Testament World*, 67.

leadership presently, but first we must return to the two general sociological approaches to our topic.

Models of First Century Religious Leadership

As noted above, two meta-theories continue to enjoy a wide following among sociologists: the structural-functionalist and the conflict models.[83] We have seen that the structural-functionalist view regards societies as comprising conservative structures whose inherent forces tend to work toward maintenance of the status quo. Social institutions remain relatively stable, and individuals empowered with the ability to shape culture operate from preservationistic motives. Change is the result of external forces, which slowly overcome the inertia of existing institutions. The conflict model, on the other hand, perceives cultures in a constant state of flux as interested parties vie for control through the exercise of various forms of power. Written histories are viewed with skepticism because, it is argued, histories remain extant only when they reflect the perspectives of the dominant or victorious party. The stories of the weak and powerless remain largely unrecorded, while the cleansed records of the empowered party mask the true picture of class conflict.

The perdurability of the circum-Mediterranean culture of antiquity suggests that a structural-functionalist model would be more adequate for describing it.[84] Yet the existence of resistance movements in first-century Palestine, such as those sustained by the Zealots, seems to support a conflict model. A discussion of the relative merits of the two meta-models is beyond the scope of the present study. It may be observed simply that both models offer the possibility for genuine insights into the first-century cultural milieu. Insights from the two models are dissimilar but not mutually exclusive. Therefore, I will propose two definitions of leadership, one from the perspective of each meta-model. From these definitions I will develop heuristic models for use in examining leadership in the first-century world.

---

83. Oakman, "The Countryside in Luke-Acts," 153. Cf. Webber, "Power," 1–73.
84. See note 2, page 18.

Definitions of Leadership

The first definition exhibits traits of the conflict model. On this view, leadership is the exertion of social power by an individual or group (i.e., leader) in such a way that a target group (i.e., followers) modifies behavior or belief in conformity with the intentions of the leader. Notice here the emphasis on the leader as an agent of change. The mechanism of such change is viewed as a function of social power, which can take several forms ranging from rhetoric to physical violence. Leadership is defined in terms of end result, rather than status or position; and in this sense the definition is phenomenological. We may call this type of leader an innovator-leader.

Alternatively, one might define leadership based on a structural-functionalist perspective: Leadership is the quality inhering in any individual (leader) who represents his or her group (followers) to outsiders, who makes administrative decisions on behalf of his or her group, or who is otherwise responsible for maintaining the well-being of a group. This definition emphasizes the qualities of a leader, not the accomplishments. It maintains an element of functionality—what the leader does—but it also incorporates an element of status. An individual can be a leader on this definition by virtue of birth or office, apart from any performance criteria. Leaders are valued for their position and their ability to sustain their group in its current state. Such leaders may be termed manager-leaders.

Models of Leadership[85]

As interesting as is the debate over whether a structural-functionalist or conflict model more adequately portrays social institutions, our present concern is the understanding of leadership for first-century individuals. Therefore, we must apply the definitions of leadership as heuristic devices for the examination of the various cultural characteristics noted above. The definitions will alert us to the presence and meaning of lead-

---

85. Rodney Stark issues an insightful challenge with regard to adequate theoretical models. He says, "If a model is to provide more than *classification*, if it proposes to *explain*, then the model must include not simply concepts, but propositions. The difference here is that between a parts catalog and a working diagram of an engine. That is, a model must include a fully specified set of interrelations among the parts" (Stark, *The Rise of Christianity*, 26, emphasis original). Whether the present models satisfy Stark's criterion for a model must be left for the reader to judge.

ership qualities or functions, but they will remain susceptible to refinement or even replacement by more adequate models.

When probing the strong group/low grid aspect of the first century from the perspective of a structural-functionalist definition of leadership, it becomes clear that persons in positions of leadership would have acted to maintain the status quo. This is true, not only because a central feature of the strong group/low grid quadrant is acquisition maintenance, but also because individuals in this quadrant tend to accept their lot in life so long as their position does not worsen. It falls to leaders, then, to assure that such worsening does not occur. In order to achieve this result, it would have been necessary for leaders to manage the means of maintenance with care. As noted above, the strong group/low grid quadrant focuses on means (strong group), not ends (grid). Therefore, first-century leaders would likely have been concerned with forms and procedures that perpetuate their group's status. Moreover, the strong group/low grid quadrant is marked by concern for boundaries and boundary-crossing rites. For this reason, leaders in this quadrant would have maintained tight control of the group's rites and ceremonies.

Considered from a structural-functionalist viewpoint, it becomes apparent that individuals who have a perception of limited good would—publicly at least—express reluctance to take on any leadership role that would draw attention to themselves, since this would expose them to charges of greed.[86] Those who do take on leadership roles would be expected to initiate and negotiate offers of balanced reciprocity. The leader would be responsible to ensure that such exchanges maintain the welfare of the group, with respect to both the goods actually exchanged and the perception of the group by outsiders.

The leader would also be responsible for the honor of the group. The leader would represent the group to outsiders and would therefore have to be conscious of the group image as portrayed to those outside.

---

86. It may be illustrative at this point to consider the statement in 1 Timothy that anyone who aspires to the office of bishop has a noble goal (1 Tim 3:1). There are two possible ways to interpret this assertion in light of our present discussion. On the one hand, it could be considered that the author was pressing for necessary leaders, providing an argument for such leadership despite cultural pressures to the contrary. Perhaps a better understanding, however, is that the view expresses a perspective from a changed circumstance, namely a successful raising of the grid. In other words, it is possible that the statement reflects a situation in which the grid has been raised, i.e., a strong group/high grid situation.

Therefore, the leader would have to be effective at playing honor "games." He would be adept at recognizing and responding to honor challenges, as well as at issuing and enforcing honor challenges.[87] Moreover, the leader would be responsible to guard the shame of the group and thus would closely monitor the activities of his followers. The leader would be responsible to see that group members' actions do not bring shame to the group.

Often the first-century leader's concern for group honor would have resulted in utilization of the patronage system. Thus, the effective leader would have required the skills to identify and assess the benefit of potential patrons and clients, as well as to connect patrons and clients as a broker. Working within the prevailing system, success would have been defined in incremental terms; change would have been slow and difficult to measure. Nevertheless, because of the development of patron-broker-client relationships, a stratified hierarchy would have been a natural development within the leadership structures of the early church.

The dyadic personalities of the first century would have placed constraints upon the self-understanding of leaders. Because dyadic personalities look to the group for affirmation, the roles played by such individuals would ordinarily fall within pre-determined, culturally accepted norms. Before an individual takes on a leadership role, the group would have to identify that individual as a leader. Once such identification had taken place, whether on the basis of innate qualities or by virtue of birth or honorable standing, the individual would take on a culturally accepted form of leadership. The first-century leadership role that is most consistent with leadership as we have been describing it is "father."[88] As a father figure, the leader would function as master of

---

87. The use of the masculine pronoun for leader here is justified within the first-century circum-Mediterranean culture, where the male imaged honor and the female was embedded in the honor of the male.

88. In this context, it is interesting to consider the command in Matthew 23:9 to call no man father. The fact that it appears exclusively in the unique Matthean material suggests that the early church maintained an ambivalent attitude toward fatherly leadership within the community. Perhaps there was a tension between the pragmatic need for leaders who functioned in the manner of traditional paternal roles for the preservation of the community, on the one hand, and an anti-paternalistic ideology, on the other. Cf. Bartchy, "Who Should be Called Father?" 135–47, esp. 138–39.

the kinship group, or in the case of the early church, the fictive-kinship group. Like a father, he would represent the group honor to outsiders.

The conflict model of leadership leads to a significantly different picture when examined in light of first-century culture. According to the conflict model, a leader is one who initiates change. In the first-century, strong group/low grid setting, this change is likely to come in the form of a societal reformation. As we have seen, the strong group/low grid quadrant can remain static over a long period of time, but when change comes, it is likely to be in the form of efforts to move up the grid (which we might call, "up-gridding"). Since conflict-model leaders are change agents, therefore, we would expect such leaders in the first-century culture to instigate plans for achieving a high grid state. For this reason, these leaders would be visionaries, ones who see a more desirable future and how to get there.

Because of the perception of limited good in the first century, the leaders' visions would likely have included methods for re-distributing wealth or power. This is the case because first-century people did not think of goods like wealth and power as produced or created, but merely accumulated from a finite stock. In order for a leader's group to increase its store of any good, that good must transfer hands. Inherent in this perspective is the conviction common to individuals in a strong group/low grid society that cultural values are unattainable in the present system. Therefore, a change is necessary in order for the group to receive the desired good. Alternatively, leaders might re-define ultimate good. Rather than struggle with the existing power structures to gain a share of the limited resources, leaders could define *good* in such a way that, while it is still a limited quantity, it is not something in high demand among the wider culture.

Examples of such re-defining of good come from the area of honor/shame. Most fundamentally, honor itself can be re-defined. What it means to be an honorable person can be given a new content. Whereas honor was sought in the wider culture by such means as funding public works projects, in the early church honor now was to be pursued through such means as living quietly and working with one's own hands. In this way, honor is still a valued good, but it is attainable by a different set of behaviors. Another way leaders could change the pursuit of honor was by re-defining kinship. As we have seen, a different logic functioned for those outside the family as compared to those inside.

While generalized reciprocity was practiced for those within the family, balanced reciprocity was the norm for those outside. By re-defining family, leaders could change common practice without changing codes of behavior. In the church, this was accomplished by establishing the members as a fictive kinship group. This explains the use of familial terms, such as ἀδελφός, to address one another.

Innovative leaders in the first century would also have been concerned to reform the patronage system, or more probably to subvert it. They would no longer be interested in the slow changes involved in "working" the patronage system. Success would be viewed instead in terms of rapid, radical change, either by doing away with the patronage system altogether or by seeking to invert the system, exchanging patrons for clients.[89] We might expect the elimination of brokers, who would be viewed as an inefficient vestige of the old order. Even if the complete elimination of brokers were not possible, leaders would attempt to minimize the number of brokers between the center and the periphery. We see just such a position being taken in the New Testament. God the Father is there viewed as the only patron, and he is immediately accessible by all believers through prayer without the need for any broker other than Jesus.[90]

Finally, despite the forward thinking of first-century innovative leaders, they would still have been subject to the strictures of dyadic personalities. Just like other first-century individuals, they would have looked to others for affirmation of their identity and role within their group. They would have, similarly, required a well-known exemplary model for the type of leadership they were to exert. In Palestine, such a model was readily available in the traditional role of prophet.[91] Prophets, of course, represented a long-standing tradition within Judaism. Jewish prophets portray many of the attributes of the innovative leader that we

---

89. Perhaps the behavior of Barnabas as described in Acts exhibits such an inversion of the patronage system. By symbolically placing the proceeds of his property sale (Acts 4:36–37) at the feet of the apostles, he revokes the rights of a patron.

90. See 1 Tim 2:5. Cf. Moxnes, "Patron-Client Relations." 257–60. Moxnes argues that the apostles also were portrayed as brokers in Acts (260–61).

91. Another role for this type of leader culturally within first-century Palestine might be "Zealot." Like prophets, Zealots sought a reformation—or revolution—of society. The role of prophet as leader is preferable here because (1) it had a longer history within the culture, (2) it lacks the overtones of violence associated with the Zealots, and (3) prophets are explicitly mentioned in the NT as participants in the early church.

have discussed: they were reformers who called people to change and who envisioned a more desirable future. In addition to these qualities, prophets also claimed direct communication with God and exhibited no concern for the status of people. We should expect, then, that first-century innovator-leaders would display these same characteristics. Table 2.2 shows the central features of the two kinds of leaders we have been discussing:

Table 2.2: Modeling Leadership in First-Century Circum-Mediterranean Culture

	Structural-Functionalist Model	Conflict Model
Strong Group/ Low Grid	• Maintain status/wealth • Exemplify contentment • Control means/forms	• Reform society • Visionary—Establish means for attaining values • Scheme for "up-gridding"
Limited Good	• Oversee balanced reciprocity • Accept leadership reluctantly	• Re-distribute wealth • Re-define ultimate good
Honor/ Shame	• Conscious of image • Effective at "games" • Control of followers	• Re-define "honorable" • Re-define kinship
Patronage	• Effective "networking" • Success = incremental improvement • Hierarchy a natural development	• Subvert patronage system • Success = rapid, radical change • Eliminate brokers—God the only patron
Dyadic Personality	• Need role affirmation • Culturally accepted role: "Father" • Master of kinship group • Represent group honor to outsiders	• Need role affirmation • Culturally accepted role: "Prophet" • Direct communication with God • No concern for persons
	Rubric: Manager-Leader	Rubric: Innovator-Leader

From this presentation, we might expect that there will be two competing types of leadership in Acts. At first sight, this assertion may appear to be merely the result of having started with two definitions of leader. Yet the expectation gains solid support from the fact that there were clearly defined cultural roles (i.e., father and prophet), which correspond to the two types of leadership we have described. If there were no culturally viable avenues for the exertion of one of the types of leadership, we should have to reject that type for the culture under investigation. Yet in the first-century Jewish culture, at least, there were established archetypes for the leadership roles we have described. The broader circum-Mediterranean culture, of course, lacked the prophetic leadership model.[92] It may well be the case that leadership roles had to be modified within the church in response to the changed cultural context as it moved from a Jewish to a Gentile environment. Whereas church leaders within a Jewish context could lead according to either a prophetic (conflict) model or fatherly (structural-functionalist) model, leaders arising from a strictly Gentile environment might have been limited by their socialization to the fatherly model. This would have exerted pressure upon the leadership structures of the church.

It has long been observed that ecclesiastical structures undergo shifts when the church enters a new culture.[93] The causes and mechanism of these changes, however, have not been adequately explored. I venture to hypothesize that one common cause of changing structures is the differences in the forms of leadership extant in the new culture. On this view, such changes as the development of hierarchical offices within the church may not simply be the inevitable result of the passage of time but of a new cultural milieu. If this is the case, to assess the publication dates of early Christian documents based on the extent of their hierarchical tendencies would appear to be ill-advised. It will be necessary to test this hypothesis as we apply the leadership models to the text of Acts throughout the study.

Summation

The goal of the present chapter has been modest. We have aimed at the development of heuristic models of first-century leadership, not at the exposition of a comprehensive theory of leadership. The development

---

92. This is not to say that the Greco-Roman world lacked innovator-leaders. One need only look at the reforms of Augustus for proof. However, as we shall see in the next chapter, the functionaries of Greco-Roman religions are more adequately described as manager-leaders than innovator-leaders.

93. Latourette, *The Thousand Years of Uncertainty*, 131–32. cf. 423.

of models has required us to probe first-century culture via insights culled from general theories of anthropology and sociology, together with research regarding leadership, authority, and power. We have observed that religious leadership structures depend on and correspond to features of their respective religious systems, and we have shown that the cultural traits of strong group/low grid, limited good, honor/shame, patron/client relations, and dyadic personality affected the options for leadership in the first century. From these sociological resources, we have developed two models of leadership, the manager-leader and the innovator-leader. We have asserted that the two models correspond to ideal types in the first century: the father and the prophet. Leaders of the father type exhibited concern for group honor by preserving the group's status through control of reciprocal exchanges with outsiders, direction of followers, and development of patron/client opportunities. Leaders of the prophet type, in contrast, operated as change agents by working for new systems of wealth-distribution, new definitions of honor and kinship, and new relationships between people as they interact with each other and God.

It should be emphasized that models of leadership remain merely heuristic. The models presented in this chapter have proved valuable for postulating an explanation of the leadership changes the church would have undergone as it moved from a Jewish to a Gentile context and for delving deeper into the portrayal of leadership in Acts. Yet their validity will continue to be tested in subsequent chapters. In the next chapter, we will use the models to explore the leadership structures of Greco-Roman religions. It will be especially important to test the hypothesis that the Greco-Roman world lacked a counterpart to the Jewish prophet. Later we will examine leadership in Second Temple Judaism. Again, the leadership models developed here will serve as a platform from which to explore the internal operations of leadership structures. It is expected that this process will lead to further refinement of the models themselves. The refined models, then, will provide the basis for a more detailed examination of the diffusion of ecclesiastical authority in Acts.

3

Authority in Greco-Roman Religions

THE PREVIOUS CHAPTER DEVELOPED THEORETICAL MODELS FOR EVALUating leadership and authority within the first-century world of the New Testament. As we continue our exploration of ecclesiastical authority in Acts, it is important to recall that the primitive Christian church grew within a larger religious context. It is necessary, therefore, to investigate authority within the first-century religious environment in order to gain a full understanding of authority in the early church. Simple logic predicts that the church was shaped by influences deriving from its environment; yet it is no simple task to describe those influences and to explain the precise mechanisms of interaction. The goal of the present chapter is to explore one aspect of the religious context, namely, the authority structures of Greco-Roman religions. To that end we shall investigate the major features of the civic religions of Greece and Rome, together with the primary mystery religions.[1] From this foundational research, we shall examine the authority structures of these religious systems in light of the models developed in ch. 2.

The present chapter makes no pretense at being a comprehensive overview of Greco-Roman religions. Instead, focus will be on those aspects that have most bearing on the question of religious authority and that are therefore most relevant to the study of the development of ecclesiastical authority in early Christianity. Other aspects of Greco-Roman religions will be passed over in silence. For example, we will not address astrological, magical, or philosophical aspects of ancient religion despite their prominence as components of the Greco-Roman religious milieu.

---

1. See note 84, below.

Greek Religion

The ancient Greek religion sustained a long history. It received its classical formulation in the poetic works of Homer and Hesiod in the eighth and early seventh centuries BCE. Their works, as we shall see, continued to offer inspiration for many centuries. Similarly, the works of Plutarch and Pausanias bear testament to the enduring significance of traditional Greek religion well into the early centuries of the Common Era. With this background in mind, we turn now to an examination of the predominant features of Greek religion.

Features of Greek Religion

Polytheism

The religion of the ancient Greeks was polytheistic with a wide array of gods and goddesses.[2] There were twelve primary deities known as the Olympians: Zeus, Hera, Poseidon, Demeter, Apollo, Artemis, Ares, Aphrodite, Hermes, Athene, Hephaestus, and Hestia. In addition to the Olympians, there were also other deities, including Chronos, said to be the father of Zeus. Moreover, there were demi-gods or heroes, such as Hercules and Asclepius, as well as chthonic (underworldly) gods. This diversity of deities can lead to the impression of great complexity within the Greek religious system, yet the complexity is magnified even further by the fact that each deity could be worshipped under a different cult name based on his or her attributes. For example, Dio Chrysostom lists and explains the following names for Zeus:

> For he alone of the gods is entitled 'Father and King', 'Protector of Cities', 'God of Friendship', and 'God of Comradeship', and also 'Protector of Suppliants', and 'God of Hospitality', 'Giver of Increase', and has countless other titles, all indicative of goodness: he is addressed as 'King' because of his dominion and

---

2. Cf. Price, *Religions of the Ancient Greeks*, 67. Price writes, "'Polytheism', in contrast to Christianity or Islam, is often seen as a tolerant and open religious system. It is associated with amateur priests, who lacked authority, and with an absence of dogma, orthodoxy and heresy. Already having many gods, it is attributed the capacity to accommodate even more at any time. This romantic view of Greek religious liberalism has little to commend it. The absence of dogmas did not entail that anything was permitted, nor was the pluralism of gods open-ended. In fact the terms 'polytheism' and monotheism' are unsatisfactory, and the issue of tolerance/intolerance is anachronistic. As a matter of state policy, religious toleration does not predate the eighteenth century."

power; as 'Father,' I think, on account of his solicitude for us and his kindness: as 'Protector of Cities' in that he upholds the law and the common weal; as 'Guardian of the Race' on account of the tie of kinship which unites gods and men; as 'God of Friendship' and 'God of Comradeship' because he brings all men together and wills that they be friends of one another and never enemy or foe; as 'Protector of Suppliants' since he inclines his ear and is gracious to men when they pray; as 'God of Refuge' because he gives refuge from evils; as 'God of Hospitality' because we should not be unmindful even of strangers, nor regard any human being as an alien; as 'Giver of Wealth and Increase' since he is the cause of all crops and is the giver of wealth and power. (*Dei cogn.*, 75–76 [Cohoon, LCL])[3]

In Greek religion, in contrast to Roman religion, the gods and goddesses were described by highly developed myths. The two poets, Homer and Hesiod, were the primary shapers of these myths. Their writings provided a literary authority for the theology of standard Greek religion. Later writers could quote Homer or Hesiod to substantiate their claims regarding the attributes of the gods and goddesses. For example, Pausanias argues by quoting Homer:

> That Asclepius was considered a god from the first, and did not receive the title only in course of time, I infer from several signs, including the evidence of Homer, who makes Agamemnon say about Machaon:—
>
> "Talthybius, with all speed go summon me hither Machaon, Mortal son of Asclepius."
>
> As who should say, "human son of a god."
> (*Descr.* 2.26.10 [Jones, LCL])[4]

Similarly, Plato discusses the "begging priests and soothsayers" (*Resp.* 2.364B [Shorey, LCL]) who appeal to the poets:

> And for all these sayings they cite the poets as witnesses, with regard to the ease and plentifulness of vice, quoting:

---

3. The primary sources cited in this chapter were originally drawn to my attention by the source books noted in the bibliography. Except where indicated, I have consulted or translated from the standard texts.

4. Notice the mode of argumentation, akin to what we would call exegesis.

> Evil-doing in plenty a man shall find for the seeking;
> Smooth is the way and it lies near at hand and is easy to enter;

But on the pathway of virtue the gods put sweat from the first step, and a certain long and uphill road. And others cite Homer as a witness to the beguiling of gods by men, since he too said:

> The gods themselves are moved by prayers,
> And men by sacrifice and soothing vows,
> And incense and libation turn their wills
> Praying, whene'er they have sinned and made transgression. (*Resp.* 2.364C–E [Shorey, LCL])

In addition to gods, Homer and Hesiod also referred to heroes, or demi-gods. The best-known hero, of course, was Heracles (=Hercules). Shrines to Heracles were common throughout Greece. Pausanias describes one such shrine at Sikyon, where Heracles received sacrifices conducted according to the rite due a god as well as that due a hero (*Descr.* 2.10.1).

Certain historical persons became honored as heroes, among whom Asclepius was probably the most well known. Although some uncertainty remains regarding the historical Asclepius, it seems likely that he was an effective, well-trained physician. Over time, Asclepius came to be thought of as a god of healing; temples were built, priesthoods were established, and cult practices were developed. Individuals seeking healing would come to a temple, present their needs to the temple personnel, and sleep over night in the presence of the cult image, in a process known as incubation. Many records of healings are extant in the form of inscriptions detailing the nature of the ailment and the occasion of the miraculous healing. For example, inscriptions from Epidaurus describe healings from an abnormal pregnancy, paralysis, blindness, dumbness, scars, and gallstones.[5] Even more detailed information about the cult of Asclepius comes from the writings of the hypochondriac, Aelius Aristides.[6] The following excerpt is especially illuminating:

---

5. Dittenberger, *Sylloge*, 3:1168–69. Cited in Grant, *Hellenistic Religions*, 56–58.

6. Cf. Festugière, *Personal Religion*, 85–104. Festugière captures some of the religious spirit of the age: "Finally, when dealing with the ancients, we must always keep in mind an important difference between the ancient and the modern religious psychology. Since we have a far higher concept of the Divinity, the notion of habitual communication between God and man seems to us unlikely. We live, generally, in a rationalist atmosphere, and when we are in need of help we usually rely on human means. In this

What happened to me was as follows: I dreamed that I stood in the entrance to the sanctuary, where also some other people were gathered, as at the time of the sacrifice for purification; they wore white garments and were otherwise festively garbed. Then I spoke about the god and named him, among other things, Distributor of Destiny, since he assigns to men their fate. The expression came to me out of my own personal experience. Then I told about the potion of wormwood, which had somehow been revealed [to me]. The revelation was unquestionable, just as in a thousand other instances the epiphany of the god was felt with absolute certainty. You have a sense of contact with him, and are aware of his arrival in a state of mind intermediate between sleep and waking; you try to look up and are afraid to, lest before you see him he shall have vanished; you sharpen your ears and listen, half in dream and half awake; your hair stands up, tears of joy roll down, a proud kind of modesty fills your breast. How can anyone really describe this experience in words? If one belongs to the initiated, he will know about it and recognize it. . . . Since the dreams agreed, we applied the remedy and I drank more of it than anyone had ever drunk before, and on the following day, at the god's direction, an equal quantity. The relief it brought me and the good it did me simply cannot be described.[7]

Festivals

Many diverse religious festivals were held throughout Greece. The most well known today, of course, is the festival of Zeus at Olympia. Then, as now, the Olympic games were held quadrennially, and truces were maintained. Yet there were many more Greek religious festivals. For example, we know of festivals at Patrae in Achaia and on the island of Myconos. Pausanias describes the festival at Patrae as follows:

> Every year too the people of Patrae celebrate the festival Laphria in honour of their Artemis, and at it they employ a method of sacrifice peculiar to the place. Round the altar in a circle they set up logs of wood still green, each of them sixteen cubits long. On

---

respect, ancient man is much closer than modern man to the divine. To him it seems entirely natural that the gods should mingle with human beings" (Festugière, *Personal Religion*, 103–4).

7. Aelius Aristides, *Sacred Orations* II: 31–32, 35, translated by Grant in *Hellenistic Religions*, 53–54.

the altar within the circle is placed the driest of their wood. Just before the time of the festival they construct a smooth ascent to the altar, piling earth upon the altar steps. The festival begins with a most splendid procession in honour of Artemis, and the maiden officiating as priestess rides last in the procession upon a car yoked to deer. It is, however, not till the next day that the sacrifice is offered, and the festival is not only a state function but also quite a popular general holiday. For the people throw alive upon the altar edible birds and every kind of victim as well; there are wild boars, deer and gazelles; some bring wolf-cubs or bear-cubs, others the full-grown beasts. They also place upon the altar fruit of cultivated trees. (*Descr.* 7.18.11–12 [Jones, LCL])

In Athens there were festivals for women (the Thesmophoria) and in honor of the dead (the Genesia, the Nemesia, and the Anethesteria). The most important of the Athenian festivals, however, was the Panathenaia. As was often the case at Greek religious festivals, games were held as part of the Panathenaia. The Panathenaian competitions included singing, playing musical instruments, foot racing, wrestling, boxing, and horse racing. There still exist some of the large jars that were filled with olive oil and presented to the winners of athletic competitions. Scenes from the victor's sport were glazed on the surface of the jars, so that today we still know for which event a particular jar was awarded. Like other aspects of Athenian religion, oversight of the Panathenaia rested ultimately with the people. As one inscription reads,

> In order that the procession may be equipped and marshalled in the best possible way each year for Athena on behalf of the Athenian people, and that all the other necessary arrangements may be made for the festival as it is being properly celebrated on every occasion for the goddess by the *hieropoioi*, **it is voted by the people, in accordance with the resolution of the council**: when the *hieropoioi* make sacrifices . . . . (Dittenberger, *Sylloge*, 1:271)[8]

Oracles

One of the well-known features of Greek religion is the interest in oracles. Oracles were indigenous to Greece, though the Romans later came to consult them. The best-known oracle, of course, was the oracle

---

8. Translated by Rice and Stambaugh in *Sources*, 119 (my emphasis).

of Apollo at Delphi. It was thought that the oracle covered a fissure in the ground known as the navel of the earth, though excavations at the site reveal that no such rift ever existed there.[9] Nevertheless, this fissure was said to emit a gas or steam, which carried the communications of Apollo. A tripod was build over the place where the fissure was purported to be, and a virgin known as the Pythia would mount the tripod and receive the communications in a trance. All manner of questions were brought to the oracle, ranging from mundane questions from individuals, such as questions regarding travel plans or interpersonal relations, to weighty matters of state, such as whether to wage war or sign treaties.[10] When a question was posed to the oracle, at the appointed time the Pythia would take her place on the tripod. Great care was taken to ensure that all sacrificial procedures were in order and that the Pythia was in the right frame of mind, for physical harm could befall her otherwise (Plutarch, *Def. orac.* 50–51; *Mor.* 437D and 438A–D). After the entranced Pythia received the communication, she would report to an assistant, known as τόν προφήτην (Plutarch, *Def. orac.* 51; *Mor.* 438B), who would translate the message. In the earlier centuries, the response was given in verse, but later the response was in prose. In *De defectu oraculorum* (*Mor.* 409E–438E), Plutarch gives an extended—one might even say convoluted—treatment of the cause of this change, as well as of why the oracle was less active in his own day than it had been in the past. Interestingly, Plutarch himself was a priest for the oracle at Delphi.

While Delphi was the most famous oracle, there were other oracles, as well, including that of Trophonius. Pausanias, the travel guide writer, tells of his first-hand experiences at this oracle (*Descr.* 9.39.5–14). According to Pausanias, the process for making an inquiry of the oracle at Trophonius was quite involved. It began with a lengthy period of

---

9. Martin, *Hellenistic Religions*, 47. Martin says, ". . . archaeological and geological investigations have uncovered no trace of a chasm at Delphi . . . ." However, Klauck refers to "the fact that sites of oracles frequently go back to ancient earth cults and are located at caves, pits or crevices in the earth" and describes steps "ending on the bare earth." He goes on to say, "In the other, larger section of the *adyton*, stood the *omphalos*, a conical stone portraying Delphi's claim to be the navel of the world, under a baldachin" (Klauck, *Religious Context of Early Christianity*, 185–86;). Cf. also Ferguson, *Greek and Roman Religion*, 120.

10. For example, see Xenophon, *Anab.* 3.1.5–7 and Herodotus, *Hist.* 1.53, respectively.

purification during which time he was resident on the oracle grounds. Then he was taken by night into the oracular shrine, where he was required to climb down into a pit, which had a narrow opening toward the bottom. He had to work his way, feet first, into the opening, but once he got his knees in, the rest of his body was drawn quickly through the opening. Pausanias compares the experience to being swept away by a great river. Once through the opening, Pausanias received the oracular response. He then returned through the same opening by which he had entered, and he was led to the "chair of Memory" (*Descr.* 9.39.13 [Jones, LCL]) where the priests questioned him about his experience. Finally he was returned to his relatives, but he was emotionally and physically exhausted and had to be carried away to rest.

We also have the record of an oracle in the second century CE associated with a god called Glycon and his spokesperson, Alexander of Abonuteichos. Our most extensive literary source for this oracle, *Alexander the False Prophet* by Lucian, provides a skeptical account of its origin (Lucian *Alex.*, esp. 12–24). According to Lucian, Alexander had acquired a large, tame snake during his youthful journeys. When he returned home, he placed a baby snake inside a hollowed goose egg, which he hid in the mud inside the foundations of a new temple construction. Then, he raised a big commotion in the marketplace by wildly reciting gibberish with occasional references to a revelation from a god. He led a crowd to the new temple and "discovered" the egg and the baby snake. The next day he invited people to a darkened room in his house to see the divine snake. He produced the full-grown, tame snake, but he hid the snake's head under his arm and arranged a model of a human head to produce the illusion that it belonged to the snake. The model head was equipped with threads whereby its mouth could be made to open and close. He had assistants to operate the mouth and provide the voice. Thus, Alexander had created a talking oracle for his god, which he called Glycon. For a small fee, persons could query the oracle. They would bring their questions in a sealed envelope and leave it with Alexander to await the god's response. Alexander would unseal the envelope, read the question, write a fitting response, and reseal the envelope in such a way that it appeared not to have been opened. He would then present the sealed envelope and the reply to the inquirer. In this way Alexander sustained a lucrative income and even employed a significant number of assistants. The cult continued to be active for more than 100 years, well after the death of Alexander.[11]

Authority in Greek Religion[12]

According to Walter Burkert, "Greek religion might almost be called a religion without priests . . . ."[13] This, of course, is an overstatement; for we read frequently in the primary literature of ἱερεῖς. Yet the point is well taken, for priests in the Greek religion were different from our conceptions of what a priest is and does. As Burkert goes on to explain, "There is no priestly caste as a closed group with fixed traditions, education, initiation, and hierarchy . . . ."[14] Instead, priesthoods assumed a wide variety of forms, and the priest was sometimes considered optional. Nevertheless, the variety was not infinite, and certain commonalities can be distinguished.

A convenient place to begin our discussion of these commonalities is with an inscription from the fourth century BCE:

> Resolved by the council and the people, on the motion of Agenor, when Meliton was presiding officer: No stranger is permitted to put in at the sanctuary of Hera; the temple attendant [*neokoros*] is to take care to keep them out. If he does not keep them out, he is to pay a fine of ten drachmas, sanctified to Hera, for each day. The superintendents [*neopoioi*] are to take care to inscribe this decree in front of the doors. (Dittenberger, *Sylloge*, 3:981)[15]

Notice first that the resolution is the product of the council and the people. In other words, the people themselves controlled the religious regulations. The same stricture was true in Athens, as might be expected given its democratic ideals. Robert Garland, in his article on priesthood in ancient Athens, has made the point forcefully. He insists that the Athenian *dêmos* retained control over religious affairs in a manner

---

11. Grant, *Hellenistic Religions*, 95.

12. We are interested here, as throughout this study, in authority as it pertains to persons wielding power in religious matters. Another type of authority, namely written authority, existed to a certain extent in Greek religion: the poetic works of Homer and Hesiod. As noted above, these authors were often cited in theological discussions to validate arguments.

13. Burkert, *Greek Religion*, 95.

14. Ibid.

15. Translated by Rice and Stambaugh, *Sources*, 124.

corresponding to its authority in all other aspects of its community life.[16] The second thing to be pointed out from the above quote is that the day-to-day administration of the sanctuary was not carried out by priests but by functionaries known as the *neokoros* and the *neopoioi*. According to Burkert, there was usually one *neokoros* for each temple and additional overseers including the *hieropoioi*, who were in charge of details relating to sacrifices, and *epimelelai* and *hierotamiai*, appointed by the state to control financial matters.[17] It is not always clear whether these functionaries held life-long appointments or shorter terms. Groups called the *orgeones* also controlled individual sanctuaries. One interesting example is an inscription detailing the lease of the sanctuary of Egretes for a ten year period. The lessee was required to maintain the sanctuary and see that it was open for worshippers. In return, he received the produce of the sanctuary lands.[18]

Priests often held their post for a one-year period. For example, an inscription from Rhodes indicates such a term when it reports the requirement that, "Each year the priest is to report to the council and convey [the treasury] to the incoming priest" (*LSCG*, 85).[19] Other priesthoods were for life, such as the priesthood on the island of Chios (*LSCG*, 77).[20] Still other priests held their post for a single, complete festal cycle.[21] Priesthoods could be received in a variety of ways. They could be purchased or the council could appoint them (*LSCG*, 77 and 85, respectively).[22] Other priesthoods, however, were hereditary and some were elected.[23]

The prerequisites for priesthood were minimal. For example, a person interested in the priesthood of Asclepius at Chalcedon could not have any physical defect and had to have the right to be clothed (i.e., to be a free citizen).[24] While in office, priests and priestesses were required to maintain certain standards of purity. The priestess of Demeter at Cos,

16. Garland, "Priests and Power," esp. 85–87 and 91.
17. Burkert, *Greek Religion*, 95–96.
18. Dittenberger, *Sylloge*, 3:1097, cited in Rice and Stambaugh, *Sources*, 125–26.
19. Translated by Rice and Stambaugh, *Sources*, 127.
20. Cited in Rice and Stambaugh, *Sources*, 129.
21. Burkert, *Greek Religion*, 96.
22. Cited in Rice and Stambaugh, *Sources*, 129 and 127, respectively.
23. Burkert, *Greek Religion*, 96.
24. Dittenberger, *Sylloge*, 3:1009, cited in Grant, *Hellenistic Religions*, 30.

for example, was forbidden to touch a grave, to enter the house where a birth had recently taken place, or to eat carrion.[25] Burkert summarizes these requirements as follows:

> As a common denominator of what is required of a priest there remains the purity, *hagneia*, befitting the sacred ... As for other requirements, the priest should above all be a worthy representative of the community. This means that he must possess full citizenship and also that he must be free from any physical defect. The mutilated and crippled are excluded. Otherwise, in contrast to more responsible positions, it is true that anyone can become a priest.[26]

Priestly duties varied widely. In one case the priest was required to open the temple daily and clean its portico regularly.[27] Elsewhere the priest collected fees, levied fines, directed the work of the *neokoroi*, and prayed over the sacrifices.[28] Other priests participated in festival processions.[29] In general, priests were responsible for the oversight of matters pertaining to sacred observances, but they were not required to possess special knowledge.

There were, however, religious functionaries who did possess special knowledge. They were known as *exegetai*. They held official positions and were responsible for expounding sacred law for particular situations. S. R. F. Price describes the *exegetai* as follows: "They are to us somewhat shadowy figures, but they were presumably important upholders and (re-)interpreters of traditional practices."[30] Their services were not compulsory nor their advice binding; their role was merely advisory.[31]

From these observations, a number of generalizations can be drawn. Although Greek religion required relatively few formal functionaries, the system of religious authority remained complex because the rules governing authority were not carefully defined. Indeed, the rules seem to have been developed on an *ad hoc* basis. However, Greek

---

25. *Archiv für Religionswissenschaft*, X:402, lines 22-27, cited in Grant, *Hellenistic Religions*, 26.

26. Burkert, *Greek Religion*, 98.

27. Dittenberger, *Sylloge*, 3:1009, cited in Grant, *Hellenistic Religions*, 30.

28. Dittenberger, *Sylloge*, 3:1004, cited in Rice and Stambaugh, *Sources*, 127-28.

29. Dittenberger, *Sylloge*, 2:736, cited in Grant, *Hellenistic Religions*, 31.

30. Price, *Religions*, 70.

31. Garland, "Priests and Power," esp. 82.

religious authority structures resembled the prevailing political structures. While Roman religious authority, as we shall see, resembled an oligarchical structure with limits of power and ultimate control by the Senate, Greek structures were less formal, tending toward a more democratic process where anyone could perform religious functions. Even when specific religious functions were required, the people who fulfilled them usually held positions for limited periods of time. Persons with specialized knowledge were valued for their advice but did not hold binding authority. Thus, the ordinary citizen was deemed competent, not only to make political decisions, but also to perform religious functions and render religious decisions.

Roman Religion

Ancient Roman religion has a history that extends across some twelve centuries, from the founding of Rome in the eighth century BCE to the triumph of Christianity in the fourth century CE. As is to be expected, the history exhibits a certain complexity, diversity, and development across that time span. Nevertheless, many of the essential features remained relatively constant. As Beard, North, and Price note, "By grouping the material thematically across the centuries, we are suggesting that (despite all the changes) the 'religions of Rome' did retain certain significant constants over their long history."[32] For this reason, while our interest for the present study is primarily in the religious milieu of the first century CE, evidence from preceding and even subsequent time periods will also be adduced both for the purposes of illustrating constants and for describing historical development.

Features of Roman Religion

POLYTHEISM AND SYNCRETISM

As is well known, the Roman religion was polytheistic. Well-known gods and goddesses indigenous to the Romans include Ceres, Janus, Jupiter, Mars, Neptunus, Quirinus, and Vesta.[33] As we shall see, the Romans also

---

32. Beard, North, and Price, *Religions of Rome*, ix.

33. Grant, *Ancient Roman Religion*, xvi. Grant notes that the interpretation of these deities as indigenous was made by Wissowa in *Religion und Kultus der Römer* and has been subject to some debate.

embraced a host of imported gods, including Diana, Fortuna, Venus, and Magna Mater.[34] The Romans considered certain abstract qualities to be governed by a corresponding deity (see Cicero, *Nat. d.* 2.60–2 and *Leg.* 2.19–22). For example, the goddess, Libertas, controlled the property of Liberty. One of the most prevalent deifications of this sort was that of chance, Fortuna. Fortuna was closely associated with the Greek goddess, Tyche, also a goddess of chance or luck, whether good or bad. Fortuna was considered a fickle goddess, and there were no guarantees of her favor despite efforts made to assure her pleasure. Thus, she expressed the fatalistic or even pessimistic outlook of the age.[35]

Unlike the Greeks, the Romans did not originally develop myths surrounding the gods. Instead, they associated the gods with certain functions. For example, the Roman god, Janus, was the god of doorways and was thus depicted in cult images as two-faced, one facing in and the other facing out. Later, many of the Roman gods became closely associated with Greek deities, and their names could virtually be used interchangeably. This association illustrates another feature of Roman religion, namely its syncretism.[36] Syncretism is perfectly understandable in a polytheistic system, but Roman religious syncretism exhibits certain noteworthy characteristics. First is its close association with Roman political and military ambitions. Not only is this seen in the sheer number of imported deities from diverse regions of the Empire, but also from the resulting theology. According to Beard, North, and Price, "Syncretism was not an innocent process. Its effect was, at least in the long term, to erode the identity of the native deity—to *sub*merge rather than merge."[37] A second notable feature of Roman syncretism is its limits. Even while new deities continued to be embraced or assimilated, active worship by

---

34. Grant, *Ancient Roman Religion*, xvii.

35. Cf. Martin, *Hellenistic Religions*, 21–23.

36. Cf. Beard, North, and Price, eds., *Religions*, 54. They say, "The expansion of the Roman empire beyond the Graeco-Roman heartland of the Mediterranean brought the Romans into contact with a yet wider range of 'native' deities. This contact between Roman and native religions often resulted in the merging of the different traditions and their various gods and goddesses. This process (now sometimes referred to as 'syncretism') was not new. The early contacts between Rome and the Greek world had, after all resulted in that range of equivalencies between Roman and Greek deities that we now take for granted . . . . But wider expansion of the empire led to a process of syncretism on a much wider scale."

37. Beard, North, and Price, eds., *Religions*, 55, (emphasis original).

individuals was being restricted to fewer gods. This eventually resulted in the worship of one god above all others, a system known as henotheism.[38] As part of this process, solar henotheism grew especially after the second century CE.[39]

Sacrifice

Sacrifice was a regular feature of Roman religion. The development of a comprehensive theory of sacrifice is beyond the scope of the present study.[40] Our purpose here is simply to describe some of the main features of Roman sacrifice. The Romans sacrificed both plant products and animals. Sacrifices regularly included libations of wine and the sprinkling of meal on the head of the victim. The usual victims were domesticated animals. A common means of sacrificing was called the *suovetaurilia* because it involved the sacrifice of a pig (*sus*), a ram (*ovis*), and a bull (*taurus*).[41] There is record of human sacrifice among the Romans, but this was generally considered barbaric.[42] The procedure for sacrifice was to parade the victim to the altar, to pour meal over its head, to expose the victim's neck by forcing its head skyward, to either stun the animal with a blunt blow to the head or kill the animal immediately with a knife blow to the neck, to cut the animal to allow for the inspection of the entrails (see below), to lay its bones covered with fat on the altar for consumption by fire, and to prepare the remaining meat for human consumption by the participants. In public sacrifices,

---

38. Ibid., 57. Henotheism differs from monotheism in that adherents of the latter insist that only one God exists, while those of the former acknowledge the existence of other gods but worship only one.

39. Grant, *Roman Religion*, xxxiv. Grant refers to solar *mono*theism, but *heno*theism seems a better term in light of Grant's elaboration: "It was really the culmination of syncretism, with its 'lords many and gods many' (1 Cor 8:5), and corresponded to the development of absolutism in government, with one supreme divine ruler in heaven and one supreme human ruler upon earth."

40 For a theoretical discussion of the prehistoric roots and existential significance of sacrificial systems, see Chilton, *The Temple of Jesus*. See also the discussion and bibliography in Klauck, *Religious Context of Early Christianity*, 37–42.

41. Cf. Beard, North, and Price, eds., *Religions*, 152.

42. Instances usually associated with human sacrifice include the killing of two Gauls and two Greeks, (Plutarch, *Quaest. rom.* 83; *Mor.* 283F), the punishment of Vestal Virgins for breaking their vows of chastity (Plutarch, *Num.* 10), and the self-dedication of a general in battle (Livy, 8.9.1–10). From this list can be deduced that the Roman sacrificial system included an element of appeasement of the gods.

a priest, who officiated with his head covered, usually oversaw the ceremony. Public slaves, indicated as such by their bare chests in Roman artwork, conducted the handling and killing of the victim.

Sacrifices were also frequently conducted for or by private individuals, with the presence of a priest desirable but not required.[43] Such sacrifices were often associated with agricultural cycles. For example, Cato gives instructions to agriculturists for conducting a sacrifice, including the giving of instructions to the slaves or servants.[44] Similarly, Horace contrasts rustic piety with public sacrifice (Horace, *Carm.* 3.23). Other times, however, private sacrifices were held for household gods, the *Lares* and the *Genius* of the head of the household. The *Lares* were the household gods for individual households. Typically, each home contained a small shrine where the cult objects for the *Lares* were kept. It was the responsibility of the head of the household to ensure that regular worship of the *Lares* was conducted.[45] Such worship included the pouring of libations and the offering of sacrificial victims. It was thought that regular worship of the *Lares* would insure their favor toward the household, yielding success for endeavors undertaken. The *Genius* was considered a divine counterpart to a household head, somewhat like our concept of a guardian angel. There was a one-to-one correspondence between the household head and his *Genius,* so it was possible to speak of the *Genius* of a particular individual.

The Imperial Cult[46]

The concept of the *Genius* facilitated the development of emperor worship and the imperial cult. In Rome, few of the emperors were worshipped as gods during their lifetimes.[47] It was possible to worship the

43. Beard, North, and Price, eds., *Religions*, 152.

44. For an example of a private sacrifice without the presence of a priest, see Cato, *Agr.* 141.

45. This fact has interesting implications for the New Testament concept of the family. Cf., e.g., Matt 23:9, Eph 6:4, and Col 3:20–21.

46. For more detailed information on the Imperial Cult, see Price, *Rituals and Power*. See also Allen Brent, *Imperial Cult*.

47. Cf. Beard, North, and Price, eds., *Religions*, 222. They say, "In Rome itself emperors were often closely associated with the gods, but only the stereotypically 'bad' emperors were said to have become gods during their lifetime; in general, emperors received divine status only after their death—and only if the senate deemed them to have deserved it."

Genius of the emperor while still considering the emperor himself to be human. Thus, a careful distinction was maintained between the concepts of deity and divinity. While living emperors were not considered gods, and thus did not employ the former term, they did use the term, divine.[48] It seems likely that the term was thought to indicate the emperor's *Genius*, not the emperor himself. Yet the distinction between the emperor and his *Genius* could become blurred, particularly for those emperors whose rule seemed praiseworthy for the widespread benefits it brought. In this respect, it was a small step from worshipping the *Genius* to worshipping the man as a god. Still, at least in Rome, a formal distinction was maintained until the time of death. Then, if the Senate approved, the emperor was declared to be a god in a ceremony known as an *apotheosis*. With great pomp, a wax effigy was processed to the funerary bier where it was burned. While the fire was yet burning, an eagle was released, flying up as from the effigy itself. The soaring eagle represented the flight of the soul into the heavens to assume its place among the gods.[49] This is the background behind the memorable joke of Vespasian, who on his deathbed reportedly said, "Woe's me. Methinks I'm turning into a god" (Suetonius, *Vespasianus* 23.4 [Rolfe, LCL]).

Outside Rome, the development of the Imperial Cult followed somewhat different lines. Especially was this the case in the east, where there had already been a tradition of worshipping rulers or other benefactors. In Athens, for example, Demetrius was worshipped as a god for his role in delivering the people from tyrannical rule (Plutarch, *Demetrius* 10.4).[50] Moreover, the cult of the goddess Roma (akin to the goddess Athena as the particular goddess of Athens) developed in the east. Temples were built and cults established for the worship of Roma. We have, for example, records of the cult of Roma in Miletus.[51] Once

---

48. See, for example, the coins issued by Octavian, pictured in Beard, North, and Price, eds., *Religions*, 224–25.

49. For a first-hand account of an *apotheosis*, see Cassius Dio, 75.4.2–5.5. See also the relief of the *apotheosis* of Emperor Antoninus Pius (reproduced in Beard, North, and Price, eds., *Religions*, 52) for a visual representation.

50. For a full discussion of the development of the deification of human beings, see Klauck, *Religious Context of Early Christianity*, 250–329. Klauck argues for the historical accuracy of the reference in Plutarch, *Lys.* 8.3–4, that Lysander was the first Greek honored as a god.

51. Sokolowski, *Lois sacrées d'Asie Mineure* 49, cited in Beard, North, and Price, eds., *Religions*, 246–47.

the cult of Roma was established, it was a small step to incorporate the worship of Rome's emperors under the auspices of Roma.

Divination and the *Pax Deorum*

Another central feature of Roman religion is that of divination and the taking of auspices by augurs. These practices stemmed, not from a desire to appease the gods, but from an effort to ascertain the current disposition of the gods. Thus, the attention to divination and augury reflects Roman concern for *pax deorum*, the peace of the gods. If the augury produced favorable results, the Romans were confident that the gods were at peace with them: the gods were favorably disposed towards them and would do nothing to disrupt or confound the activities to be undertaken. On the other hand, if favorable omens could not be produced, this was taken to indicate the disfavor of the gods. Business, government, war-making, and other activities were to be postponed until the *pax deorum* could be assured. Auspices were required to be taken for a wide variety of activities, including the meetings of the Senate, public elections, and military campaigns. They even had to be taken before every crossing of the *pomerium*, the boundary of the ancient city of Roman set up, according to legend, by Romulus, the founder of Rome. Throughout all such ceremonies, great care was taken to ensure that exact procedures were followed. The rationale was somewhat analogous to that of controls in science: if there were a mistake in the ceremony, there could be no certainty in the validity of the outcome. Pliny the Elder described the formulaic prayers as follows:

> We see also that our chief magistrates have adopted fixed formulas for their prayers; that to prevent a word's being omitted or out of place a reader dictates beforehand the prayer from a script; that another attendant is appointed as a guard to keep watch, and yet another is put in charge to maintain a strict silence; that a piper plays so that nothing but the prayer is heard. (Pliny the Elder, *Nat.* 28.3.11 [Jones, LCL])

The auspices could be taken in a variety of ways. Initially, auspices were taken by watching the activities of birds. For example, the augur might indicate a portion of the sky and a direction for the flight of birds. If birds flew through the indicated portion from the indicated direction, this signaled a good omen. Later, domesticated fowl were kept for the purposes of augury. Grain would be placed in front of the birds; if they refused to eat the proffered grain, this was considered a sign of the failure of *pax deorum*.

Another common way for assessing the state of the *pax deorum* was the use of Etruscan haruspices for reading the entrails of sacrificial victims, especially the heart and the liver. The Museo Civico in Piacenza owns a bronze replica of a liver probably dating from the third or second century BCE.[52] The replica is divided into sections with various inscriptions, presumably for use as a guide for examining entrails. Literary evidence alludes to the presence or absence of a "head" on the liver, as well as the presence and condition of the heart. In one extreme case, a liver was said to have dissolved after the sacrifice (Livy, 41.14.7 and 41.15.1–4). When the condition of the entrails failed to indicate a favorable omen, the sacrifice would be repeated. This led skeptics to complain of the greediness of the gods, who seemingly were unsatisfied with a single sacrifice.

Because Etruscans were considered foreigners in ancient Rome, the Romans seem to have been ambivalent toward them. From time to time, opinions were expressed doubting their efficacy. In one famous event, a Roman consul certified the election of two incoming consuls despite the objection of the haruspices. He claimed that he himself had adequately taken the auspices, and that they were favorable. Thus, he judged his own activity to be superior to that of the foreigners. Significantly, the same magistrate later realized he had failed to take the auspices at every requisite point, and that therefore the results of the election were indeed invalid. The elected officials resigned and new elections were held (Cicero, *Nat. d.* 2.10–11).[53]

The condition, or more exactly the failure, of the *pax deorum* could also be indicated by the occurrence of prodigies. Prodigies were unusual natural events, such as the spontaneous ignition of a soldier's spear, the appearance of two moons, or the birth of abnormal offspring. When such events occurred, steps had to be undertaken to restore the *pax deorum* by expiating the prodigies. In addition to regular sacrifices,

---

52. For a photographic reproduction, see Beard, North, and Price, eds., *Religions*, 177.

53. The *vitium*, i.e., the mistake in the taking of the auspices, was the failure to perform the test on both crossings of the *pomerium*. He had taken them when he entered the city but failed to repeat the ceremony when he exited.

a sacred spring might be declared. The declaration of a sacred spring required that all the animals born in the spring of a given year were to be sacrificed to the gods. One such spring was declared in 217 BCE, though it was not fulfilled until twenty-one years later. In this case, the vow included provisions for circumventing foreseeable *vitia*, i.e., ritual mistakes in the execution of the vow. For example, the decree included the caveat that accidental deaths or animals inadvertently sacrificed incorrectly were nevertheless to be considered as having met the conditions of the sacred spring. Despite such precautions, however, the sacred spring had to be repeated the following year because it was determined that it had not been adequately performed (Livy, 22.10.1–6 and 34.44).[54]

The Sibylline Books and the *Quindecimviri*

In extreme cases, the Senate would authorize the consultation of the Sibylline Books to learn how to expiate a prodigy and restore the *pax deorum*. The Sibylline books, composed in Greek verse, were thought to have been the written records of a prophetess known as the Sibyl. In fact, a certain sense of mystery enveloped—then as now—the identity of the Sibyl. The ancients seem to have believed that the books had been preserved from time immemorial and to have originated from a single hand. As more Sibylline books appeared, however, speculation arose that there might in fact have been multiple Sibyls. The most likely explanation for this confusing state of affairs is that there had been a female seer who left a kernel of prophetic writings. Around this kernel grew up a variety of pseudepigraphical books. A fascinating legend relates how the Sibylline Books first came into the possession of the Romans. A mysterious woman (the Sibyl herself?) approached Tarquin, traditionally said to be Rome's fifth king, and offered to sell him nine books for a tremendous sum. When Tarquin declined, the woman departed and destroyed three of the books. She then offered the remaining books for the original price. Tarquin scoffed, noting that if he had refused more books at that price he certainly would not take the reduced number. However, when she returned later with even fewer books at the same price, the official *augures* determined that the gods were offering these books to the Roman people for their benefit. The

---

54. For the dates, see Beard, North, and Price, eds., *Religions*, 155–56.

remaining books were then bought for the asking price (Dionysius of Halicarnassus, *Ant. rom.* 4.62).

When the Senate authorized the consultation of the Sibylline Books, a college of experts known as the *quindecimviri* would scour the texts for information pertaining to the crisis at hand.[55] These experts would interpret the relevant passage(s) and recommend a course of action to the Senate. Thus, in a sense, the *quindecimviri* were what we would consider a committee of the Senate, authorized for a specific function but without the power to enact its recommendations apart from the actions of the whole body. In fact, the *quindecimviri* were not allowed to peruse the Sibylline Books except on those occasions when they were specifically told to do so by the Senate. The recommendations of the *quindecimviri* varied, of course, but one course of action sometimes advised was the conducting of a *lectisternium*.[56] A *lectisternium* was a feast held in honor of the gods in which the cult images of the gods were literally present at the feast. The images would be brought out of their temples and placed on couches at the feast, thus symbolically participating in the festivities. Another course of action sometimes advised was the importing of a foreign cult to Rome. During the war with Hannibal, the cult of Magna Mater was imported from Asia Minor under such circumstances. Envoys were sent to retrieve the cult object, in this case a stone thought to have fallen from heaven. They also brought religious functionaries to establish the cult in Rome (Livy, 29.11.5-8 and 14.5-14). However, the sordid details of the cult offended the sensibilities of the Romans, and the Senate forbade Roman citizens from participating, at least initially.[57]

Foreign cults were imported under other conditions, as well. For example, when the Romans were besieging a foreign city, a formal ceremony could be performed in which the indigenous deities were offered better treatment in Rome—such as the provision of a more luxurious temple—than they received from their present adherents. The gods were thus invited to abandon the city and its inhabitants and to assist the Romans instead. One thusly acquired deity was Juno from the

---

55. The name, *quindecimviri*, refers to the fifteen members of the college. Cf. Klauck, *Religious Context of Early Christianity*, 33.

56. For reference to the declaration of the first *lectisternium*, see Livy, 5.13.4-8.

57. See further the section on the mystery religion of Cybele and Attis, below.

Etruscan city of Veii (Livy, 5.21.1–7 and 5.22.4–7).[58] Macrobius records the formula for this ritual, known as *evocatio*:

> This is the formula by which the gods of a besieged city are called out:
>
> "If it is a god or if it is a goddess who has taken under his or her protection the people and state of Carthage, and thou above all who hast taken this city and this people into thy keeping: I pray, I implore, I plead with thee to grant me this favor—abandon the people and the state of Carthage, their lands, their temples, their sanctuaries, and their city; depart, and leave them. Inspire this people and city with fear, terror, forgetfulness. Leave them and come to Rome, to me and my people. Our land, our temples, sanctuaries, and city will be more pleasant to thee and dearer. To me, to the Roman people, and to my soldiers be graciously disposed, and let us know and be aware of it. If thou wilt do this, I vow to thee a temple and games!" (Macrobius, *Sat.* 3.9.7–8)[59]

The Calendar and Religious Festivals

Preventative measures were also undertaken to assure the favorable conditions of the *pax deorum*. In addition to the sacrificial system, the Romans paid a great deal of attention to the religious dimensions of the calendar. As is well known, Julius Caesar regulated the Roman calendar. He coordinated lunar and solar cycles by borrowing knowledge from the Egyptians, but he also continued religious traditions that stretched far back into history, even into the prehistoric period. Days on the Roman calendars were marked according to whether they were *fastus, comitialis, nefastus,* or *endotercisus. Fastus* days were those on which all kinds of business could be transacted without threat to the *pax deorum*, on *nefastus* days no business could be conducted, and on *endotercisus* days only part of the day was available for business. Days

---

58. It is interesting to note that the Romans themselves considered relocating to this city they had just conquered when under pressure from the Gauls. Only a passionate speech, recalling the importance of Rome's traditional religious rites and the necessity that they be performed at the present site of Rome, dissuaded the people from moving.

59. Translated by Grant, *Roman Religion*, 22–23. "Carthage" here is used as the quintessential Roman enemy.

marked as *comitialis* were available for public assemblies (Macrobius, *Sat.* 1.16.2–6).[60]

Also included on the calendar were festival days and days for the celebration of games, both of which were held in honor of the gods. The major festivals on the Roman calendar included the Parilia, the Saturnalia, the rituals of the *Salii*, and the Lupercalia. The Parilia (later also called the Romaia, in honor of the founding of Rome) was held on April 21 and dealt with assuring the welfare of the city's livestock. The Saturnalia was held on December 17. Social roles were inverted during this festival, and slaves seized the opportunity to indulge. The rituals of the *Salii* were held twice a year, in March and October. These rituals were associated with the traditional times for the departure and return of the armies.

Arguably the most memorable festival was the Lupercalia, held on February 15. The Lupercalia seems to have been a purificatory festival, but its significance was much disputed even in antiquity. Some argued that the significance of this rite was a commemoration of Remus and Romulus being raised by wolves, while others considered it a festival of the dead or of purification (Plutarch, *Rom.* 21.3–8 and Varro, *Ling. Lat.* 6.34).[61] Part of the festival included the running of naked boys (or young men) through the streets carrying strips of goatskin. It was thought that if the goatskin touched a young woman, she would be guaranteed fertility, and for this reason the runners where not avoided. The Lupercalia gained notoriety when Mark Antony, as one of the runners, brought a royal wreath to Julius Caesar (Plutarch, *Caes.* 61.3–4).[62]

Games were also scheduled as part of the religious activities listed on the calendar. Games included both athletic and musical competitions, as well as the performance of dramatic compositions. The most fully attested of the games were the *ludi saecularum*, which were established by Augustus as part of his religious reformation for the re-establishment of the *pax deorum*. Other games included the Megalesian Games, the

---

60. Cited in Beard, North, and Price, eds., *Religions*, 61. Especially helpful for explaining these days is Beard, North, and Price, eds., *Religions*, 62–63, n. 5.

61. Cf. Grant, *Roman Religion*, xi. He says, "Varro, whose book on ancient Roman religion, *Antiquitates rerum divinarum* (*Sacred Antiquities*), survives in fragments quoted by St. Augustine, acknowledges that he could only guess the meaning of much of the primitive ritual [of the ancient Roman religion]."

62. Julius Caesar, of course, declined the wreath at that time.

Roman Games, and the Capitoline Games. Notice the religious component of the games in the following description by Livy: "We have added Capitoline Games to the other annual festivals, and by authority of the senate have established a new college [of priests] for this purpose" (Livy 5.52.11 [Foster, LCL]).[63]

Religion in the Military

Roman religion was very important to the military. We have already seen how auspices were taken before military action and how a ceremony invited the deities of besieged cities to come over to the Romans. There was also a religious component to the declaration of war. When a grievance occurred, an envoy was sent to the offending territory. When he crossed the border, he would state the grievance and the Romans' demands. As he continued toward the city center, he would repeat these statements to the first person he met, when he entered the city gates, and once again when he arrived at the marketplace. If the demands were not met, a fetial priest (a member of the priestly college dedicated to propriety regarding declarations of war and peace) was chosen to go to the border and hurl a spear into the enemy territory as an official declaration of war. When the empire grew too large to enact these ceremonies literally, a plot of ground in Rome itself would be designated as enemy territory, and the spear would be cast therein (Livy, 1.32.5–14).

The gods were also looked to for aid in the midst of battle itself. Not infrequently a general would make vows of temples or other gifts to the gods for efficacious aid. One especially memorable instance involved the dedication of a commander himself to the gods. When his troops were being defeated by the enemy, he called a priest to perform a ceremony dedicating himself to "Janus, Jupiter, Father Mars, Quirinus, Bellona, Lares, divine Novensiles, divine Indigites, ye gods in whose power are both we and our enemies, and you, divine Manes" (Livy, 8.9.6 [Foster, LCL]). He then informed his fellow commander of his resolve and charged headlong into the enemy troops whom he fought with great intensity. When his own troops saw what he was doing, they redoubled their efforts and routed the enemy (Livy, 8.9.1–14).

---

63. Cf. Ferguson, *Greek and Roman Religion*, 76.

Authority in Roman Religion

Roman religious authority is fairly well documented in the extant literature and epigraphic evidence. There was a wide variety of religious functionaries, each with particular titles, roles, and responsibilities.[64] Some priesthoods were organized into priestly colleges, while others seem to have functioned more independently. Three of the priestly colleges stood out from the others by virtue of their importance: the *pontifices*, the *augures*, and the *quindecimviri sacris faciundis*.[65] Members of these colleges were usually elected by the vote of the people, though during some periods vacancies were filled by consensus within the colleges themselves. Only men from the elite class were eligible for these positions, and they had to be nominated by influential members of the college for which they were under consideration (cf. Cicero, *Ep. Brut.* 20 [1.7]).

We have already seen that the primary functions of the *quindecimviri* and the *augures* were the consultation of Sibylline Books and the taking of the auspices, respectively. But members of these colleges fulfilled additional roles, as well. For example, the *augures* were also responsible for defining sacred space (Cicero, *Leg.* 2.8.21 and Varro, *Ling. Lat.* 7.8–10).[66] Similarly, we read of the *quindecimviri* limiting the period of mourning for free women in connection with the Augustan reformation and the *ludi saecularum* (*ILS* 5000).[67] We also read of the *quindecimviri* approving an individual for priesthood in a Roman colony:

---

64. Mary Beard, in her essay on priests in Rome, offers a comprehensive list of these functionaries for Rome (Beard, "Priesthood," Table 1).

65. According to Augustine, these three colleges formed the organizational framework for the first three books of Varro's work on divine antiquities (Augustine, *Civ.* 6.3). Beard, North, and Price added a fourth, the *tresviri epulonum*. The *tresviri epulonum* were responsible for overseeing the feasts (Beard, North, and Price, eds., *Religions*, 199 and 368).

66. The discussion in Varro is about the word *templum*, which is related to, but not identical to our word, temple. The *augures* set off certain portions, whether in the sky or on earth, as sacred, thus "inaugurating" them. Cf. Beard, North, and Price, eds., *Religions*, 86–87.

67. Cited in Ferguson, *Greek and Roman Religion*, 82. It should be noted, however, that the *Saecularium Celebratorum* was itself instituted under the direction of the Sibylline Books. Thus, the edict of the *quindecimviri* regarding mourning can be viewed as an extension of their usual function.

> The *quindecimviri sacris faciundis* greet the *praetores* and other magistrates of Cumae. We learn from your letter that you have created as priest of the Mother of the Gods Licinius Secundus in place of the late priest Claudius Restitutus. By your wish, we have conceded to him the right to wear the armlet and crown, but only within the boundaries of your *colonia*. (ILS 4175)[68]

The *pontifices* were primarily responsible for assuring the accuracy of public religious events, such as sacrifice. Livy, describing the founding of the office of *pontifex* by Numa, gives the following description of their role:

> ... and to him [the *pontifex*] he [Numa] intrusted [sic] written directions, full and accurate, for performing the rites of worship; with what victims, on what days, in what temple, sacrifices should be offered and from what sources money was to be disbursed to pay their costs. All other public and private sacrifices he likewise made subject to the decrees of the *pontifex*, that there might be someone to whom the commons could come for advice, lest any confusion should arise in the religious law through the neglect of ancestral rites and the adoption of strange ones. And not merely ceremonies relating to the gods above, but also proper funeral observances and the propitiation of the spirits of the dead were to be taught by the *pontifex* as well, and also what prodigies manifested by lightning or other visible sign were to be taken in hand and averted. (Livy, 1.20.5–7 [Foster, LCL])[69]

Another important order with religious authority was the Vestal Virgins. They were the priestesses of the goddess Vesta, and they formed a group similar to the other priestly colleges. They enjoyed privileges not normally accorded to unmarried women, such as the right to make wills and to conduct business independently. They were to be chosen as children from an elite family and to have both parents living. They were to serve thirty years, the first ten as apprentices, the second ten performing the duties of the office, and the last ten teaching their expertise to new Virgins (Plutarch, *Num.* 10). Their primary duty was to attend to the eternal flame of the sacred hearth, but they had other duties as well. For example, they conducted the sacrifice at the women-only festival

---

68. Translated by Beard, North, and Price, eds., *Religions*, 249.

69. For epigraphic evidence of the role of the *pontifices* in matters relating to burials, see *ILS* 8380, cited in Beard, North, and Price, eds., *Religions*, 201. See also epistolary evidence in Pliny the Younger, *Ep.* 10.68–69.

of Bona Dea (Cicero, *Att.* 1.13).⁷⁰ In addition to such formal activities, they also acted as high-status patrons by virtue of their office. An inscription honors one Vestal Virgin for her assistance:

> To Campia Severina, senior Vestal Virgin, most holy and most kind. In gratitude for the benefits of equestrian rank and a military post of the second rank that she obtained for him, Aemilius Pardalas, honoured at her request with the command of the first cohort 'Aquitanica', erected this. (*ILS* 4929)⁷¹

Other priestly colleges include the *Luperci*, the *Salii*, and the *Fratres Arvales*. The *Luperci* were responsible for overseeing the festivities of the *Lupercalia*, described above.⁷² They performed the sacrifices and other rituals, especially the running of the "sacred race" (Plutarch, *Caes.* 61.3 [Perrin, LCL]). The *Salii* were "a kind of dancers and singers of hymns in praise of the gods of war" (Dionysius of Halicarnassus, *Ant. rom.* 2.70.1 [Cary, LCL]).⁷³ Livy describes their founding by Numa as follows:

> He likewise chose twelve *Salii* for Mars Gradivus, and granted them the distinction of wearing the embroidered tunic and over it a bronze breastplate, and of bearing the divine shields which men call *ancilia,* while they proceeded through the City, chanting their hymns to the triple beat of their solemn dance. (Livy, 1.20.4 [Foster, LCL])⁷⁴

The *Fratres Arvales* were charged with performing rituals for the agricultural productivity of the fields (*arva*) surrounding Rome.⁷⁵ They conducted ceremonies and official business in a grove outside Rome dedicated to Dea Dia, and each spring they processed about the fields.

---

70. Cf. Beard, North, and Price, eds., *Religions*, 198.

71. Translated by Beard, North, and Price, eds., *Religions*, 204.

72. The *Luperci* were actually divided into two colleges, the *luperci Quinctiales* and the *luperci Fabiani*. However, the features that differentiate between the two colleges are uncertain.

73. Cf. Varro, *Ling. Lat.* 5.85 (Kent, LCL): "The *Salii* were named from *salitare* 'to dance,' because they had the custom and the duty of dancing yearly in the assembly-places, in their ceremonies."

74. The *ancilia* were figure-eight shaped shields, the first of which was thought to have fallen from heaven into Numa's palace (Dionysius of Halicarnassus, *Ant. rom.* 2.71.1–2).

75. Cf. Varro, *Ling. Lat.* 5.85 (Kent, LCL): "*Fratres Arvales* 'Arval Brothers' was the name given to those who perform public rites to the end that the ploughlands may bear fruits: from *ferre* 'to bear' and *arva* 'ploughlands' they are called *Fratres Arvales*."

We have extant inscriptions detailing the activities of the *Fratres Arvales*.[76] One inscription includes a song, which may be dated to the sixth century BCE:

> Help us, O household gods! (repeat three times)
> Let no harm or danger, O Marmar, attack our people!
> (three times)
> Be thou satisfied, O fierce Mars!
> Leap over the threshold!
> Stand still! Beat [the ground]! (three times). (*ILS* 5039)[77]

The priestly colleges developed simple, internal hierarchical structures. The *Fratres Arvales*, for example, had a master or chairman, a vice-chairman, and a *flamen*. The *Fratres* themselves appointed these leaders for one-year terms.[78] The leadership structures were somewhat different in the college of the *pontifices*. It was headed by the *pontifex maximus*. He was elected by the people and usually held his position for life. As could be expected, the *pontifex maximus* held a considerable degree of personal power. Naturally, the duties of the pontifical college were uniquely present in the person of the *pontifex maximus*. In addition, he appointed the *flamen Dialis*, the priest of Jupiter (see below). He was also responsible for overseeing the Vestal Virgins. He had the final say on who was to be a Vestal Virgin and was responsible for their day-to-day work, as well as for meting punishment as appropriate. Plutarch's account of the punishment of the unchastity of a Vestal Virgin notes his unique role:

> When the litter [carrying the bound Virgin] reaches its destination [for her live interment], the attendants unfasten the cords of the coverings. Then the high-priest, after stretching his hands toward heaven and uttering certain mysterious prayers before the fatal act, brings forth the culprit, who is closely veiled, and places her on the steps leading down into the chamber. After this he turns away his face, as do the rest of the priests . . . . (Plutarch, *Num.* 10.7 [Perrin, LCL])

---

76. See Grant, *Roman Religion*, 233–38.

77. Translated by Grant, *Roman Religion*, 17–18.

78. W. Henzen, *Acta Fratrum Arvalium*, clii, translated by Grant as follows: "Next they appointed Titus Julius Candidus Caecilius Simplex to be chairman from these Saturnalia to the next Saturnalia" (Grant, *Roman Religion*, 235).

FLAMINES

Whereas the priestly colleges had authority over certain religious functions or festivals, another class of priests, the *flamines*, was dedicated to particular deities. These included the *flamen Martialis*, the *flamen Quirinalis*, and twelve minor *flamines*. The most important *flamen*, however, was the *flamen Dialis*. The *flamen Dialis* held a unique position. Unlike the other functionaries, the *flamen Dialis* had extensive restrictions on his behavior, which practically precluded any political career.[79] These restrictions included the prohibition of reviewing troops outside the *pomerium*, the requirement to sleep on the same bed every night—no more than three consecutive nights away were allowed, and an alternate bed was proscribed because the bed had to have specially prepared clay around each of its legs—and the necessity of wearing a distinguishing hat at all times (even indoors during the earlier years) (Aulus Gellius, *Noctes atticae* 10.15). Similar requirements were made of the *flamen's* wife. Whereas other priesthoods were viewed as desirable for the advancement of political clout, the office of *flamen Dialis* was something of a dead end street, especially in view of the fact that the *flamen Dialis*, like all *flamines* in Rome, held his post for life.[80] As priest of Jupiter, he was responsible for the maintenance of the cult of Jupiter, but he was also required to perform additional public duties, such as participating in marriage ceremonies.

THE AUGUSTAN REFORMATION

It should be apparent from the preceding discussion of religious authority in Rome that authority was widely dispersed among various functionaries. Mary Beard, in her illuminating article on priests in the Roman Republic, has argued that religious authority rested ultimately

---

79. The *flamen Dialis* was second only to the *rex sacrificulus* or *rex sacrorum* in terms of respect of position. Aulus Gellius, *Noct. att.* 10.15.21 (Rolfe, LCL) says, "No other has a place at table above the *flamen Dialis*, except the *rex sacrificulus*." However, the *rex sacrorum* was absolutely prohibited from political office, and therefore the position was not sought after. The *rex sacrorum* does not figure as prominently in the literature as the *flamen Dialis*.

80. In the Roman provinces the *flamines* did not hold the office for life. Nevertheless, certain honors were still accorded them. See *ILS* 6964, cited in Beard, North, and Price, eds., *Religions*, 252–53.

with the Senate itself.[81] Each of the colleges was responsible to the Senate, and the Senate had final say in such matters. For this reason, she argues that the Senate was actually the mediator between humans and gods and that the priests acted only in an advisory capacity.

This state of affairs changed dramatically with the rise of Augustus and the Augustan Reformation. As we have seen, Roman religion was concerned with the *pax deorum,* but prior to Augustus civil wars and prodigies indicated that this *pax* was broken. Augustus set about to rectify the problem. He restored the functioning of the *Fratres Aravales,* which had been neglected, and he built or restored numerous temples (Augustus, *Res gestae* 19–21). Significantly, he also changed the balance of religious power. Whereas authority had been dispersed to different colleges and *flamines,* Augustus began to acquire multiple priesthoods. Augustus himself details his acquisitions: "I have been *pontifex maximus, augur,* a member of the *quindecimviri sacris facuindis,* of the *septemviri opulonum,* an Arval Brother, a *sodalis Titius,* and a fetial priest . . ." (*CIL* 3:769–99).[82] In this way, Augustus concentrated not only political power, but also religious authority in a single person. This concentration was to be emulated by subsequent emperors right down through Constantine and the first Christian emperors.[83]

Mystery Religions[84]

Ancient mystery religions were optional religious affiliations that required secret initiatory rites for membership. The mystery religions

81. Beard, "Priesthood," 31.

82. Translated by Grant, *Roman Religion,* 170. Cf. Augustus's describes in his memoirs of how he became *pontifex maximus:* "I declined to be made Pontifex Maximus in succession to a colleague still living, when the people tendered me that priesthood which my father had held. Several years later I accepted that sacred office when he at last was dead who, taking advantage of a time of civil disturbance, had seized it for himself, such a multitude from all Italy assembling for my election, in the consulship of Publius Sulpicius and Gaius Valgius, as is never recorded to have been in Rome before" (Augustus, *Res gestae* 10 [Shipley, LCL]). Note the remarkable confluence of ambition, respect, and contempt.

83. For an essentially reconstructionistic perspective on the relation between religious and political authority in the Roman Empire during this period, see Potter, *Prophets and Emperors.*

84. Walter Burkert has argued that "mystery *cults*" is a better term than "mystery *religions.*" He says, "[This book] abandons the concept of mystery *religions* from the

attracted a wide following, and individuals sometimes sought initiation into more than one religion.[85] It is sometimes thought that the primary appeal of mystery cults is that they offered their initiates the possibility of life after death. It seems more likely, however, that it was not the existence of life after death, but an improved quality of that existence which the mysteries offered.[86] Be that as it may, as we shall see, it is even more likely that mystery religions catered to an existential, felt need, in addition to any metaphysical one. In other words, the appeal of the mysteries was not merely some vision of an idealized after-life, but also

---

start. Initiation at Eleusis or worship of Isis or Mithras does not constitute adherence to a religion in the sense we are familiar with, being confronted with mutually exclusive religions such as Judaism, Christianity, and Islam. Whereas in these religions there has been much conscious emphasis on self-definition and on demarcating one religion as against the other, in the pre-Christian epoch the various forms of worship, including new and foreign gods in general and the institution of mysteries in particular, are never exclusive; they appear as varying forms, trends, or options within the one disparate yet continuous conglomerate of ancient religion" (Burkert, *Ancient Mystery Cults*, 3–4). He goes on to say, "The use of the term 'mystery religions,' as a pervasive and exclusive name for a closed system, is inappropriate. Mystery initiations were an optional activity within polytheistic religion, comparable to, say, a pilgrimage to Santiago di Compostela within the Christian system" (Burkert, *Ancient Mystery Cults*, 10). The point is well taken. In the present study, however, "religion" is used in a broader sense than Burkert envisions. Moreover, the term "religion" itself seems to be gaining a broader connotation in our increasingly pluralistic culture. (Burkert seems to concede this point. He notes, "Religion meant knowledge about ultimate reality to more dogmatic ages; it meant history of ideas to the nineteenth century; for moderns, poised between nihilism and linguistics, it has become 'constructing worlds of meaning' " [Burkert, *Ancient Mystery Cults*, 30].) For these reasons, we shall use "mystery cults" and "mystery religions" interchangeably in the present study.

85. We see this, for example, in the case of Apuleius, who claimed to have been initiated into numerous different mysteries. (Apuleius, *Apol.* 55.4–5), cited in Klauck, *Religious Context of Early Christianity*, 134.

86. Klauck, *Religious Context of Early Christianity*, 104. Klauck here is speaking specifically of the Eleusinian mysteries. He says, "Let us at any rate hold fast to the point that Eleusis made an important contribution to the development of individual eschatology among the Greeks. The hope which finds expression in the mysteries is orientated to a better destiny in the afterlife." Cf. Turcan, *Cults of the Roman Empire*, 25–26. Turcan asserts, "But the idea of 'salvation' was very early enriched by the concern to be preserved even after death from the punishments of hell or punitive and distressing reincarnations (in Orphism and Pythagoreanism). In truth, the preoccupations of present life were often linked to those of the life hereafter. . . . Eastern religions offered their followers various forms and concepts of 'salvation'. But their liturgies and especially their initiations were deemed to ensure protection in this world and the next, without breach of continuity."

the meeting of needs for personal connections, both between individuals and between the individual and his or her god or goddess, which were not readily met in the civic religions.[87]

Our knowledge of the ancient mystery religions is somewhat limited because their initiates were required to maintain strict codes of silence. Nevertheless, there were significant public aspects to the cults. Thus, our knowledge comes primarily from two types of sources: (1) descriptions of the public displays and (2) accounts of the secrets by Christian opponents who sought to discredit the mysteries. As a result, a certain degree of uncertainty remains, since we cannot be sure either to what extent the public displays corresponded to the secret rites or to what degree the Christians accurately portrayed their opponents.

Eleusinian Mysteries

Contrary to a common misconception, not all mystery religions originated in the east.[88] Actually, the most ancient mysteries were indigenous to Greece. The most famous Greek mystery cult was centered in the town of Eleusis near Athens and is commonly called the Eleusinian mysteries. It is speculated that the Eleusinian cult was originally based on the agricultural cycle.[89] According to the explanatory myth *Homeric Hymn to Demeter*, however, the goddess Demeter instigated the mysteries. Demeter's daughter, Persephone or Kore, had come to earth and was abducted by Hades, Zeus's brother and god of the underworld. When Demeter discovered Persephone missing, she was disconsolate and began roaming the earth in search of Persephone. Incognito, she came to Eleusis where she offered herself as nurse for an infant prince. She intended to immortalize the prince by nightly placing him in the fire to burn away his mortality. For a time this plan seemed to be working, but it was foiled when the mother discovered Demeter placing the boy in the flames and cried out in horror. Demeter then revealed her identity as a goddess and instructed the people how to worship her, thus instigating the Eleusinian mysteries. In the meantime, Zeus brokered a compromise between Demeter and Pluto whereby Persephone would

---

87. Cf. Meyer, *Ancient Mysteries*, 9.

88. Cf. Burkert, *Ancient Mystery Cults*, 2.

89. Meyer, *Ancient Mysteries*, 5. See also the discussion of the Eleusinian mysteries' cult object, below.

remain with Hades four months out of the year and with Demeter for the remaining eight months. This is the reason that the earth flowers and is fruitful for eight months but lies dormant for four. Ultimately, then, the myth lends credence to the hypothesis of agricultural underpinnings, while at the same time reflecting the incorporation of a deeper, spiritual sense.[90]

The Eleusinian mysteries were celebrated with two annual ceremonies. The first, known as the lesser mysteries, was held in the spring. It took place in Athens and was open to the public. During this ceremony, sacrifices were held, and candidates for initiation fasted and underwent purificatory rites. The celebration of the greater mysteries, as the name implies, was considered the major ceremony. Celebrants came from all over the Mediterranean to attend the greater mysteries. Held in September, the ceremony began in Athens with public celebrations and concluded in Eleusis with a closed-door ceremony. The festivities in Athens, held over multiple days to accommodate late arrivals, were similar in content to those of the lesser mysteries. At the conclusion of the Athenian portion of the ceremony, a formal procession made its way to Eleusis. The climactic conclusion of the greater mysteries incorporated the secret initiation of new members. Initiates came from all walks of life. They were men and women, slave and free, native and foreigner. Even prominent Romans, including Cicero and a number of emperors, sought initiation into the Eleusinian mysteries. The initiation ceremony ended with the revelation of the cult object. According to the Christian, Hippolytus, the cult item revealed to the initiates was an ear of corn (Hippolytus, *Haer.* 5.3 [*ANF* 5:55]). If this is correct, it adds additional weight to the notion that the Eleusinian mysteries were originally related to agricultural rites. However, Tertullian insisted that the item revealed was a phallus (Tertullian, *Val.* 1 [*ANF* 3:503]).

Dionysiac Mysteries

Another mystery religion associated with the Greeks, in this case from as early as the second millennium BCE,[91] was the cult of Dionysus. Like the Eleusinian mysteries, the Dionysiac mysteries were grounded in an ancient etiological myth suggesting connections to an agricultural

---

90. Tripolitis, *Religions of the Hellenistic-Roman Age*, 19.
91. Ibid., 22.

prehistory. Dionysus was a god of nature, vivifying plants and animals. Eventually, Dionysus's power was associated specifically with the vine. As might be expected for such a god, ceremonies incorporated a celebration of the fruit of the vine and were orgiastic in nature. Unlike the Eleusinian mysteries, however, the Dionysiac mysteries were not tied to a single locality; instead, the religion spread across the Greco-Roman world.

In Rome, the Dionysiac mysteries were celebrated under the god's Roman name, Bacchus. In a well-known incident recorded both in literature and inscription, the Bacchanalia (rites of the Bacchus mystery religion) were severely limited by action of the Roman Senate.[92] Livy describes the Roman impression of the cult that produced the negative response:

> To the religious element in them were added the delights of wine and feasts, that the minds of a larger number might be attracted. When wine had inflamed their minds, and night and the mingling of males with females, youth with age, had destroyed every sentiment of modesty, all varieties of corruption first began to be practised, since each one had at hand the pleasure answering to that to which his nature was more inclined. There was not one form of vice alone, the promiscuous matings of free men and women, but perjured witnesses, forged seals and wills and evidence, all issued from this same workshop: likewise poisonings and secret murders, so that at times not even the bodies were found for burial. Much was ventured by craft, more by violence. This violence was concealed because amid the howlings and the crash of drums and cymbals no cry of the sufferers could be heard as the debauchery and murders proceeded. (Livy, 39.8.5–8 [Sage, LCL])

It is easy to see why the Romans would want to suppress such activities. Yet they did not outlaw the cult absolutely; they severely restricted it, limiting the number of people who could gather together for rituals. Nevertheless, the cult survived and eventually became popular among the Roman elite.

Also associated with the Dionysiac mysteries were the Orphic mysteries, so called after Orpheus, its founder and an alleged double of Dionysus. The Orphic aspects of the cult are known predominantly

---

92. Livy, 39.8–14, esp. 39.14.8–10; and *ILS* 18, cited in Beard, North, and Price, eds., *Religions*, 290–91.

through the Orphic Hymns and inscriptions on gold plates found in graves. The Orphic Hymns consist of a collection of eighty-seven poetic works pseudonymously attributed to Orpheus.[93] The hymns are of only "marginally Orphic character."[94] Addressed to various gods, they are syncretistic in nature. In contrast, the gold plates show that the initiates into the Orphic mysteries believed people were doomed to continuous cycles of reincarnation because they did not know how to navigate their way through the underworld. It was thought that with the proper instruction, initiates upon their death could bypass the usual route, which led back to earth, and arrive at the preferred destination. For this reason, the gold plates included navigational instructions. For example, one inscription reads,

> In the house of Hades, at the left hand, you will find a spring
> And, just a few steps beyond it, a single white cypress.
> But take care not to come near the spring;
> Instead you will find other cooling waters, streaming forth
> From Mnemosyne's lake—but here watchers are at hand.
> Say to them: "I am a son of Earth and of starry Heaven,
> [I am of heavenly descent;] this ye yourselves know.
> I am languishing from thirst, and about to pass away; quickly then give me to drink
> Cooling water from the spring, swelling from the lake of Mnemosyne [Memory]."
> Gladly then will they give you to drink from the divine spring,
> And thenceforth with other heroes you will reign.[95]

CYBELE AND ATTIS

The cult of Cybele and her consort, Attis, was widespread in the Greco-Roman world. Various names were given to the goddess, including Cybele (in Asia Minor and Greece), Magna Mater (Rome), and Atargatis (Syria). As may be expected from such diversity, the myth of the universal goddess took various forms. According to Hans-Josef

---

93. Klauck, *Religious Context of Early Christianity*, 120; Meyer, *Ancient Mysteries*, 101. Grant, however, puts the number of hymns at eighty-eight (Grant, *Hellenistic Religions*, 109).

94. Meyer, *Ancient Mysteries*, 102.

95. Kern, *Orphicorum Fragmenta* 32a, translated by Grant, *Hellenistic Religions*, 108.

Klauck, the myth usually followed one of two main forms.[96] In the first version, a jealous Zeus dispatches a wild boar to kill Attis. In the second and dominant version, Cybele becomes jealous of Attis, who expresses interest in another. She causes him to go insane and castrate himself, and he dies from his wounds. In some accounts, Attis does not in fact die; in still others Zeus reanimates the body so that it does not decay, its hair keeps growing, and one finger moves.

Initiates into the mysteries of Cybele and Attis ate herbs from a drum and drank milk from a cymbal, replicating the behavior of one reborn.[97] For this reason, the drum and cymbal were considered sacred cult objects. Moreover, the drum and cymbal were used in the worship of Cybele and Attis, sounding the rhythms that accompanied the crescendo of orgiastic frenzy and self-inflicted cuttings. At the height of frenzy, some males would enter a trance-like state and castrate themselves in an apparent reenactment of the myth. These self-castrated eunuchs were known as *galli* and lived subsequently in service of the cult.

Another spectacular ceremony was the *taurobolium*. In this ceremony, the high priest would enter a pit specifically constructed for the occasion. Over the pit was a wooden lattice with many openings to the pit below. With the priest in the pit, a bull was led onto this lattice and its throat slit. The blood flowed through the holes in the lattice and down onto the priest in a ceremony that Christian apologists considered a perverted parody of true baptism.[98] The priest would let the blood flow onto his hair, into his open eyes and mouth, and over his body. When the blood ceased flowing, the priest would present himself to the congregants for whom he had vicariously undergone this purificatory ritual.

Isis and Osiris

The mystery religion of Isis and Osiris developed out of an Egyptian religious myth. This myth had competing versions, and no complete account is extant from Egypt itself. A full version exists in Greek, produced by juxtaposing the various Egyptian narratives (Plutarch, *Is. Os.*;

---

96. Klauck, *Religious Context of Early Christianity*, 121–22.

97. Ibid., 124–26.

98. It is a matter of historical debate whether the advent of the *taurobolium* postdates that of Christian baptism.

Mor. 351C–384C). According to the myth, Isis and Osiris were sibling deities and consorts. Seth, a rival for the affections of Isis, attacked Osiris, confined him in a wooden box, and cast him into the sea. In a scene reminiscent of Demeter's wanderings in search of Persephone, Isis searched for Osiris and eventually found his body. However, Seth obtained the body again, this time dividing it into small pieces and sending them throughout Egypt. A tomb was constructed for each piece, thus accounting for the multiple graves of Osiris.

Arguably the most intimate, sympathetic account of the mystery religion of Isis and Osiris comes from the novel, *Metamorphoses* (also called *The Golden Ass*) by Apuleius. Although it is necessary to maintain the requisite caution due to the genre of the text as fiction rather than autobiography, much can be learned about the cult of Isis through *Metamorphoses*.[99] The novel narrates the spiritual quest of the protagonist, Lucius. Lucius begins as an over-curious youth, who turns into a donkey through his unskilled dabbling in magic. He becomes a fulfilled initiate of Isis with his human form restored by following the instructions of the goddess.[100] Apuleius offers a memorable account of Lucius's initiation. He had offered himself as a candidate, but the priest warned him that he would have to wait until the time at which he would be chosen. The novel at this point conveys the sense of expectation and impatience of Lucius. When the time finally arrived for Lucius to be initiated, he approached the event with zeal. Although declaring his inability to relate much of what he had done and seen because of vows of secrecy, he goes on to provide substantial detail. He tells, for instance, about the sacred robe he wore:

> ... I came forth wearing twelve robes as a sign of consecration. This is a very holy attire, but no obligation prevents me from talking about it, since at that time a great many people were present and saw it. Following instructions I stood on a wooden platform set up in the very centre of the holy shrine in front of the goddess's statue, the focus of attention because of my garment, which was only linen, but elaborately embroidered. An expensive cloak hung down my back from my shoulders

---

99. Cf. Festugière, *Personal Religion*, 72–77. Festugière concludes, "It is, then, certainly Apuleius who speaks" (76).

100. Along the way, Lucius experiments with a variety of religious options. For this reason the novel has served as the framework for one modern author's exposition of Greek religion (Martin, *Hellenistic Religions*, 16).

all the way to my heels. Moreover, from whichever direction you looked I was conspicuously marked all round with vari-coloured animals: on one side were Indian dragons and on the other Hyperborean gryphons which look like winged birds and are produced in another world. Initiates call this garment the Olympian stole. In my right hand I carried a torch alight with flames, and my head was beautifully bound with a crown made of leaves of shining palm, jutting out like rays of light. After I had thus been decorated in the likeness of the Sun and set up in the guise of a statue, the curtains were suddenly opened and the people wandered round to view me. (Apuleius, *Metam.* 11.24 [Hanson, LCL])

Following the initiation, Lucius has a deep emotional connection to the goddess. He says,

O holy and eternal saviour of mankind, you who ever bounti-fully nurture mortals, you apply the sweet affection of a mother to the misfortunes of the wretched. . . . But my talent is too feeble to speak your praises and my inheritance too meagre to bring you sacrifices. The fullness of my voice is inadequate to express what I feel about your majesty; a thousand mouths and as many tongues would not be enough, nor even an endless flow of inexhaustible speech. I shall therefore take care to do the only thing that a devout but poor man can: I shall store your divine countenance and sacred godhead in the secret places of my heart, forever guarding it and picturing it to myself. (Apuleius, *Metam.* 11.25 [Hanson, LCL])

Lucius undergoes two additional initiation ceremonies and eventually becomes a priest of Isis. As Klauck rightly points out, however, the multiple initiations do not imply stages of initiation but rather renewals of initiation in new cult centers or for new personal needs.[101] The narrative is remarkable in two respects. First, it gives a sense of the emotional depth of Lucius's personal commitment to Isis. This is a quality not readily found in the ancient civic religions. Second, it reveals the pastoral care of the priest of Isis. It was unusual for priests in the Greco-Roman world to exhibit such a high degree of personal concern. Here, the priest advises, admonishes, and encourages Lucius. He is called "a father to me" (Apuleius, *Metam.* 11.25 [Hanson, LCL]).

---

101. Klauck, *Religious Context of Early Christianity*, 136.

Mithraism

Mithraism was a popular mystery cult, especially among Roman soldiers. For this reason, most of the extant Mithraic shrines, today called Mithraea (singular, Mithraeum) by scholars, are located in areas where there were significant communities of soldiers. These Mithraea are all similarly constructed. They are underground, in the form of caves, and they all have stone benches and an altar at one end. There is also always a stylized image of Mithras killing a bull.[102] The iconography also includes figures of Cautes and Cautopates (holding a torch up and down, respectively), a scorpion, a snake, and a dog. As suggested by these depictions, the cult had connections to astrology. It was thought that the immortal soul descended through the spheres of the planets, acquiring an additional vice with the passing of each sphere. The initiations of Mithras enabled the soul to eliminate these vices and to re-ascend past the planetary spheres to the realm of light. With this soul journey in mind, John Ferguson aptly summarizes the internal significance of the religion: "For this is what Mithraism is about, the battle between light and dark, day and night, life and death, summer and winter, good and evil. The Mithraist was in the most literal sense on the side of the angels."[103]

There were seven levels of initiation in Mithraism: raven, male bride, soldier, lion, Persian, sun-runner, and father (Jerome, *Epist.* 107.2).[104] The highest level was the father, who was the head of an individual Mithraic community. Like other mystery religions, the secrets of initiation into the Mithraic mysteries remained well guarded. Still, iconographic evidence suggests that the initiation ceremonies included such activities as rites of purification (including the use of honey rather than water for two of the levels), the performance of feats of courage or endurance, and the ritual consumption of bread and water. The initiates into each level were presented with distinctive headgear specific to that

---

102. For a photograph of a Mithraic relief, see Beard, North, and Price, eds., *Religions*, 307.

103. John Ferguson, *Religions of the Roman Empire*, 121.

104. Information regarding several of these levels is rather obscure. For example, even the translation of the second level is disputed. Some translate, "male bride," while others translate, "larva of the bee" (see Klauck, *Religious Context of Early Christianity*, 142). Some translators prefer "Embryo" (Martin, *Hellenistic Religions*, 117). For this translation, Martin cites Merkelbach, *Mithras*, 88–90. Others offer textual emendations to "*cryphius* (the hidden one) or *gryphus* (vulture)" (see Klauck, *Religious Context of Early Christianity*, 143, n. 45.)

level.¹⁰⁵ Later the initiates refused to wear the headgear in public, declaring that Mithras was their crown (Tertullian, *Cor.* 15.3 [*ANF* 3:103]).

Authority in Mystery Religions

The assessment of Beard, North and Price with respect to the priests of certain mystery cults is well taken. They say,

> It is even harder to reconstruct any clear picture of the character of these ["oriental"] priesthoods than of the traditional priesthoods of the city [Rome]. They were in any case very varied, with individual cults having many different types of officials—full-time, part-time, male, female, and so on. But even more problematic is how to assess the wild, dangerous, 'odd' image of these priests often presented in Roman literature, and to judge how far that image reflects the 'real life' character of the priests.¹⁰⁶

Nevertheless, certain observations can be made. The first thing to note about authority in the mystery religions is the highly hierarchical nature of the mysteries. The Eleusinian mysteries had initiates into the lesser and greater mysteries, implying two levels of initiation. In addition, of course, there were higher levels of authority as required by the need for someone capable of conducting the initiation ceremonies. Similarly, as we have seen, Mithraism had a seven level hierarchy. Interestingly, these levels seem to have been divided into two tiers. The members of the first three initiation levels were known as attendants, while those of the last four were known as participants.¹⁰⁷ Thus, full initiation seems to have begun with the rank of lion. This implies that the hierarchy of persons in positions of authority comprised at least three levels.

The second thing to notice is that many mystery religions had a great many functionaries. For example, an inscription of the Bacchic cult lists the following:

> [To] Agripinilla the mystae whose names appear below [erected this statue]: Macrinus, the hero [*heros*], Kathegilla the torch-bearer [*dadouchos*], priests [7 names], priestesses [2 names], hierophant Agathopous, god-bearers [*theophoroi*, 2], assistant and tirer of Silenus [*hypourogos* and *seilenokomos*, 1], chest-bearers

---

105. Klauck, *Religious Context of Early Christianity*, 144–45.
106. Beard, North, and Price, eds., *Religions*, 209.
107. Tripolitis, *Religions of the Hellenistic-Roman Age*, 52.

[*kistaphoroi*, 3 women], chief herdsmen [*archiboukoloi*, 3], holy herdsmen [*boukoloi hieroi*, 7], leaders of bacchants [*archibassaroi*, 2; *bassaroi* were Thrassian bacchants], acolytes [*amphithaleis*, 2], bearers of the winnowing fan [*liknaphoroi*, 3 women], bearer of the sacred phallos [*phallophoros*, woman], fire-bearers [*purphoroi*, 2], secretary [(?) *hieromnemon*, 1], youth leaders [*archineaniskoi*, 1], women leaders of bacchants [*archibassarai*, 4], herdsmen [*boukoloi*, 11] . . . .[108]

As Frederick C. Grant points out, we do not know the precise functions of most of these officials.[109] The case is somewhat different with the Eleusinian mysteries where, surprisingly, control of the cultus was under the direction of the people of Athens. Two families, the *Kerykes* and the *Eumolpidai*, had a certain degree of authority over the mysteries and the initiates, and *hieropoioi* were in charge of finances within Athens.[110] Likewise, we have a degree of knowledge regarding the role of the father in the Mithraic communities. As the community's high priest, his responsibilities included overseeing the processes of initiation, teaching the new members, and defending the community's concerns.[111]

Finally, one of the distinguishing marks of authority figures in the mystery religions is their high degree of personal concern. As we have seen, this is especially true of the priest of Isis in Apuleius's novel. Similarly, according to Tripolitis, "More than in any other cult, the Mithraic initiate was a member of a closely knit family that aided each other; each member was protected by his victorious god both in this life and the next."[112] Over this "family" stood the member with the highest rank, the father. We see, then, that the mystery religions were somewhat connectional. However, the sense of connection did not extend multi-locally, as can be seen by the fact that Lucius, the main character in Apuleius's novel, was required to be re-initiated upon arrival in Rome.[113]

---

108. Vogliano, "La grande iscrizione," 215–31, esp. plate XXVII. Translated by Grant, *Roman Religion*, 57. Bracketed comments original to Grant.

109. Grant, *Roman Religion*, 58.

110. Cited in Rice and Stambaugh, *Sources*, 184–85.

111. Tripolitis, *Religions of the Hellenistic-Roman Age*, 54.

112. Ibid., 52.

113. Cf. Burkert, *Ancient Mystery Cults*, 51. He writes, "Ancient mystery cults did not form religious communities in the sense of Judaism or Christianity."

It is easy to see why, from a history of religions perspective, mystery religions are sometimes considered to offer precedent for the authority structure of early Christianity. Not only are they hierarchical, they also demonstrate personal, pastoral care. Historians argue about which religious group to credit for such innovations. More importantly, however, it must be acknowledged that the widespread longing for personal religion in the ancient world accounts for the phenomenal success of these religious systems. In that vein, it is possible to argue that the spread of religious innovations was not so much the result of inter-faith borrowings as of similar solutions to common personal needs.[114]

Greco-Roman Religions and Ecclesiastical Authority

When we analyze Greco-Roman religious leadership in the terms developed in the previous chapter, we may conclude that the dominant forms are those that we said should hypothetically be linked with Empire. The quintessential example of this, of course, is the religious reformation of Augustus. As we have seen, it is difficult to assess whether Augustus was motivated by political or religious sentiments. One likely reason for this is that both political and religious activities served the same end, namely the extension of the Roman Empire.

The other dominant forms of religion in the Greco-Roman world also served to maintain the status quo. The proliferation of Emperor worship was an extension of sentiments that had earlier come to expression in the Hellenistic world in response to the perception of having

---

114. Some of the mystery cults may be regarded as a belonging to a larger phenomenon of the ancient world, namely, the so-called voluntary associations (See, for example, Beck, "The Mysteries of Mithras," esp. 179. Cf. S. Ascough, "Voluntary Associations," 180). As is common recognized, even the voluntary associations without overt religions purposes normally incorporated unmistakable religious elements (cf. Kloppenborg, "Edwin Hatch," 213: "[Professional, athletic, literary, dining and cultic associations] shared, at least nominally, a 'religious' character and most, even those of a professional nature, had a tutelary deity."). The degree to which these associations influenced the structure of the early Christian church is an interesting question still under debate (See especially Ascough, "Voluntary Associations," 149–50). The scope of the present investigation precludes adequate exploration of this important question. For our present purposes, we must be content to concur with the observation of Stephen G. Wilson: "The impulse to reform, to speak for the unheard, to advance the cause of liberty and democracy, are not aims that we immediately associate with ancient associations—understandably so when we cast things in this modern way." Wilson, "Voluntary Associations," 2.

encountered a super-human entity. Although this religious expression grew over time, it continued to propagate the influence and power of the Roman Empire. Likewise the Greek civic religion functioned toward the stability of the present system. The purchase of priesthoods was firmly embedded in the dominant honor culture, and the major festivals served to stamp time with a certain predictability that functioned to facilitate diachronic continuity. One need look no further than the writings of Plutarch, a self-proclaimed priest at Delphi, to see how at least one religious functionary consistently urged a conservative stance with respect to traditional values and cultural institutions. Thus, while it is true that individuals vied for the honor associated with priesthoods (and thus through their conflict perpetuated the priestly institutions), it seems that religious institutions placed conservative constraints upon individuals who pursued leadership in the Greco-Roman world.

Even the mystery religions were predominantly conservative cultural institutions. This was especially true of the Eleusinian cult, with its semi-annual mysteries. These regularly recurring events were associated with well-placed families in Athens and had a stabilizing effect on the culture. Similarly, each of the mystery cults provided a means of maintaining cultural continuity. Even in the case of the cult of Magna Mater coming to Rome, the process was conducted in such a way as to incorporate this foreign cult into the larger Roman religious milieu. Thus, the mystery cults were embedded in the larger religious system in the Greco-Roman world.

From a typology of religion perspective, as we might expect, the religions of the Greco-Roman world tended to follow the ritual performance pattern. The interest in omens on the part of both Greeks and Romans, for example, betrays a concern for ritual propriety. As we have seen, when the Romans took the auspices, the purpose was to ascertain the fitness of a particular activity at the given time, not primarily to appease the gods. Greco-Roman religious leadership usually consisted of priests, who would have emphasized correct procedures and proper timing. On the other hand, where we see a certain degree of pastoral concern within the leadership (as in the cult of Isis, for example) there does seem to be a degree of emphasis on deeds of devotion. Even here, however, ritual performance seems to be dominant. Initiations had to take place according to an explicit (Eleusis) or implicit (Isis) timetable, rituals were performed according to exacting details, and leadership often followed a hierarchical pattern.

To be sure, there were elements of shamanic mediation in the Greco-Roman religious world. The healing cult of Asclepius seems to fall into this category. Individuals would come to Asclepius for a particular concern at the time of their need, and religious functionaries would prescribe certain activities to be performed by the ailing individual. However, the abundance of magical tablets and curses shows that the need for individual empowerment was not met by the organized religions of the Greco-Roman world. Thus, there was an undercurrent of religious activity that catered to the aspirations of countless people whose dreams and despairs remain unrecorded. In the nature of the case, however, this shamanic religious leadership remained informal. For this reason, it does not seem to have had a direct impact on the development of leadership in the early church.

Several noteworthy features emerge from the present portrayal of the central contours of religious authority in Greco-Roman religious systems. First, religious authority tended to mirror the structures of the prevailing political scene. The ancient Athenian religious structures manifested democratic leanings, and those of the Romans shifted from oligarchical to monarchical in nature. Second, developments in religious authority responded to needs for greater religious stability and desires for personal religious direction. This is demonstrated both by the Augustan concentration of religious power out of concern for the *pax deorum* and by the success of stratified mystery religions. Finally, in general, the different functionaries were not hierarchically arranged but instead fulfilled roles requiring different areas of expertise. To some extent this was true even in the mystery religions. For example, each of the grades of initiation into the Mithraic mysteries had distinctive duties to perform.

These observations lead to a provisional assertion, which will have to be tested in the remainder of the study: In the earliest authority structures of the church, differences in office reflected a separation of religious expertise rather than degrees of religious authority and power. On this view, for example, when the apostles affirmed seven for 'waiting tables' in order to devote themselves to concentrate on the word of God (Acts 6:1–7), they were establishing themselves as experts in the interpretation of Scripture and deacons as experts in maintenance of proper order. Only later, under the influence of the same forces that had caused the concentration of religious authority in Greco-Roman religions, were the various religious functions unified in the person of a monarchical bishop. Careful examination of the text of Acts, informed also by a study of the authority structures of Second-Temple Judaism, will be necessary to assess the validity of this hypothesis.

4

Authority in Second Temple Judaism

THE TERM, SECOND TEMPLE JUDAISM, IS A CONVENTION FOR DENOTING Judaism between the construction of the second temple after the return of certain exiles from Persia in 538–39 BCE until its destruction in 70 CE. However, this six-century period is not marked by uniform religious beliefs or practices. The present study investigates the leadership patterns and structures within Judaism during the Second Temple period, with special emphasis on the situation in the first century of the Common Era. The first century, of course, coincides with the rise of Christianity and with at least the beginnings of the so-called parting of the ways between Judaism and Christianity.[1] The contours of first-century Judaism before 70 CE have the greatest likelihood of influencing the developing forms of primitive Christianity. After 70 CE, parallel developments in Christianity and Judaism are most likely the result of similar responses to common external forces, not of direct influence or dependency.

The study begins with a brief historical overview of the Second Temple period. This overview sets the context for a more thorough analysis of the institutions and groups of first-century Judaism. We shall begin by examining the three Jewish institutions that seem to have been founded during the Second Temple period, namely, the *gerousia*, the sanhedrin, and the synagogue. Next, we will turn to Jewish groups that were prominent during the first century. Here we will study the Pharisees, the Sadducees, and the Essenes. In each case, we shall assess the nature and function of leadership as understood within each

---

1. For a discussion of the contours of the debate over the timing and mechanism of the separation of Christianity from Judaism, see Dunn, *The Partings of the Ways*. For an extended, detailed look at the process as it occurred in Antioch studied from the perspective of sociology, see Zetterholm, *The Formation of Christianity in Antioch*.

institution or group. From this vantage point, we will draw general conclusions regarding leadership in Second Temple Judaism.

Historical Overview of the Second Temple Period

Second Temple Judaism may be divided into roughly four time periods: the Persian period, the Hellenistic period, the Hasmonean period, and the Roman period. The Roman period can be further subdivided to include a Herodian period. It should not be supposed, however, that these divisions mark socio-historical discontinuities. As Lawrence Schiffman points out regarding the transition from the Persian to the Hellenistic period,

> As the Persian period drew to a close, the signs of Greek influence on the material culture of Palestine steadily increased. Greek mercenaries, traders, and scholars were visiting the country in ever larger numbers, making a distinctive mark on its character. Thus the dawning of the Hellenistic period . . . came as the completion of a cultural process long under way.[2]

With this caveat in mind, we turn our attention to the first period of Second Temple Judaism.

The Persian Period (538–332 BCE)

The Bible itself records the beginnings of the Persian period in the books of Ezra and Nehemiah. These books describe the return of some exiles from the Persian Empire and their reconstruction of the temple and city wall. Certain themes prevalent throughout the Second Temple period begin to emerge already in these books. For example, Nehemiah exhibits a close connection between temporal and religious leadership. Although he was the governor, Nehemiah performed religious functions such as purging the temple (Neh 13:4–9) and appointing priests to specific tasks (Neh 13:13). As we shall see, the connection between the two types of leadership is a complicating factor throughout the Second Temple period.

---

2. Schiffman, *From Text to Tradition*, 42–44.

The Hellenistic Period (332–63 BCE)

Direct information regarding the Hellenistic period is scarcer than that of the previous period, since we do not have any contemporary historical descriptions. We do, of course, have literature from this period, yet this literature narrates few contemporary events. For example, the Astronomical Book of Enoch (1 En. 72–82) seems to have been written during the Hellenistic period.³ Such works supply limited information regarding the attitudes, beliefs, and behaviors characteristic of Second Temple Judaism, even though their subject matter does not deal directly with the history of the Hellenistic period. Our principal sources for the historical events of the Hellenisitic period, therefore, are the writings of Josephus (especially *Jewish Antiquities*) and 1 and 2 Maccabees.

From the primary sources, we learn that throughout the Hellenistic period, the fortunes of the Jews were fashioned in large part by the maneuverings of the Ptolemies to the south and the Seleucids to the north. Evidence suggests that different Jewish factions favored one or the other of the neighboring powers. The welfare of each Jewish faction seems to have waxed or waned relative to the success of its preferred foreign overlord. For example, Hyrcanus, a nephew to the high priest with ties to the Ptolemies, killed himself when the Seleucids gained control over the Land of Israel (*Ant.* 12.236). Later, Onias III lost the high priesthood when his brother, Jason, purchased the office from Antiochus IV (2 Macc 4:7–10). Onias III was later killed (2 Macc 4:33–34) and his son, Onias IV, fled to Egypt (*Ant.* 12.387). Onias IV then founded the temple at Leontopolis with the intention of establishing a rival to the Jerusalem temple (*J.W.* 7.423–32).⁴

The Oniad temple was not the only alternative to the Jerusalem cult during the Second Temple period; there were at least three others: the Elephantine (Egypt) temple, the Tobiad temple in Transjordan, and the Mount Gerizim temple.⁵ The existence of these temples demonstrates that Judaism in the Second Temple period was more diverse than the conventional traditions would imply. The Judaism represented

---

3. VanderKam, *Introduction to Early Judaism*, 89.
4. Cf. Ibid., 19 and 50.
5. Ibid., 203.

by the temple at Elephantine, in particular, exhibited a high degree of syncretism and accommodation to the host culture.[6]

The Hasmonean Period (c. 140–63 BCE)

Toward the end of the Hellenistic period, a Jewish family, the Hasmoneans, succeeded in gaining independence from the Hellenistic overlords. Nevertheless, the Hasmoneans, or Maccabees, were unable to stop the spread of Hellenism in the Land of Israel. For this reason, the period of Hasmonean rule is usually considered part of the Hellenistic period. The internecine intrigues of the Hasmoneans are complex and often confusing. Nevertheless, the fact that the roots of some of the groups we will encounter in the first century are planted in Hasmonean soil requires us to touch on these intrigues briefly.

One of the more important developments from this period is the conjunction of temporal and spiritual power in a single person. Although the Hasmoneans were not of Zadokite stock (1 Macc 2:1), they procured the high priesthood. Thus, the Maccabees were able both to gain Jewish independence from the Seleucid rulers and to acquire control of the dominant religious institution. The extent of the power granted to the Hasmoneans is suggested by the following passage in 1 Maccabees:

> The Jews and their priests have resolved that Simon [son of Mattathias] should be their leader and high priest forever, until a trustworthy prophet should arise, and that he should be governor over them and that he should take charge of the sanctuary and appoint officials over its tasks and over the country and the weapons and the strongholds, and that he should take charge of the sanctuary, and that he should be obeyed by all, and that all contracts in the country should be written in his name, and that he should be clothed in purple and wear gold. None of the people or priests shall be permitted to nullify any of these decisions or to oppose what he says, or to convene an assembly in the country without his permission, or to be clothed in purple or put on a gold buckle. Whoever acts contrary to these decisions or rejects any of them shall be liable to punishment. (1 Macc 14:41–45 NRSV)

---

6. Ibid., 9.

The concentration of temporal and spiritual authority in the hands of one individual was to have enduring effects on the subsequent history of the Jews. We have argued above that religious authority structures mirrored political organization in the Greco-Roman world (see pages 100–103). If that is the case, perhaps the amalgamation of temporal and spiritual authority among the Jews in the Hasmonean period was a natural result of the Hellenizing forces evidenced throughout the circum-Mediterranean world during that period. From the Hasmonean period on, it becomes difficult to compartmentalize the two types of power or authority in the Jewish world. Indeed, it seems more difficult to separate the two than in the Greco-Roman context.

Two other developments in the Hasmonean period require comment. First, the Pharisees and Sadducees emerged during this period. The impetuses and mechanisms of their founding and initial growth remain obscure. We do know, however, that the two parties[7] were influential during the reign of John Hyrcanus (124–104 BCE). We read about the court intrigues between the Pharisees and Sadducees as they jockeyed for power. According to Josephus, the Pharisees lost their standing with John Hyrcanus when he asked the Pharisees for their opinion of him (*Ant.* 13.288–96). Although the Pharisees as a group placated him by telling him how well he measured up to their standards, one Pharisee by the name of Eleazar spoke out against him. The predictable result was that John Hyrcanus turned against the Pharisees and embraced the Sadducees instead. Though this story may not be entirely historical, it likely contains a historical kernel, namely, that the Pharisees and Sadducees were prominent groups by the time of the Hasmoneans and that they vied for dominance with each other. This historical judgment gains further support from another story related by

---

7. We use "party" as a convenient word merely to designate an identifiable sociological grouping. Cf. Neusner, "Mr Sanders' Pharisees and Mine," 75: "The Pharisees formed a social entity, of indeterminate classification (sect? church? political part? philosophical order? cult?), in the Jewish nation in the Land of Israel in the century or so before A. D. 70." It should be noted that Josephus uses the term αἵρεσις to classify the Pharisees, Sadducees, and Essenes. Αἵρεσις can be translated "party," but it has other meanings as well. According to Rengstorf's concordance, Josephus uses αἵρεσις thirty-one times (Rengstorf, ed., *A Complete Concordance to Flavius Josephus* 1:35). It appears that αἵρεσις is used in conjunction with the Pharisees, Sadducees, and Essenes only seven times (Josephus, *J.W.* 2.162, *Ant.* 13.171, 288, 293, *Life* 12, 191, 197), where it is translated variously with "sect" or "school" by Thackeray (LCL). In addition to αἵρεσις, Josephus also uses τάγμα and φιλοσοφία to refer to these groups.

Josephus (*Ant.* 13.399–407). In this story, Alexander Janneus (reigned 103–76 BCE) told his wife, Salome Alexandra, on his deathbed that she should curry the favor of the Pharisees, since they had the support of the populace. Salome Alexandra then inherited the throne from her husband. Following Alexander Janneus's advice, Salome Alexandra backed the Pharisees and was a highly successful ruler as a result. According to Josephus, τὸ μὲν οὖν ὄνομα τῆς βασιλείας εἶχεν αὐτή, τὴν δὲ δύναμιν οἱ Φαρισαῖοι (*Ant.* 13.409).[8]

A second development in the Hasmonean period is the probable foundation of the Qumran community. Despite their highly esoteric nature, the Dead Sea Scrolls contain enough hints to allow the tracing of the formation of the community. The difficulty in interpreting the relevant passages stems, in large part, from questions regarding the identity of unnamed individuals, such as the Wicked Priest and the Teacher of Righteousness.[9] One possible interpretation is to identify these individuals with a Hasmonean ruler and a Zadokite priest, respectively. Reading the Scrolls in this way, the central issue that led to the formation of the Qumran community was the usurpation of the high priesthood by a non-Zadokite.[10] Thus, the texts would reflect the struggle of a leader who was losing his authority to a powerful rival. This rival may have been Jonathan or Simon, who ruled from 152–142 and 142–134 BCE, respectively.[11] The Teacher of Righteousness, then, would have made his case that the Hasmoneans ought not to have taken both the temporal and spiritual leadership roles. The temple cult became impure because its leadership was improper. Therefore, the Teacher of Righteousness would be a dispossessed claimant to the high priesthood, who formed a rival community in opposition to the official Hasmonean ruler.[12] If this interpretation is correct, the Hasmoneans

---

8. Ralph Marcus translates as follows: "And so, while she had the title of sovereign, the Pharisees had the power" (Josephus, *Ant.* 13.409 [Marcus, LCL]).

9. Early hypotheses regarding the identity of these individuals included Jesus, Paul, John the Baptist, and James as candidates for one or the other. Cf. García Martínez, *Dead Sea Scrolls*, xlvii.

10. Cf. Schiffman, *From Text to Tradition*, 116.

11. VanderKam, *Introduction to Early Judaism*, 164.

12. Archaeology supports this interpretation, since the excavation of Khirbet Qumran indicates the community began occupation there shortly before or during the reign of John Hyrcanus (134–104 BCE). Paleographic analysis of the manuscripts, which indicates that some were copied as early as the third century BCE, also supports

must have forced the Zadokite priest, along with others who supported the old order, out of the city. These individuals together formed the new community where they concentrated on maintaining their state of purity under the conviction that one day God would restore them to leadership of the Jerusalem temple cult.

The Groningen Hypothesis offers a reconstruction preferable to the one just outlined.[13] One main feature of this hypothesis is that the Qumran community was a splinter group of Essenes that left the main group for the desert some twenty years after the initial founding. Therefore, there was a close connection in origin, belief, and practice between the Qumran community and the larger Essene party, but the two groups were not coterminous. In other words, while the Qumran community was Essene, not all Essenes were of the Qumran community. The Groningen Hypothesis has the advantage of accounting for both the commonalities and the differences between the Qumran community and what we know of the Essenes from classical sources. It also accounts for archeological and paleographical evidence by maintaining an early date for the founding of the community. Moreover, the hypothesis accounts for the inconsistencies in the description of the Wicked Priest—the designation refers to the succession of Hasmonean rulers, not to a single individual—and explains the distinctive halakhah as well as the polemical nature of many Qumran documents. The identification of the Qumran community as Essene also gains support from a classical source. According to Pliny the Elder, there was a community of Essenes near the Dead Sea (*Nat.* 5.73). For these reasons, the Groningen Hypothesis is the most likely solution of the puzzles of the Qumran community and its literature. We will discuss the leadership of the groups mentioned in this section (the Pharisees, Sadducees, and Essenes) below.

The Roman Period (63 BCE–70 CE)

The Hasmonean period ended in 63 BCE when the Roman, Pompey, conquered Jerusalem and defeated the Hasmonean, Aristobulus II (*Ant.* 14.64–76). For a time, the Hasmoneans maintained a certain level of influence, sometimes with the backing of powerful Romans, other

---

this interpretation (García Martínez, *Dead Sea Scrolls*, xxxix and xlvii).

13. García Martínez, *Dead Sea Scrolls*, liii–lvi.

times with the support of the Romans' rivals, the Parthians. Meanwhile the Idumean, Antipater, gained the confidence of the Romans and wielded considerable power. He appointed his son, Herod, governor of Galilee. Soon Herod was maneuvering himself into positions of power. In 40 BCE, the Roman senate appointed Herod as king, and in 37 BCE, Herod consummated his appointment by conquering the Hasmonean loyalists in Jerusalem (*Ant.* 14.385–87, 468–91). Herod maintained the position of king until his death in 4 BCE.

Herod's tenure is infamous. He was implicated in the death of numerous enemies and potential enemies. He even killed members of his own family, including two of his sons whom he suspected of plotting against him (*Ant.* 16.394). Herod continued what was to become the normal Roman practice of appointing and removing the Jewish high priest. One instance ended tragically when the young Herod-appointee drowned. According to Josephus, Herod arranged the death because the young man's popularity with the people and his Hasmonean lineage made him a threat (*Ant.* 15.50–56). Herod was called before Mark Antony to account for his role in the affair, but he avoided censure.

Clearly, there was a dark side to Herod, yet he seems to have been an effective ruler. He was able to maintain a greater level of peace and stability over a larger region for a longer period than any of his successors for the next century. He conducted extensive building projects, both at home and abroad (*Ant.* 15.318–41). Undoubtedly some of his success at home stemmed from the favor he curried in the broader Greco-Roman world through his underwriting of lavish projects. His most notable building projects within his realm include the port city of Caesarea and the renovation of the Jerusalem temple. A remarkable artist's conception of Herod's temple may be found in E. P. Sanders's work, *Judaism: Practice and Belief, 63 BCE–66 CE*.[14] As is clear from that sketch, Herod's temple would have been impressive even by today's standards.

One might get the impression from Herod's interest in upgrading the temple that he had a genuine concern for the Jewish religion. It is more likely, however, that he conducted this building project, like his others, in order to achieve personal honor.[15] Undertakings for the

14. Sanders, *Judaism*, 308.

15. My assessment of Herod's motivation accords with the evaluation of Josephus: "But because of his ambition (φιλοτιμίας) in this direction and the flattering attention

public weal were a common way of promoting self-honor, the dominant value in circum-Mediterranean culture.[16] Thus, the temple reconstruction was not a sign of Herod's interest in the Jewish temple, but a predictable participation in a common, culturally predicated practice. Strengthening this interpretation is the fact that Herod's other projects included pagan temples and civic buildings, such as a theater, which would have been anathema to a devout Jew (*Ant.* 15.267 and 339). If Herod had been interested in following the Jewish religion, he likely would have followed its strictures even outside Judea.

After Herod's death, his kingdom was divided into three parts, each ruled by one of his sons. Actually, this depiction is a simplification of a process that included opposing claims to the throne and mediation by Augustus in Rome (*Ant.* 17.219–49). In the end, Archelaus received Judea, Idumea, and Samaria; Antipas received Galilee and Perea; and Philip received Batanea, Trachonitis, Aurantitis, and Panias (*Ant.* 17.317–320). Archelaus acquired the title, ethnarch (ruler of the people), while both Antipas and Philip received the title, tetrarch (ruler of a fourth). Archelaus proved to be an ineffective ruler, and in 6 CE he was replaced by direct Roman rule after just ten years. Antipas and Philip retained their positions until 39 CE and 33/34 CE, respectively.[17]

As just noted, when Archelaus lost his position, Rome took over direct rule in Judea under the authority first of prefects (until the kingship of Agrippa I, 41–44 CE), and later of procurators (after the reign of

---

which he gave to Caesar and the most influential Romans, he was forced to depart from the customs (of the Jews) and to alter many of their regulations, for in his ambitious spending (φιλοτιμίας) he founded cities and erected temples—not in Jewish territory, for the Jews would not have put up with this, since we are forbidden such things, including the honouring of statues and sculptured forms in the manner of the Greeks,—but these he built in foreign and surrounding territory. To the Jews he made the excuse that he was doing these things not on his own account but by command and order, while he sought to please Caesar and the Romans by saying that he was less intent upon observing the customs of his own nation than upon honouring them. On the whole, however, he was intent upon his own interests or was also ambitious (φιλοτιμούμενος) to leave behind to posterity still greater monuments of his reign. It was for this reason that he was keenly interested in the reconstruction of cities and spent very great sums on this work" (Josephus, *Ant.* 15.32830 [Marcus, LCL]).

16. See the discussion of honor/shame, pages 44–47.

17. VanderKam, *Introduction to Early Judaism*, 39.

Agrippa I).[18] Most of these Roman rulers had only a short tenure. The average was only four years, and nine of the fourteen ruled for three years or less. The rulers and their tenures are indicated in Table 4.1:

Table 4.1: Roman Rulers of Judea, 6–66 CE[19]

	Dates (CE)	Duration (years)
Coponius	6–9	3
Marcus Ambibulus	9–12	3
Rufus Tineus	12–15	3
Valerius Gratus	15–26	11
Pontius Pilate	26–36	10
Marcellus	36–37	1
Marullus	37–41	4
Cuspius Fadus[20]	44–46	2
Tiberius Julius Alexander	46–48	2
Ventidius Cumanus	48–52	4
Antonius Felix	52–60	8
Porcius Festus	60–62	2
Albinus	62–64	2
Gessius Florus	64–66	2

18. According to Schiffman, "[The Roman governors] are customarily called procurators by modern scholars, but initially their true title was prefect, and it was only during the reign of the emperor Claudius (41–54 CE) that the term procurator came into use to designate them" (Schiffman, *From Text to Tradition*, 146). It is tempting to dismiss the distinction as mere semantics, yet the distinction remains important for assessing the care with which ancient historians worked. Pilate is correctly called prefect, as substantiated by an archaeological discovery in Caesarea with Pilate's name and title still visible (Schiffman, *From Text to Tradition*, 151). Josephus uses the Greek terms ἡγεμών and ἐπίτροπος (*Ant.* 18.55 and *J.W.* 2.169, respectively) for Pilate; the Loeb edition translates both these as "procurator." The NT uses ἡγεμών for Pilate (Matt 27:2—Luke 3:1 uses the cognate verb), Felix (Acts 23:24, 26), and Festus (Acts 26:30).

19. Schiffman, *From Text to Tradition*, 148. The stated durations are the result of simple subtractions of the dates given.

20. During this three year gap, Judea was ruled by a king, Agrippa I. The Romans suspended direct rule during this period in favor of rule by Agrippa I, who thus extended his jurisdiction over the entire realm once ruled by his grandfather, Herod the Great. After the death of Agrippa I (narrated in Acts 12:20–23), the Romans resumed direct rule (VanderKam, *Introduction to Early Judaism*, 39–41).

During this same period, the following individuals held the Jewish high priesthood:

Table 4.2: Jewish High Priests, 6–66 CE[21]

	Dates (CE)	Duration (years)
Ananus son of Sethi (Annas)	6–15	9
Ishmael son of Phiabi	15–?	c. 1
Eleazar son of Ananus		c. 1
Simon son of Camithus	?–18	c. 1
Joseph Caiaphas	18–36	18
Jonathan son of Ananus	36–?	c. 2
Theophilus son of Ananus	?–41	c. 3
Simon Cantheras son of Boethus	41–?	c. 1
Matthias son of Ananus		c. 1
Elionaeus son of Cantheras	?–44	c. 1
Joseph son of Camei	44–?	c. 2
Ananias son of Nedebaeus	?–48	c. 2
Ishmael son of Phiabi	50–?	c. 3
Joseph Cabi son of Simon	?	c. 3
Ananus son of Ananus	?	c. 3
Jesus son of Damnaeus	?	c. 3
Jesus son of Gamaliel	?	c. 2
Matthias son of Theophilus	?–66	c. 2

Under direct Roman control, the rulers continued to follow the precedent set by Herod of appointing and removing the high priest at will. There were several consequences of this state of affairs. First, there was a relatively high degree of instability. When we consider the two offices (high priest and Roman ruler) together, the longest period without change in one or the other was ten years, from 26 to 36 CE (during the tenures of Pilate and Caiaphas). Undoubtedly the lack of stability contributed to the sense of unrest, which ultimately resulted in the revolt and subsequent destruction of the temple. Second, the retention of the high priesthood became increasingly dependent upon one's

21. VanderKam, *Introduction to Early Judaism*, 179. Except for Ananus and Caiaphas, the dates are only approximate. They depend on the dates of the ruler who appointed them.

political skills. A high priest who could convince successive Roman rulers of his utility could preserve his position for quite some time. Such political shrewdness seems to have been the forte of Ananus, who served through the administration of three Romans (Coponius, Marcus Ambibulus, and Rufus Tineus). As the high priesthood devolved into a politically dependent institution, its function naturally gravitated toward the more political aspects of the institution. Since strong political skills became a prerequisite for the high priesthood, we can expect that the high priests would have played to this strength. Finally, the nature of religious leadership underwent changes at the highest levels. We would expect, therefore, that lower level religious leaders would emulate their superiors, replicating their political maneuverings. On the other hand, there could also be a conservative backlash against the changes in the nature of religious leadership. Such a backlash seems to have driven some of the partisan maneuverings in the first century.

Second Temple Institutions

This brings us to the end of our brief historical survey of the Second Temple period. There remains for us to discuss, however, the case of three elusive institutions, which seem to have had their start during this period: the *gerousia*, the sanhedrin, and the synagogue.[22]

The Gerousia

The *gerousia* was a counsel of elders that functioned at least since the early part of the Second Temple period.[23] The exact history, constitution, and function of the *gerousia* remain largely obscure. There were also *gerousiai* in the diaspora. According to James T. Burtchaell, each Jewish community had a council of elders known as its *gerousia*.[24] Like

---

22. It is curious to note that all three of these terms are derived from the Greek, not the Aramaic or Hebrew. The proximate reason for this is that the terms come to us via Greek-language sources, such as Josephus and Philo. It poses an interesting problem, however, since one wonders how much has been shifted in the translation. For example, was a higher degree of order imposed on the facts than was warranted? Were there comparable titles in Aramaic or Hebrew, which would have been recognized as such by native speakers? Were these institutions standing bodies, as the Greek titles suggest, or were they informal, ad hoc gatherings of notables? Cf. Sanders, *Judaism*, 542, n. 62.

23. Safrai, "Jewish Self-government," 381; Sanders, *Judaism*, 319.

24. Burtchaell, *From Synagogue to Church*, 237.

the *gerousia* in Jerusalem, these bodies appear to have been comprised of the heads of leading families. Still, how families were deemed 'leading' is unclear. According to R. Alastair Campbell,

> We may take it for granted that there was in all of these Jewish communities a γερουσία, but if so, then it is not likely to have been a body with defined membership or fixed constitutional rights and duties. In light of what we have seen of the Sanhedrin in Jerusalem, it is more likely to have met as required to rule on matters of dispute in the community, and to have consisted of the senior representatives of the leading families. Its members could be referred to as 'the elders', but this was everywhere an imprecise term of honour of fairly widespread application.[25]

The *gerousiai*, therefore, likely consisted of the heads of honorable families. The process of assembling the *gerousiai* was probably an informal one whereby potential participants were invited to "show up" at the meeting time. Conversely, it is unlikely that individuals were officially excluded from the *gerousiai*. Instead, anyone who had lost favor with the group simply was not informed of the next assembly. Gaining sufficient honor to break into the rank of *gerousia* families would have been difficult, but it would have been relatively easy to lose honor. As a result, the size of the *gerousiai* would have tended to become smaller over time. Moreover, elders would have experienced a great deal of pressure to retain their place. They would have had to be constantly on the guard against dishonoring themselves or their family. This personal wariness would have tended to make the *gerousiai* a relatively conservative institution.

Headed by the high priest, the Jerusalem *gerousia* would have been responsible for both religious and temporal leadership. This body helped institute the celebration of Hanukkah (2 Macc 1:10—2:18). The elders of the *gerousia* also facilitated the defense of Judea (Jdt 4:6–8, 5:1) and arranged treaties with outsiders (1 Macc 12:5–18). As stated above, the *gerousia* would have been a conservative body, so it is unlikely that it would have initiated major cultural changes, whether religious, ethical, or behavioral. It would have worked to maintain the status quo, even if that required certain concessions.

---

25. Campbell, *The Elders*, 52–53.

Sanhedrin

The Sanhedrin appears to have been a governing body during the Herodian period and later, for which the Jerusalem *gerousia* was the organizational predecessor during the Maccabbean period. The Sanhedrin figures in many primary sources, from Josephus to the Mishnah. As James C. VanderKam and others have noted, the descriptions of the Sanhedrin in these various sources do not agree with each other in every detail, leading some scholars to posit the existence of multiple institutions.[26] The scholarly consensus, however, is that all sources refer to a single body; the differences in the sources are the result of different emphases or of changes over time. Sanders succinctly summarizes the majority view as follows:

> Most scholars have thought that the evidence can all be conflated into a one-sanhedrin theory. Josephus' *boulē* is the Mishnah's Sanhedrin and also the New Testament's Synedrion. It consisted of seventy or seventy-one men, and it served as both a legislative assembly and a supreme court. Pharisees were admitted to it during the reign of Salome Alexandra. Since it contained both Pharisees and Sadducees, it was a 'representative national body.' From time to time the majority changed. After the reign of Salome Alexandra, the Pharisees were increasingly recognized as the only 'religious' authorities. Some hold that by then the priests had lost all interest in the law. Therefore when the issue was 'religious,' a Pharisee presided (as in the Mishnah); when the issue was 'governmental' the high priest presided (as in the New Testament, where the court decides on the *religious* question of blasphemy!) The Sanhedrin always existed, at least from about 135 BCE to 66 CE; its members were appointed for life; and they continued in office even when there was a change in the head of state.[27]

Yet Sanders and others have questioned the very existence of the Sanhedrin as a standing institution during the first century.[28] They do, of course, admit that the Sanhedrin figures in the primary sources for the period, but they insist that it was an ad hoc institution, called into existence at the instigation of a higher authority for the purpose

---

26. VanderKam, *Introduction to Early Judaism*, 184.

27. Sanders, *Judaism*, 474, emphasis original. The quoted paragraph neatly summarizes the position of Safrai, "Jewish Self-government," 379–92.

28. Campbell, *Elders*, 30–31; Sanders, *Judaism*, 475–78.

of rubber-stamping that authority's will. According to Sanders, scholars wrongly insert the Sanhedrin into stories where it does not exist.[29] He offers two compelling examples. First, the Sanhedrin is mentioned nowhere in Josephus's story of Salome Alexandra, despite scholarly reconstruction of the Sanhedrin as a representative body whose balance of power shifted toward the Pharisees because of Salome Alexandra's endorsement. Second, the Sanhedrin plays no part in the story of Herod conquering Jerusalem. The Sanhedrin is only mentioned once previously in Josephus, and Sanders finds it unlikely that a body as durable and powerful as scholars assert would have done nothing to warrant mention before Herod ascended the throne. Moreover, he finds it unlikely that Herod would have killed just enough members of the Sanhedrin (the forty-five mentioned in *Ant.* 15.6) to create a majority in his favor, especially since *Jewish War* says he "exterminated the partisans" of his rival (*J.W.* 1.358).

Sanders's arguments seem to me to be quite persuasive. To his observations, I might add that there were other sanhedra in the Land of Israel during the first century. After Pompey conquered Judea, he installed Scaurus as ruler. Scaurus's successor, Gabinius, divided Judea into five sections, each governed by a sanhedrin (*Ant.* 14.91). Jerusalem was the site for one sanhedrin, while the others were at Gadara, Amathus, Jericho, and Sepphoris. If the Jerusalem council was only one of five, it is unlikely that the Sanhedrin in Jerusalem had the status and authority attributed to it by the majority of scholars. Yet Josephus describes the resulting government as an aristocracy (ἀριστοκρατία, *Ant.* 14.91).[30] This designation suggests that the members of the sanhedra came from a limited number of families.

In light of the sociological realities of the first century, therefore, it is likely that the Jerusalem Sanhedrin consisted of a relatively well-defined body of specific individuals, the elders. Moreover, even if the Sanhedrin existed as such only when called into existence for a particular purpose, its composition would have been relatively stable from one assembly to the next. Here we must part company with Sanders and Campbell, who assert that the ruler could choose whomever he or she

---

29. Sanders, *Judaism*, 475–8.

30. According to Ralph Marcus, the editor of the Loeb edition, "By 'aristocracy' Josephus means priestly rule, as he explains in *Ant.* xi.111" (Josephus, *Ant.* 14.91, note g [Marcus, LCL]).

liked to fill the Sanhedrin.³¹ It is rather more likely that a more complex situation existed, in which a more or less stable group of well-regarded elders regularly served as the Sanhedrin. Any modification to the composition of the Sanhedrin would have been an honor challenge, with all the associated risks that entailed.

The elders must have constituted a specific group of people, but they only became the Sanhedrin when they assembled for official business. Yet the convening authority—whether the high priest, the Herodian ruler, or anyone else—could not choose whomever he wished to be part of the Sanhedrin; he would have had to draw from the elders. These elders would have been identifiable as such by virtue of the honor in which the people held them. Therefore, despite Sanders's assertion to the contrary, the Sanhedrin would have had the power to contradict the will of the convening authority.³² At the same time, however, the complex relationships produced by the position of the elders as intermediaries between the convening authority and the people at large would have restricted the choices of the Sanhedrin.

The foregoing discussion relates the ordinary functioning of the Sanhedrin; it does not preclude, however, the complete reconstitution of the Sanhedrin by bold and powerful individuals who were willing to accept the risks of extreme challenges to the status quo. Herod was certainly such an individual. Gabinius, as a victorious military officer, would also have been in a position to make wholesale changes to the constitution of the council. We can surmise, therefore, that there was discontinuity between the *gerousia* and the Sanhedrin, even though the two institutions likely functioned in similar ways. However, we must reject the notion that each ruler would have formed his or her own council.³³ Discontinuities in the constitution of the Sanhedrin would have been the exception, not the rule.

---

31. Sanders says, "... rulers could nevertheless empanel a group of their supporters for a trial" (Sanders, *Judaism*, 488). Campbell likewise argues, "... the ruler in convening the court was also likely to determine its membership" (Campbell, *Elders*, 32).

32. Sanders, *Judaism*, 480–81.

33. Sanders does not say that each ruler formed his or her own council, only that he or she would have wanted to do so (Sanders, *Judaism*, 477). This assertion, of course, we can affirm.

The Synagogue

The origins of the synagogue are largely lost to us, though there are certain clues from archaeology. Sites in Egypt suggest that the synagogue might have originated there as early as the Hellenistic period.[34] At that time, however, it was known by the Greek term προσευχή, or place of prayer.[35] The earliest known προσευχαί begin appearing in the third century BCE.[36] In the Land of Israel, the vast majority of synagogues date from the third century of the Common Era or later; only four can be dated to the Second Temple period.[37] It is likely, however, that more synagogues existed in the first century. One reason archaeologists do not find them is that in the first century synagogues usually met in private homes, not in dedicated buildings.[38] Another possible explanation is that the dearth of pre-70 synagogue structures is the result of a wider phenomenon in which the turmoil of the Jewish revolts or the reconstruction of subsequent centuries destroyed archeological evidence of all types.[39] In any case, there is no reason to doubt the historicity of the

---

34. According to Carsten Claussen, "Sixteen inscriptions and four papyri mention or seem to imply the existence of synagogues in Egypt between the third century BCE and the early second century CE . . . However, up to the present date no ancient synagogue building has been discovered in Egypt" (Claussen, "Meeting, Community, Synagogue," 147–48). Some earlier scholars surmised that the origins of the synagogue lay in the Persian period, but this is only speculation. See Gutmann, "Synagogue Origins," 1. See also Schiffman, *From Text to Tradition*, 166.

35. Following Campbell, who says, "It would not be wide of the mark to say that in general προσευχή is a Diaspora συναγωγή, and that συναγωγή is a Palestinian προσευχή" (Campbell, *Elders*, 46). Joseph Gutmann, like other scholars, views the προσευχή as something different from the synagogue (Gutmann, "Synagogue Origins," 3). While Gutmann's position is possible, it seems more likely that the προσευχή was the institutional predecessor of the synagogue. This judgment rests on the similarity of function between the two: both are gathering places for the worship of Jewish communities. Similarly, as Gutmann himself concedes, both institutions embodied responses to the pressures of Hellenization (Gutmann, "Synagogue Origins," 3–4). Despite the use of προσευχή in Acts in such a way as to suggest that it differs from the synagogue (Acts 16:13, τῇ τε ἡμέρᾳ τῶν σαββάτων ἐξήλθομεν ἔξω τῆς πύλης παρὰ ποταμὸν οὗ ἐνομίζομεν προσευχὴν εἶναι—no synagogue building seems to be in view), it is more likely that προσευχή was used to connote an unincorporated or small synagogue that lacked a permanent structure.

36. Gutmann, "Synagogue Origins," 3.

37. Levine, "Revolutionary Effects," 171.

38. Cf. Campbell, *Elders*, 48.

39. Levine, "Revolutionary Effects," 171.

New Testament references to synagogues in the Land of Israel already during the life of Christ.[40] The most likely reconstruction of the history of the synagogue, therefore, is that it started as a Diaspora institution in Egypt but soon gained popularity among Jews in many places. The discovery of one inscription (the so-called Theodotus inscription, which concerns a synagogue in Jerusalem for worshippers coming from the Diaspora[41]) suggests that pilgrims coming to Jerusalem during the festivals brought the idea of the synagogue with them, from whence it spread into other parts of the Land of Israel and back into still other parts of the Diaspora. This interpretation finds further support from the statement in Acts regarding the Synagogue of the Freedmen, which served pilgrims from Cyrene, Alexandria, Cilicia, and Asia (Acts 6:9).

The leadership of the synagogues seems to have evolved into a complex diversity of offices. James Tunstead Burtchaell argues that there was large number of offices in the synagogues of the late Second Temple period.[42] He describes the following as officers of the synagogue: elders (πρεσβύτεροι, πρεσβιτερής), notables (ἄρχοντες), senior elder (γερουσιάρχης), community chief (ἀρχισυνάγωγος, ἀρχισυναγωγίσσα), assistant (νεωκόροι, ὑπηρέτης), father and mother of the synagogue (πατήρ/μητήρ συναγωγῆς), scribe (γραμματεύς), priests (ἱερεῖς), commissioner (φροντιστής), teacher (διδάσκαλος), and reader. Campbell, however, insists that the evidence for these officers is later than the Second Temple period. He says,

> Burtchaell's list of synagogue officers is taken from Frey's *Corpus Insciptionum Judaicarum,* and this evidence, as well as being entirely epigraphic, is also for the most part later by some centuries than the period of earliest Christianity. . . . It is unlikely that the whole elaborate pattern of office and honour on which Burtchaell relies would have been appropriate to the earliest Christians, or even at that time available for their imitation.[43]

---

40. Cf. Riesner, "Synagogues in Jerusalem," 209.

41. Deissmann, *Light from the Ancient East,* 440. Cf. Acts 6:9, τινες τῶν ἐκ τῆς συναγωγῆς τῆς λεγομένης Λιβερτίνων καὶ Κυρηναίων καὶ Ἀλεξανδρέων καὶ τῶν ἀπὸ Κιλικίας καὶ Ἀσίας.

42. Burtchaell, *From Synagogue to Church,* 228–59.

43. Campbell, *Elders,* 203–4.

Table 4.3: Leaders in Synagogue Inscriptions[44]

TITLE	LOCATION	DATE
ἄζζανα	Apamea, Syria	4th Century
ἀρχισυνάγωγος	Aegina, Greece	4th Century
	Teos, Ionia	3rd Century
	Myndus, Caria	n.d.
	Akmonia, Phrygia	1st Century
	Side, Pamphyia	4th Century
	Apamea, Syria	391 CE
	Caesarea Palestine	6th Century
	Sepphoris-Diocaesarea, Palestine	5th Century
	Jerusalem, Palestine	1st Century?
	Constantia-Salamis, Cyprus	3rd Century
ἄρχων	Magne, Greece	3rd Century
	Olbia, Euxini	n.d.
	Akmonia, Phrygia	1st Century
	Constantia-Salamis, Cyprus	3rd Century
	Berenice Cyrenaica	n.d.
	Elche, Spain	n.d.
βουλευτής	Sardis, Lydia	3rd Century
γερουσιάρχης	Apamea, Syria	4th Century
διάκων	Apamea, Syria	4th Century
ἐπιστάτης	Athribis, Egypt	2nd Century BCE
ζυγοσάτης	Side, Pamphyia	5th Century
ἱερεύς	Jerusalem, Palestine	1st Century?
	Berenice Cyrenaica	n.d.
προστάτης	Alexandria, Egypt	n.d.

The evidence compiled from Baruch Lifshitz's work on Jewish synagogue inscriptions (see Table 4.3) supports Campbell's position. His book transcribes synagogue dedications and gives dates for most inscriptions. By comparing the various titles and their dates, one can readily see that most titles are both uncommon and late. While we can never have an exhaustive accounting of all ancient synagogues, the

44. Compiled from Lifshitz, *Donateurs et fondateurs dans les synagogues juives*.

relative scarcity of titles besides ἀρχισυνάγωγος and ἄρχων before the third century suggests that the diversification of synogogal offices did not become common until about that period.⁴⁵

We must conclude, therefore, that Campbell has a superior grasp of the material as it relates to our period. His reconstruction of the Second Temple synagogue leadership may be summarized as follows:

> The synagogue had two functionaries, the ἀρχισυνάγωγος and the ὑπηρέτης. The ἀρχισυνάγωγος was responsible for deciding who would read at the Sabbath service and for maintaining order during the service. The ὑπηρέτης was in charge of the physical building—where such existed—as well as discipline and the instruction of children. Any other leadership functions were performed, not by synagogal officers, but by officers of the Jewish community itself.⁴⁶

In sharp contrast with Burtchaell, Campbell argues that elders were officers of neither the synagogue nor the community. Instead, elder was an honorary term for individuals of distinction and influence, whatever their exact role or office might have been.⁴⁷

---

45. Cf. Brooten, *Women Leaders*, 57: "There exist two Greek inscriptions in which the title *mētēr synagōgēs* occurs (reconstructed), one Greek inscription in which a woman bears the title *mētēr*, two Latin inscriptions in which the title *mater synagogae* occurs, and one Latin inscription in which a woman bears the unusual title *pateressa*. All six of the inscriptions are from Italy, three being from Rome, two from Venosa in Apulia and one from Venetia in Brescia. They range in date from around the second century CE until perhaps as late as the sixth century." Cf. also Levine, "First Century CE Synagogue," 1: "The overwhelming bulk of information regarding the synagogue stems from Late Antiquity (third to seventh centuries)."

46. Surprisingly, many of the officials mentioned in this connection by Campbell are the same ones Burtchaell lists as synagogue officials: γερουσιάρχης, ἄρχοντες, φροντιστής, γραμματεύς, and πατήρ/μητήρ συναγωγῆς. If the evidence for these titles is late, surely that applies to the designations regardless of whether they refer to the synagogue or to the community generally. Especially considering the close connection in the ancient world between temporal and religious leadership, Campbell may be guilty of the same anachronistic error of which he accuses Burtchaell. This has no bearing, however, on the conclusions regarding the status and function of elders or the primary synagogal functionaries, the ἀρχισυνάγωγος and the ὑπηρέτης.

47. Campbell, *Elders*, 49–54.

Second Temple Groups

Pharisees

The Pharisees appear prominently in many first-century Jewish sources. It is surprising, therefore, that such a large range of uncertainty and debate exists concerning this group. The nature of our sources is the root of this ambiguity. We have no primary sources written by the Second Temple Pharisees themselves,[48] except perhaps the *Psalms of Solomon*.[49] Their treatment in other sources varies from tangential to hostile. In the case of the NT, the writings are antagonistic toward the Pharisees. In the gospels they appear as the foil to Jesus. For this reason, the descriptions of the group are one-sided. While they must contain recognizable traits of the Pharisees (otherwise the writings as a whole would have seemed incredible to the first-century audience), they do not supply an exhaustive perspective.

The works of Josephus offer another important source of information regarding the Pharisees. Josephus claims to have lived as a Pharisee himself (*Life* 12), so we may have an insider's perspective. Nevertheless, the relevant passages functioned as summaries for outsiders, not exhaustive treatments or detailed expositions for insiders. Moreover, Josephus may have desired to portray the Pharisees in an overly favorable light. If it is true that the post-70 Rabbis were the inheritors of the Pharisees, then Josephus may have been trying to identify himself with the winning party while at the same time justifying that party's dominance. Together, these factors mean that Josephus must be assessed carefully for any tendentiousness. One cannot accept his writings at face value as historical when it comes to his descriptions of the Pharisees.

Additional major sources for the beliefs and practice of the Pharisees come from the second century and later, namely, the Mishnah and other rabbinic Jewish documents. A crucial question regarding these sources is their degree of historical reliability: do they accurately reflect the realities of the first century, or do they reflect the concerns of the time in which they were written? Even where it is determined that

---

48. Neusner, "Sanders' Pharisees," 75.
49. Evans, *Noncanonical Writings*, 38.

a given pericope derives from the first century, one must still assess the extent of ahistorical accretions.[50]

Despite the questions regarding the historicity of our sources, the picture of the Pharisees that emerges from the sources is relatively consistent.[51] According to Anthony J. Saldarini, "The rabbinic laws and stories which can be somewhat reliably dated to the first century . . . show that the Pharisees had a strong interest in tithing, ritual purity and Sabbath observance."[52] Such concerns are consistent with the depiction of the Pharisees in the NT. For example, in Mark 2:24 (τί ποιοῦσιν τοῖς σάββασιν ὃ οὐκ ἔξεστιν;) the Pharisees question Jesus about his activities on the Sabbath, and Mark 7:1-5 (. . . διὰ τί οὐ περιπατοῦσιν οἱ μαθηταί σου κατὰ τὴν παράδοσιν τῶν πρεσβυτέρων, ἀλλὰ κοιναῖς χερσὶν ἐσθίουσιν τὸν ἄρτον;) demonstrates a Pharisaic concern for purity. Preoccupation with purity is common among groups whose identity is threatened and who therefore place a great deal of emphasis on boundary issues.[53] Such concerns are natural in a low-grid, high-group society like that of the first-century Jew, where there was pressure from competing compatriot groups and pressure from foreign overlords (see pages 40-42).

The sources also agree that the Pharisees held a belief in the afterlife (Acts 23:6-8; Josephus *Ant.* 18.14; *J.W.* 2.163). Some scholars contend that this belief was the result of contact with Hellenistic culture, not a

---

50. See Neusner, *Formative Judaism*, 71.

51. Contrast Neusner, *Formative Judaism*, 72: "The simple fact, which I wish to stress, is that there is a striking discontinuity among the three principal sources which speak of the Pharisees before 70, the Gospels, and the rabbinic writings of a later period, on the one side, and Josephus on the other." While Neusner is undoubtedly correct as it pertains to particulars, there, nevertheless, seems to be broad areas of agreement in all three sources, which we pursue here.

52. Saldarini, *Pharisees, Scribes and Sadducees*, 290. Cf. Neusner, "Sanders' Pharisees," 82: "One primary mark of Pharisaic commitment was the observance of the laws of ritual purity outside of the Temple, where everyone kept them. Eating one's secular, that is, unconsecrated, food in a state of ritual purity as if one were a Temple priest in the cult was one of the two significations of party membership." Here Neusner touches on a heated debate between himself and E. P. Sanders regarding the exact character of the Pharisaic party in the first century. Although the two agree on many points, they disagree sharply over the issues of whether the Pharisees ate secular food in ritual purity, whether the Pharisees espoused a normative Oral Law, and whether the Pharisees should properly be called a sect.

53. Cf. Saldarini, *Pharisees, Scribes and Sadducees*, 215.

product of a careful reading of Jewish scriptures.[54] Whether or not immortality is a native Jewish conception, there can be little doubt that the Pharisees believed it to be consistent with their sacred writings. Given their concern for boundaries noted above, it would be unlikely that they would have knowingly borrowed a belief they considered contrary to their own religion.

In addition to belief in the afterlife, Josephus reports that the Pharisees also believed in fate as well as in free will (*Ant.* 13.172, 18.13; *J.W.* 2.163). There is nothing inherently unlikely that the Pharisees held this view, even though other sources do not explicitly attributed this trait to the Pharisees.[55] Moreover, the description occurs in the context of an exposition of the four Jewish "philosophies." It is most likely, therefore, that the assertion that the Pharisees believed in fate was Josephus' attempt to explain the Pharisees' perspective in categories that would have been accessible to his audience, the Greco-Roman world. Still, it is unlikely that Josephus just made this up; rather, it is his interpretation of the Pharisees' views. The Pharisees probably did not talk explicitly about their views of fate within their own worldview. But neither would they have refuted Josephus' assertion had they read it.

Despite this full picture of the Pharisees, a number of crucial questions remain: how many Pharisees were there, where were they found, and how influential were they among their countrymen? With respect to the first question, Josephus gives the answer that there were 6000 Pharisees (*Ant.* 17.42).[56] If there were approximately 2,265,000 people in the Land of Palestine in the first century, 6000 Pharisees would be less than three tenths of one percent of the population.[57] Such a small percentage seems out of proportion with prominence given them in

---

54. Cf. Saldarini, *Pharisees, Scribes and Sadducees*, 304: "The Sadducees' belief is the traditional Biblical view; ideas of resurrection, immortality and afterlife entered Judaism in the second century BCE and only gradually dominated Judaism over the next four or five centuries."

55. Feldman, however, notes similar Talmudic sayings at *'Abot* 3.19, *Ber.* 33b, and *Nid.* 16b (Josephus, *Ant.* 18.13, note e [Feldman, LCL]). Thackeray also notes a similar saying by R. Akiba (Josephus, *J.W.* 2.163, note d [Thackeray, LCL]).

56. Of Josephus's figures for the Sadducees, Essenes, and Pharisees, Sanders correctly notes, "We cannot assume that these numbers are precise, but we should accept what they imply: that relatively few Jews belonged to one of the parties and that the Pharisaic party was the largest of the three, followed by the Essenes" (Sanders, *Judaism*, 14).

57. Byatt, "Josephus and Population," 56.

our sources. Still, in the ancient world, power was not had in numbers; power resided in the privileged class and its retainers. If the Pharisees were retainers of the rulers, 6000 may not be too small a number.

The Second Temple sources agree that the Pharisees were present in Jerusalem; the Synoptic Gospels alone picture the Pharisees also as active in Galilee as opponents of Jesus. Questions regarding the historicity of the Synoptic depiction have been raised, not only because the Pharisees are not mentioned as present in Galilee in other sources, but also because form criticism has suggested that references to the Pharisees are later additions to the Synoptic accounts.[58] However, as Saldarini notes, the Gospel of Mark was written before the destruction of the Temple at a time when its readers could have disputed its claims for the Pharisees.[59] He suggests that Pharisees in Galilee may have been retainers of the Jerusalem establishment, assisting in efforts to extend Temple authority and the tithe-collecting base outside Judea.[60] Although Saldarini himself remains non-committal ("In the end, whether the Pharisees were present in Galilee and what their roles there might have been remain uncertain and obscure."[61]), there seems to be no compelling reason to doubt their influential presence in small numbers in Galilee.

The extent to which the Pharisees were an influential group in the first century continues to draw scholarly debate. The traditional view, influenced particularly by Josephus's statement that the Pharisees were the most popular of the three philosophies (Pharisees, Sadducees, Essenes), is that the Pharisees were the dominant group throughout the first century. They were politically active, and their views dictated religious behavior among Jews from the temple leadership to the 'am ha-aretz throughout the Land of Palestine and beyond.[62] This perspective has been challenged, especially by E. P. Sanders and Jacob Neusner. Though these two scholars disagree on many points, they agree in

---

58. Saldarini, *Pharisees, Scribes and Sadducees*, 291.
59. Ibid., 291–92.
60. Ibid., 296.
61. Ibid., 297.
62. The term, 'am ha-aretz, is used here to denote the common people. In later rabbinic usage, 'am ha-aretz became a pejorative term for unschooled individuals who could not be counted on to have followed purity codes (Oppenheimer, '*Am Ha-Aretz*, 1–4).

arguing that the Pharisees were less prominent than has traditionally been thought.[63] Observations used to support this position include (1) the Pharisees largely drop out of Josephus's narrative after the account of Salome Alexandra, except for a brief appearance in the history of Herod, and (2) their prominence in the sources reflects the concerns of a later period, when the Pharisees had gained a certain degree of prominence and had returned to political activity. However, the explicit statements of Josephus regarding the Pharisees' prominence should weigh more heavily than his silence regarding their specific activities.[64] Moreover, even if the prominence of the Pharisees reflects the interests of a later period, the fact that the Pharisaic perspective endured the upheaval of the revolt strongly suggests that the Pharisees had a certain vitality to enable their endurance. Nevertheless, it seems likely that the situation was more complex than either the traditional view or the view of Sanders and Neusner. The Pharisees were indeed an important and influential group in the first century, but there were other powerful groups as well. Such groups included the Sadducees and the Jerusalem chief priests, whom Sanders stresses.[65]

Having established that the Pharisees functioned as leaders in the Judaism of the first century, it remains to evaluate the nature of that leadership. One helpful heuristic tool is Dale Cannon's religious typology (see pages 37–40). As we have seen, Cannon postulates six fundamental ways of being religious: the way of sacred rite, of right action, of devotion, of shamanic mediation, of mystical quest, and of reasoned inquiry. A reading of the primary sources suggests several possibilities for the Pharisees' primary way of being religious. Their well-known penchant

---

63. Neusner, "Sanders' Pharisees," 75; Sanders, *Judaism*, 401. Cf. Hengel and Deines, "Sanders," 4. Cf. also Saldarini, *Pharisees, Scribes and Sadducees*, 128, 132. It should be noted, however, that Sanders acknowledges a complex situation involving the parties of first-century Judaism. He says, "We have before us two extreme positions: that the Pharisees exercised general supervision of all aspects of life and Neusner's counter-proposal, that they dropped out of society altogether to form private eating clubs. Both extremes are unrealistic and can readily be shown to be so. The history that we have just surveyed shows that the Pharisees did not withdraw from society" (Sanders, *Judaism*, 389).

64. Contrast Sanders: "But [Morton] Smith's basic insight has been accepted by all four of us [Jacob Neusner, Shaye Cohen, Martin Goodman, and Sanders]: if one *studies cases*—reads Josephus' accounts of individual events—one can and must correct his often misleading summaries" (Sanders, *Judaism*, 401, emphasis original).

65. Sanders, *Judaism*, 317–40, 487. Cf. Hengel and Deines, "Sanders," 52.

for detailed rules suggests the way of right action, and their concern for Torah study suggests the way of reasoned inquiry. The centrality of the Temple to all groups during the Second Temple period suggests that the Pharisees also adhered to the way of sacred rite.

On Cannon's model, the ways of being religious can be combined into a more complex, multidimensional approach.[66] Yet typically one way will predominate, and the other approaches will be understood in terms of the dominant one. In the case of the Pharisees, there is evidence that the sacred rite was the primary way of being religious. As Neusner rightly points out, the Pharisees' interest in purity is in fact grounded in concern for sacred rites—despite Sander's protests to the contrary.[67] It was not until well after the first century that Judaism developed an understanding of rational inquiry as a means of spiritual encounter in its own right.[68] What, then, was the role of rational inquiry for the first-century Pharisees? The Pharisees likely understood their study to be undertaken for the purpose of rectifying ritual performance. Their study was not considered a direct means to God; rather, they thought study would yield a better understanding of the proper mechanisms necessary for proper conduct of the rituals. The proper performance of sacred rites was what would bring them into closer relationship with God. Similarly, social action,[69] while understood as commanded by God and therefore a way of pleasing him, was ultimately subordinated to the way of ritual performance.[70]

---

66. Cannon, *Six Ways*, 39.

67. Neusner, "Sanders' Pharisees," 94.

68. Ibid., 91.

69. I borrow here the vocabulary employed by Bartchy (Bartchy, "Lectures."). I find Bartchy's terminology to be clearer than Cannon's at certain points. In particular, where Cannon has "right action," Bartchy uses "social action." The latter term accurately reflects Cannon's meaning, while the former term is misleadingly vague.

70. The discussion of the Pharisees between Sanders and Neusner hinges on whether the Pharisees were interested in ritual. Sanders agrees that the Pharisees, like most people in the ancient world, valued ritual, but he redefines ritual in terms of "commemorative" and "ethical" components (Sanders, *Jewish Law*, 245). Neusner argues that the Pharisees valued ritual for ritual's sake (Neusner, "Sanders' Pharisees," 94). According to Neusner, Sanders's motivation is to shield the Pharisees from denigration by liberal Protestants, who have an aversion to ritual. Neusner rightly points out that rituals are important to Judaism, then as now (Neusner, "Sanders' Pharisees," 93–95). Cf. Swartz, "Sage, Priest, and Poet," 101.

If, as we have been arguing, the Pharisees were religious leaders whose primary way of being religious was ritual performance, then we should expect that the Pharisees would have been priests, the characteristic leaders for this way of being religious (see pages 37–40). Yet clearly not all Pharisees were priests. Whereas priests usually have expertise in proper performance of ritual, the Pharisees specialized in cognitive expertise. Most Pharisees were barred from actual performance of temple rituals because of their non-priestly descent; there were non-priestly Pharisees and priestly Pharisees, as well as non-Pharisaic priests. This fact suggests that the strictures of the Pharisees regarding the right performance of temple rituals must have differed from those of the average priest in identifiable ways. We can conclude, therefore, that the Pharisees' functional religious leadership entailed the study and promulgation of proper ritual procedures, yet only the Pharisaic priests had the ability to enforce their conclusions or put them into practice. Whatever power most Pharisees had with the people must have consisted of advising the *'am ha-aretz* in the proper preparation for ritual deeds. Therefore, the preparations advised by the Pharisees must have been acceptable to the temple priesthood, since otherwise they would have rejected the people's offerings. The leadership exerted by the Pharisees, then, was primarily of an advisory and exemplary type. As a group, the Pharisees would have held positions of respect and honor, with all the rights and responsibilities that such honor entailed in the first-century honor/shame culture.

Priests and Sadducees

It is common in the secondary literature to view the chief priests and the Sadducean party as virtually synonymous. For example, Martin Hengel and Roland Deines refer to "... the priestly aristocrats and the largely identical Sadducees...."[71] However, as Saldarini points out, the primary sources say neither that all Sadducees were priests nor that all priests were Sadducees.[72] The identification seems to have become a sort of scholarly shorthand, whereby distinctions between the two groups are left in the background without adequate justification. Nevertheless, there surely was significant overlap between the two groups, and much

---

71. Hengel and Deines, "Sanders," 55. Cf. Steve Mason, "Chief Priests," 156.
72. Saldarini, *Pharisees, Scribes and Sadducees*, 117, 121, 154, and 298.

Authority in Second Temple Judaism 131

of what is said of the one applies likewise to the other. Therefore, in the following discussion, the two groups will be treated in turn, but it should be realized that there will be some overlap analogous to that of the two groups themselves. Yet we must not assume that what is predicated of one group is necessarily representative of the characteristics of a particular individual from the other group.

The Sadducees, like the Pharisees, appear in many of the Second Temple sources. However, less is known about them because their beliefs and practices are not explained as fully.[73] In the NT, they appear largely as the allies of the Pharisees against Jesus. Whether this alliance was historical has been questioned.[74] However, Saldarini rightly observes that the two groups would have been natural allies when faced with a threat to their authority such as that which Jesus posed.[75] Both groups had gained a degree of status above that of the average person; they were similarly placed between the Roman rulers and the 'am ha-aretz. There is no reason to doubt, therefore, the NT description of the Sadducees as allies with the Pharisees against Jesus.

Elsewhere in the NT, the Sadducees are contrasted with the Pharisees. Specifically, the Sadducees are characterized as disbelieving in resurrection (Matt 22:23 and parallels, Acts 23:8). Josephus affirms this belief of the Sadducees in his description of the Jewish "philosophies" (*Ant.* 18.16, *J.W.* 2.165). Josephus also contrasts the two groups' views of fate. Whereas, as we have seen, the Pharisees are said to believe in free will in concert with fate, the Sadducees are said to believe in absolute free will (*Ant.* 13.173, *J.W.* 2.164). Again, this description may reflect Josephus's attempt to translate the viewpoint of the Sadducees into categories recognizable in the Greco-Roman world.[76]

It is difficult to reconstruct the nature of leadership among the Sadducees from this limited information. Certainly, we have no

---

73. Cf. Saldarini, "Though the Sadducees appeared, mostly along with the Pharisees, in Josephus, the New Testament and rabbinic literature, the sources give so little information about the Sadducees that great care and restraint is needed in characterizing them" (Ibid., 298).

74. Ibid., 166–67.

75. Ibid., 167.

76. The Sadducees also appear briefly in rabbinic literature. There, they are caricatured as the opponents of the Pharisees. It is unlikely that the descriptions contribute anything of historical value beyond what we know from other sources (Ibid., 301–2).

knowledge of their internal workings—other than the fact that some Sadducees were sufficiently prominent to warrant recognition by name in Josephus, e.g., Jonathan the Sadducee (*Ant.* 13.293)[77] and Ananus the Younger, a high priest (*Ant.* 20.199).[78] It seems likely that, as a group, the Sadducees had a certain degree of authority, but this is speculation based on knowledge of the sociology of the first century, coupled with the similarity of the Sadducees to the Pharisees with respect to social location. According to Josephus, "[The Sadducees] are men of the highest standing. They accomplish practically nothing, however. For whenever they assume some office, though they submit unwillingly and perforce, yet submit they do to the formulas of the Pharisees, since otherwise the masses would not tolerate them" (*Ant.* 18.17). Although few scholars have accepted this statement at face value, it nevertheless indicates that the Sadducees were but one group among others in the power structures of leadership in the first century.

The priests and Levites also had a certain degree of power and prestige within the leadership structures of Second Temple Judaism. When the author of the *Letter of Aristeas* described the service in the temple, he noticed the silence with which the priests went about their business (*Let. Aris.* 92, 95).[79] The absence of conversation strongly suggests that each priest understood his task without the need for direction or correction in his duties. As the letter says, "There is no one to give orders with regard to the arrangement of the sacrifices" (*Let. Aris.* 94), and none seems to have been necessary. The degree of proficiency is especially striking since the priests did not serve in the Temple year round but only one week in twenty-four.[80] Undoubtedly, the hereditary nature of the priesthood contributed to the competence of the priests, since fathers would have passed on their expertise to their sons. The

77. See the story of John Hyrcanus, above (page 108). This story demonstrates that the Hasmonean high priests were not Sadducees in Josephus's view, since John Hyrcanus vacillated between favoring the Pharisees and the Sadducees without being a part of either.

78. Saldarini wrongly says that Josephus refers to an individual Sadducee only once (Saldarini, *Pharisees, Scribes and Sadducees*, 301–2).

79. Cited in Sanders, *Judaism*, 80–81. According to Craig Evans, the *Letter of Aristeas* was written "between 130 and 70 BCE, with additions as late as first century CE" (Evans, *Noncanonical Writings*, 31). It seems likely, therefore, that the description of the priestly activity accurately reflects first-century practice.

80. Sanders, *Judaism*, 78.

result would have been a highly competent priesthood, which efficiently managed the correct performance of ritual.

The preceding paragraph describes "ordinary priests,"[81] but there were also "chief priests." The exact identity of the chief priests has been hard to substantiate, though it seems likely that they were the members of the elite families from whom the Romans and Herodians appointed the high priests.[82] For this reason, we may surmise that the chief priests received their position by virtue of their social standing, not as the result of their position in a hierarchy of priests. The chief priests do not seem to have had institutional authority over the daily operations of ordinary priests. Two observations support this claim. First, as we have already seen, the priests went about their business in silence. This implies that each priest had his own duties and could perform them without the oversight of a supervisor, or higher authority. Second, evidence suggests that the temple functioned regularly apart from the involvement of the high priest, who might appear only on the major feast days to perform rituals specifically assigned to that office.[83]

We should not imagine, however, that the priesthood was some sort of democratic body. Although the average priests conducted their duties without the direct oversight of an authoritative hierarchy,[84] the strictures of first-century Jewish culture would have dictated that priests would have been responsible to others in three ways. First, they would have been responsible to their elders, specifically to their biological forebears, who would have instructed them in their duties. Since the priesthood was hereditary, sons would have been obligated to follow the direction of their fathers. Second, the constraints of the honor/shame system, together with the expectations from one's dyadic personality (see pages 49–51), would have dictated the regular behavior of most priests. Finally, the common priests would likely have responded to the directives of the high priest, not because he had direct religious authority over them, but because of his position over the people as a whole. One example of such compliance on the part of the priests is their

81. Cf. Ibid., 77–102; VanderKam, *Introduction to Early Judaism*, 182–83.
82. VanderKam, *Introduction to Early Judaism*, 181.
83. Sanders, *Judaism*, 326.
84. Although there were priests with administrative duties, including a temple treasurer, they do not seem to have organized into a hierarchical structure. Cf. Sanders, *Judaism*, 83.

continued performance of cultic ritual incorporating the reforms of Caiaphas.[85] In this case, Caiaphas implemented the innovation to have moneychangers and sacrificial animal salesmen in the temple precinct itself. There is no evidence that regular priests refused to perform their religious duties in protest. Therefore, even though there was no religious hierarchy in the usual sense, the priests did follow the leadership of the high priest. The leaders of the Temple, then, were ritual experts who performed their complex duties with minimal direction from a relatively small hierarchical structure.

Essenes

Of the three Jewish "philosophies" described by Josephus, the Essenes are the least well known, primarily because they do not appear in the NT. However, they are the group most fully described by Josephus. Like the Pharisees, Josephus says the Essenes believe in life after death (*Ant.* 18.18, *J.W.* 2.154–158); but in contrast to both the Pharisees and the Sadducees, the Essenes believed in fate ruling all human behavior (*Ant.* 13.172, 18.18). They held strict views regarding Sabbath observance (*J.W.* 2.147) and purity rules (*J.W.* 2.129, 149). Josephus praised them for keeping their property in common (*Ant.* 18.20, *J.W.* 2.122) and for their generosity (*J.W.* 2.134). The Essenes swore no oaths (*J.W.* 2.135) and conducted many of their activities in silence (*J.W.* 2.130, 133).

As noted earlier, the Qumran community was most likely Essene. Examination of Josephus's description of the Essenes strengthens this assessment. For example, Josephus's account of the initiation process (*J.W.* 2.137–142) compares favorably, though not in every detail, with the description in the Scrolls (1QS 6.13–23). Josephus also asserts, "There is yet another order of Essenes, which, while at one with the rest in its mode of life, customs, and regulations, differs from them in its view on marriage" (*J.W.* 2.160). Since Josephus was aware of at least one Essene sub-group, it seems reasonable to posit the Qumran community as another such group. Therefore, we may consider the Dead Sea Scrolls and Josephus as independent but complementary sources for studying the leadership structures of the Essenes.

According to Josephus, the Essenes had a hierarchical structure. There were four grades (*J.W.* 2.150), and the group members were

---

85. Chilton, *Temple of Jesus*, 107–9.

obedient to their superiors (*J.W.* 2.129, 134). Despite this hierarchy, Josephus says the Essenes elected their leaders.[86] Moreover, there was a priestly aspect to the Essene leadership. The group sent offerings to the Jerusalem temple and conducted their own, separate sacrifices (*Ant.* 18.19). Priests also said grace before their communal meals (*J.W.* 2.131).

A similar picture emerges from the *Rule of the Community* (1QS), the Dead Sea Scroll that is most helpful for understanding the organization and leadership of the Qumran community. Like Josephus, this scroll portrays a priestly component. Priests and Levites are mentioned frequently, as are synonyms such as sons of Aaron (at 5.21, for example) and sons of Zadok (e.g., 5.2, 9). The duties of priests include reciting the liturgies (1.21–23), saying grace (6.4–6), interpreting God's will (5.9), and forming judgments (9.7). Whenever ten men from the community council gathered, a priest had to be present (6.3). The priests seem to have resided at the top of a hierarchy that also included the Instructor, the Inspector, and the members of the community council. The community members were ranked according to seniority and maturity, and each member was obedient to the member higher than him (5.23, 6.2). Nevertheless, there was a certain degree of flexibility within the hierarchical order, as each member was re-evaluated annually and could be moved up or down in the order (5.24). The *Rule* does not say who performed the evaluation, but it may have been done democratically. The scroll speaks often of the Many and refers also to the majority (5.22, 6.19) and the authority of the multitude (5.2).

From Josephus and the *Rule of the Community*, a general picture of the leadership of the Essene sect emerges. The community held a democratic ideal, but the leadership usually functioned according to a strict hierarchy. Priests held a special position within the sect, and the whole system seems to have promoted ritual performance and the maintenance of ritual purity. The community evaluated progress toward

---

86. Some scholars see a dual leadership implied here. According to Louis H. Feldman, the translator of the Loeb edition of *Antiquities* 18, "Those who see a dual leadership in the Qumrân sect, one priestly, the other non-priestly, may discern here a parallel, which, to be sure, depends on adopting the reading of the Epitome (though it may perhaps be deduced from the manuscript A)" (Josephus, *Ant.* 18.22, note d [Feldman, LCL]).

individual attainment of spiritual virtues, and members could advance in the organization through good conduct.

Leadership in Second Temple Judaism

In some respects, Second Temple Jewish leadership patterns are surprisingly similar to patterns of Greco-Roman religious leadership. For example, both were comprised largely of functionaries of the manager-leader type (see Table 2.2, page 57). These were mostly priests with a conservative outlook who exerted a stabilizing cultural force. Another similarity is that the religious leaders tended to be also leaders in the community. We have seen how priesthoods in Greco-Roman religion were often purchased as a means of elevating one's standing in the community. In the same way, the Jewish religious functionaries, especially in the temple and the diaspora synagogues, functioned as community leaders.

Still, Second Temple Jewish leadership differed from Greco-Roman leadership in striking ways. Unlike in the Greco-Roman world, Jewish priesthoods were not for sale—despite the occasional maneuvering evident, for example, among the Hasmoneans. There was also a stronger sense of centralization of authority. Although Burkert has noted a degree of centralization in the cult of Mater Magna,[87] this does not seem to have been the usual pattern for Greco-Roman religions. Jewish leadership also exhibited a greater emphasis on the authority of written sources and the study thereof, suggesting an element of rational inquiry as a way of being religious. Finally, there was a greater concern for the purity of the people, not just of the priests.

We do not see in Second Temple Jewish leadership, however, the kind of conflict-oriented leadership expected in an occupied land. This lack is likely due to the fact that the temple leadership was allied with the Roman occupiers.[88] Because of their status as intermediaries, the temple priests had a vested interest in maintaining the status quo. Similarly, the

87. Burkert, *Ancient Mystery Cults*, 36.

88. It is also possible that there was a greater incidence of innovative leadership in Second Temple Judaism that simply failed to make it into the historical record because of its subversive nature. We do hear a great deal, of course, about the *sicarii*, but the extent to which such revolutionaries are properly characterized as religious leaders is debatable. Moreover, it seems unlikely that their leadership structures had a notable impact on authority in the early church.

diaspora Jews, by virtue of their minority status, would have benefited from the kind of stability afforded by managerial leadership. Even the Essenes, who withdrew from regular society in apparent protest, did not develop innovative leadership (see Table 2.2, page 57). Instead, they deferred expectations for substantive change to an imminent future to be cataclysmically instituted by God.

Our study of the institutions and groups of Second Temple Judaism suggests a number of generalizations about Jewish religious leadership in the first century. First, temporal and spiritual leadership were closely connected. The Sanhedrin dealt with temporal matters, but the high priest was often the convening authority. Similarly, the Sadducees seem to have concerned themselves with temporal affairs, but many of them were priests. The Pharisees exhibit a primary emphasis on spiritual matters, but this outlook resulted in pronouncements regarding temporal issues, such as food harvest and storage procedures. The extreme instance of the link between spiritual and temporal realms comes from the Essenes, for whom spiritual oversight governed all of life. Leaders in the first century did not draw a firm line between the spiritual and temporal. For them, leadership meant influencing all areas of life.

A second generalization is that leaders emphasized rituals and the Temple. This emphasis is obvious in the case of the priests and likely for the Sadducees. The Pharisees and Essenes also valued ritual and sacrifice, as we have seen. It is also possible to understand the ἀρχισυνάγωγοι as overseers ensuring the proper conduct of those rituals that transfered from the Temple practices to the synagogue. The leaders of first-century Judaism seem to have valued accurate ritual performance. When they were not directly involved in the performance of rituals, they studied and taught proper procedure and advised their followers on how to fulfill ritual requirements.

Third, first century Jewish leaders often were community elders. The designation, elder, was based not on age alone, but also on one's standing in the community. Honorable individuals became elders who led their communities. The authority of the elders, however, seems usually to have been traditional and not official. Although there were religious officials, such as the high priest, and religious functionaries, such as the ordinary priests and Levites, the leaders of the Pharisees and Essenes seem not have held actual offices which would have been filled by successive leaders. Even in the synagogue, most of the offices were not established until after our period.

Fourth, despite areas of broad agreement, there remained a range of options in terms of specific leadership structures. As we have just seen, leaders tended to be elders with standing in the community. What constituted an honorable standing, however, was variously construed. For example, the elders in the *gerousia* and Sanhedrin seem to have been chosen based on their honorable birth, while leaders at Qumran received their position based on merit as well as seniority. There was also a range of options between democratic and autocratic leadership. The Essenes purported to value at least some level of democratic decision-making, while the high priest functioned autocratically. Similarly, some groups were hierarchical, while others were non-stratified. For example, the Essenes developed an elaborate hierarchy, yet the Pharisees seem to have been largely egalitarian in structure.

We may conclude, therefore, that various leadership styles existed in first-century Judaism. A concern for sacred rites and for the maintenance of ritual purity informed all these styles. Honored individuals wielded authority and offered valued advice on ritual matters pertaining to every day life. While the forms of leadership varied, the aim and scope of leadership remained constant. The aim was to lead the people of Israel closer to God through the proper performance of God-pleasing practices, and the scope encompassed the entirety of life.

5

Authority in the Jerusalem Church

WE HAVE SET OUT IN THE PRECEDING CHAPTERS TO EXPLORE FIRST-century religious leadership from a sociological perspective. We have attempted both to present general models of first-century religious leadership (ch. 2), as well as to apply those models in exploration of Greco-Roman religions (ch. 3) and Second-Temple Judaism (ch. 4). The purpose has been to develop a "thickened" understanding of first-century religious leadership from which to evaluate the specific portrayal of leadership in the early church as described in the book of Acts. To this end we now turn.

The present chapter will focus on ecclesiastical authority in the primitive Jerusalem community. Our attention, therefore, will center upon three passages from the first part of Acts, namely, 1:15–26, 6:1–7, and 12:1–25. As we shall see, each of these passages offers important information regarding the nature of leadership in the Jerusalem church. In each instance, it will be seen that cultural expectations influenced the actions of church leaders and their constituents. Yet the church exhibited a growing departure from the cultural norms for religious leadership in the first century. As we shall see, the early church, while initially bound by contemporary cultural scripts, soon transcended these constraints in remarkable ways.

Selection of the Twelfth Apostle (1:15–26)

Acts 1:15–26 relates the story of the demise of Judas and his replacement as one of the apostles. The pericope is important for understanding Luke's view of ecclesiastical authority because (1) it gives the requirements of an apostle; (2) it shows the selection of a church leader; (3) it demonstrates a leader in action; and (4) it provides the job description of an apostle, at least in part.

According to this passage, after Jesus ascended into heaven and before the Holy Spirit came at Pentecost, Peter addressed the believers, explaining why according to the Scriptures it was necessary to replace Judas as a disciple. After a Lukan aside relating the demise of Judas, Peter proposes a process for selecting a replacement. He gives the criteria for the choice, and two men are brought forward as candidates. After prayer for God's selection, lots are drawn and Matthias is chosen.[1]

Commentators often argue that the text shows that the selection of Matthias was conducted in such a way that it was not the choice of the believers but of Jesus himself.[2] They draw attention to the ἔδει (v. 16) and δεῖ (v. 21) in the text to show that Scripture, at least so far as Luke is concerned, required events to take place as described.[3] Therefore, the emphasis among commentators has been on divine control throughout the narrated events. Although the theological importance of such a viewpoint is surely vital to the Luke's narrative in Acts, the present study will focus on another, underappreciated aspect of the narrative. To that end, we shall explore Acts 1:15–26 from a sociological perspective in order to examine ecclesiastical authority in the Jerusalem church. It shall be necessary first, however, to consider the critical question of the historicity of this passage.

Historicity of Acts 1:15–26

The question of historicity in Acts is a tangled one with a long history. A full discussion of the issues involved, of course, goes well beyond the scope of the present study. Nevertheless, it is necessary to discuss some of the issues involved and to sketch my own position in order to indicate the frame of reference within which I will be working. The central

---

1. According to Richard Pervo, the use of lots was relatively common in the first-century Mediterranean world. He says that drawing lots "would not have struck the Theophiluses of the day as an example of religious fanaticism, for lots were in general use as a means for selecting officers, jury-members, and other functionaries" (Pervo, "Meet Right," 47).

2. Barrett, *Acts I–XIV*, 94, 97, 103, and 105; Bruce, *Acts*, 112. Cf. Dowd, "Ordination," 208; Fitzmyer, *Acts,* 220 and 228; Haenchen, *Acts,* 164.

3. Barrett, *Acts I–XIV*, 96 and 100; Bruce, *Acts*, 108; Gaventa, *Acts,* 72; Zwiep, *Judas,* 136–55.

questions relating to the historicity of Acts are the date of composition and the use of sources. Clearly, a late date for the composition of Acts tends to call into question its historical reliability, while an early date has the opposite effect. The use of sources is complicated by a number of factors. Aside from the form-critical methods employed by Gospels scholars, source critics of Acts also have to contend with questions regarding the so-called "We-sections," which may reflect a travelogue source. Moreover, source critics must address the question of the historicity of the speeches in Acts. The opinions of scholars range from complete dismissal to confident acceptance of their historical reliability.[4]

The position undergirding the present study is that, while not representing the *ipsissima verba* of the alleged speakers, Acts does represent the substantial content of the actual speeches. Support for this position comes from the fact that the practice of placing speeches in the mouths of historical figures was common among first-century writers of history and biography, while at the same time attention seems to have been paid to capturing the import of such speeches.[5] Moreover, the testimony of the author of Luke-Acts himself lends credibility to this claim. According to Luke 1:3, the author composed his work παρηκολουθηκότι ἄνωθεν πᾶσιν ἀκριβῶς ("after having diligently investigated everything again") and presented it καθεξῆς ("in order"). These claims, while surely

---

4. Contrast, for example, Conzelmann, who summarily dismisses Peter's speech as a Lukan composition, with Witherington, who argues for a generally positive view toward the historicity of this and all the speeches in Acts (Conzelmann, *Acts*, 10; Witherington, *Acts*, 116–20). See also Bruce, "Speeches in Acts." Bruce, contrasting his own view with that of "the Dibelius-Haenchen-Conzelmann line," insists that "The situation in Acts is analogous to that in Thucydides . . . . The speeches in Acts are not mere rhetorical exercises, nor are they introduced simply as vehicles for the author's own reflections or interpretations . . . . But, if the Thucydidean analogy be valid, we should also expect Luke to 'give the general purport of what was actually said' and not to ascribe to the speaker sentiments or utterances out of keeping with his true beliefs and teachings" (Bruce, "Speeches in Acts," 54–55).

5. See Witherington for a defense of this assertion. He says, "What can be gathered from Thucydides and Polybius and those who followed their lead is that unless there was documentary evidence, writers could seldom produce verbatim a speech which had been heard. Rather, they offered up summaries which conveyed various of the major points of what was spoken, not just the gist or main point . . . . If Luke was, as I think, a careful historian in the mold of Thucydides and Polybius, we may expect from him adequate and accurate (so far as his sources allowed) summaries of what was said on one or another occasion . . ." (Witherington, *Acts*, 117).

conventional, do suggest that Luke wrote with the same level of historical accuracy expected of other first-century historians.

When the question of the historicity of Acts impinges on the question of ecclesiastical authority, a further layer of complexity is introduced: Luke himself was a leader within his community. Gerd Theissen has persuasively argued this point with respect to the Gospel writers in "Evangelienschreibung und Gemeindeleitung: Pragmatische Motive bei der Abfassung des Markusevangeliums."[6] According to Theissen, the relationship between community and Evangelist is complex. On the one hand, the evangelists were *bona fide* theologians, making theological statements by the manner in which they ordered, worded, and supplemented their material. At the same time, however, the Evangelists would have been constrained by their community. Much of their theology would have been received from the people with whom they lived, yet they also had a message for their community that sought to move it in directions of the Evangelists' choosing. In other words, the Evangelists both received their theology from the community and created theology for that community in a dialectical relationship. The term Theissen uses to describe the Evangelists in this relationship is "leader."[7]

The fact that Luke should be regarded as a leader of his community has important implications for the study of the historicity of Acts. First, since Luke wrote within the context of a community, we should expect that blatant fabrications by Luke would have been rejected. Clearly, this factor alone would not be sufficient to establish historicity, as the existence of spurious gospels amply attests. Yet the constraint supplied by the community nevertheless remains one point in favor of the historical reliability of both the narrative and the speeches of Acts. Second, recognition of Luke as leader leads to the reasonable conclusion that he would have shaped his narrative (both the Gospel and Acts) to accentuate those features of the story that would have promoted his own understanding of leadership. For this reason, we should expect that Luke would have had a definite purpose for any unhistorical material he introduced into the narrative. In the case of Acts 1:15–26, however, we encounter the selection of an individual, Matthias, who never figures again in the narrative. Moreover, we are introduced to another

---

6. Theissen, "Evangelienschreibung und Gemeindeleitung," 389–93.

7. German: *Leiter*. Theissen, "Evangelienschreibung und Gemeindeleitung," 390 and passim.

individual, Joseph Barsabbas, who is not even selected. It is difficult to imagine that Luke created these characters simply to make some point about leadership or theology without basing them on sources he deemed reliable. Therefore, there seems to be is no compelling reason to doubt the selection of Matthias for substantially the reasons enumerated in Peter's speech.[8]

Authority of the Apostles

Discussion regarding the role of the apostles in Acts 1 has been dominated by investigation into their theological significance for Luke. For example, one commentator argues that Judas's vacated place had to be filled in order to restore the "sacred number" in preparation for Pentecost.[9] Another commentator asserts, "The Twelve are reconstituted so that they can confront Israel assembled in Jerusalem on the first great feast day following Passover, the feast of Assembly or (in Greek) Pentecost."[10] The notion that the twelve apostles both symbolize and judge the twelve tribes of Israel is the traditional view.[11] This theologi-

---

8. Some commentators take the opposite view. Ernst Haenchen offers one of the most succinct arguments. He asserts that (1) the explanations regarding Judas's death and the name of the field would have been out of place within a community so close in time and space to the events narrated, (2) the quotations depend upon the LXX text of Psalms, which would not have been used by the Jewish audience Peter was addressing, and (3) the conception of apostle implied in the qualification listed in verses 21–22 represents a later development, differing as it does from the tradition recorded in Mark 1:16–20 (Haenchen, *Acts*, 163). We concede that verses 18–19 are the narrator's interpolation and that the exact apostolic qualifications may represent a later conception. Yet Haenchen seems to have overstated the case when arguing that the Psalms passages could not have been used with Peter's Jewish audience because they rely on the text of the LXX. The most substantive change specifically dependent upon the LXX involves replacing a plural third person plural pronoun with a singular one (see Haenchen, *Acts*, 161, n. 5). There seems to be no logical difficulty in assuming that the pre-Pentecostal community could have viewed the plural curse as uniquely applicable to Judas. (Cf. Witherington, *Acts*, 125.) Moreover, it is difficult to imagine that the early believers held no qualification for apostleship substantially similar to the requirement expressed in vv. 21–22, namely, that the candidate had been with Jesus during the majority of his public ministry. Thus, while admitting that the speech as recorded in Acts has been adapted in certain respects for the implied readers, we may continue to affirm that the logic of the speech reflects the shape of Peter's original argument.

9. Haenchen, *Acts*, 164. Cf. Johnson, *Acts*, 38–39.

10. Fitzmyer, *Acts*, 221.

11. See, for example, Bruce, *Acts*, 112; Fitzmyer, *Acts*, 220–21; Gaventa, *Acts*, 72; Scott, "Luke's Geographical Horizon," 524; Spencer, *Journeying through Acts*, 39. For

cal view gains support from such NT passages as Matt 19:28 and Luke 22:30 (where Jesus says the Twelve will judge the twelve tribes) and Rev 21:10–14 (where the names of the twelve tribes are inscribed on the gates of the new Jerusalem and the names of the twelve apostles on the foundation stones).

As important as these theological perspectives are, our present interest is in a sociological perspective regarding the authority of the Twelve in Acts 1. It should be noted, first, that the idea of the Twelve as representing the tribes does not seem to be a dominant Lukan theme.[12] If it were, we should expect Luke to have made some reference to the tribes in the Acts 1 passage. Instead, we find the scriptural justification for the replacement of Judas relating more to prophetic reasoning to replace a traitor than theological justification for exactly twelve apostles. The quotations Peter offers to support his advice (γενηθήτω ἡ ἔπαυλις αὐτοῦ ἔρημος καὶ μὴ ἔστω ὁ κατοικῶν ἐν αὐτῇ, and τὴν ἐπισκοπὴν αὐτοῦ λαβέτω ἕτερος, v. 20, quoting Ps 68:26 [LXX] and Ps 108:8 [LXX], respectively) come from deprecatory Psalms condemning evildoers, not from passages related to the importance of twelve tribes or twelve rulers. For this reason, the purpose for filling the vacancy created by Judas's abdication seems to be the removal of the stigma of his betrayal, rather than specifically to reconstitute the Twelve. We may conclude, therefore, that Luke's interest in the Twelve is historical and sociological, not purely theological.

What role, then, do the apostles play according to Acts 1:15–26? To begin answering this question, we turn our attention to v. 22. The phrase μάρτυρα τῆς ἀναστάσεως αὐτοῦ σὺν ἡμῖν γενέσθαι ἕνα τούτων is used in Peter's speech to describe the role Judas's replacement would fulfill. As indicated by the phrase σὺν ἡμῖν, Peter indicates here that the role intended for the replacement is the same as that envisioned for all the apostles. Therefore, the phrase is crucial for understanding Luke's view of apostleship.

---

a rigorous defense of this view, see the recent monograph by Arie W. Zwiep. Zwiep regards Acts 1:15–26 as an example of Greco-Roman and Jewish succession stories intended by Luke to justify Jesus' claim that in the eschaton the Twelve apostles would sit on the twelve thrones of Israel (Zwiep, *Judas*). The notion that Luke intends Acts 1 to be read as the fulfillment of Luke 22:30 (which does not have the phrase, "twelve thrones") is capably refuted in Estrada, *From Followers to Leaders*, 176–78.

12. Cf. Barrett, *Acts I–XIV*, 94.

Especially important in this regard is the word μάρτυς. The central meaning of μάρτυς, of course, is witness, that is, one who reports what he has seen or heard.[13] The word occurs thirty-five times in the NT, twice in Luke and thirteen times in Acts. Clearly, the word μάρτυς is important in Acts. In the present context, the word recalls two earlier occurrences in Luke-Acts, namely, Luke 24:48 and Acts 1:8. In Luke 24:48, the risen Jesus declares that the disciples are μάρτυρες of his suffering and resurrection. He goes on to say in v. 49 that they are to remain in Jerusalem until they receive power from on high—a clear foreshadowing of the events of Acts 2. The context strongly suggests, however, that it is not only the eleven who are called witnesses here. In Luke 24:33 we find that the referent is the two Emmaus disciples, the eleven, and τοὺς σὺν αὐτοῖς. However, the context of Acts 1:8, which appears to be a duplicate account of the same event described in Luke 24, seems to envision only the eleven as present. Acts 1:2 refers only to the apostles whom Jesus had chosen, not to any other disciples. Other believers are not mentioned until v. 14, after the eleven are listed by name as the ones returning to Jerusalem following Jesus' ascension. The implication is that these eleven were the only ones who heard the commission of Acts 1:8.[14] Yet when the fulfillment of the promise comes in chapter 2, all the disciples received the Holy Spirit (v. 1, ἦσαν πάντες ὁμοῦ). Still, it is the Twelve (Peter and the eleven) who stand up as witnesses in 2:14. It seems, therefore, that the role of μάρτυς is one of testimony to outsiders. All the believers are empowered as witnesses, but the Twelve have a heightened visibility in this regard. Thus, with respect to μάρτυς, the role of the apostles differs in degree from the rest of the community, but not in kind.

Several other verses in this passage have bearing on the question of Luke's perception of the apostles' role in the Jerusalem church. The second part of Acts 1:20 quotes from Psalm 109:8: τὴν ἐπισκοπὴν αὐτοῦ λαβέτω ἕτερος ("Let another take his supervision"). Our attention here focuses on the meaning of ἐπισκοπή, which is clearly related to the English term "bishop." Thus, for example, the King James

---

13. Cf. BDAG, "μάρτυς," 619–20.

14. Nevertheless, we should hasten to add that the church from the beginning accepted this commission, together with that in Matthew 28, as directed to the whole church and not just the eleven. This can be seen already in Acts 8:4, when those scattered by the persecution went about (διέρχομαι) preaching.

translates ἐπισκοπή as "bishoprick," while the NASB has "office," and the NIV has "place of leadership." According to BDAG, the term can mean simply a visitation, rather than carrying any ecclesial signification.[15] The meaning here, however, is complicated by the fact that it occurs within a quotation from the OT, being a LXX translation of פְּקֻדָּה (pᵉquddâ). According to G. André in the *Theological Dictionary of the Old Testament* (TDOT),

> The term pᵉquddâ exhibits several semantic nuances. It can refer to the mustering of soldiers, or to the task or office of a pāqîd, e.g., responsibility for the tabernacle and its accoutrements.... The term pequdda also refers to the fate set for human beings .... Ps. 109 also exhibits juridical overtones, which is why the translation "his fate—he should receive another" fits better than "another should receive his office."[16]

It seems likely, therefore, that the usage of the word in Ps 109 has to do with the power of the individual to impact negatively the circumstances of the speaker, rather than to any office in the formal sense.

A second verse which has bearing on the role of the apostles is Acts 1:25, where the significance of λαβεῖν τὸν τόπον τῆς διακονίας ταύτης καὶ ἀποστολῆς is central to our present concern.[17] The phrase

---

15. BDAG, "ἐπισκοπή," 379.

16. André, "פָּקַד," TDOT 12:61. Cf. the entry in the *Theological Wordbook of the Old Testament* (*TWOT*), which describes פָּקַד as having the basic meaning, "to exercise oversight over a subordinate, either in the form of inspection or of taking action to cause a considerable change in the circumstances of the subordinate, either for the better or for the worse" ("פָּקַד," *TWOT* 2:731). Similarly, the entry for פְּקֻדָּה reads, "Its commonest use is to express the primary idea of [pāqad]—intervention by a superior power (usually God or a king) in order to make a great change in the situation of a subordinate" ("פָּקַד," *TWOT* 2:732). Care must be taken in the use of this entry of *TWOT* to illuminate the Greek word ἐπισκοπή. It seems likely that the semantic range of the Greek word ἐπισκοπή has influenced the editors of the *TWOT*. (Notice, for example, the prevalence of the ἐπισκοπή word group in the bibliography listed for פָּקַד.) Such a procedure, of course, can be valuable, but it introduces circularity into any attempt to understand ἐπισκοπή on the basis of the *TWOT* description of פְּקֻדָּה. In particular, it seems more likely that the idea of office would be imported first from later ecclesiastical usage into a reading of the NT use of ἐπισκοπή and thence into the meaning of פְּקֻדָּה.

17. A textual variant occurs in v. 25 that has some bearing on the understanding of ecclesiastical authority in this passage. Textual issues in Acts are among the most complex in the NT. According to Coppens, "Plus d'un exégète a trouvé son Waterloo dans sa tentative d'expliquer le caractère propre de la recension occidentale des Actes" (review of *Theological Tendency of Codex Bezae Cantabrigiensis*, 274; quoted in Martini, "La tra-

can be understood to mean that "apostle" was an office of the church from the very first and that Matthias filled the office formerly held by

---

dition textuelle des Actes des Apôtres, 21). Interestingly, Coppens has loosely translated the original English, which reads, "The researcher approaching this enigmatic area of New Testament textual criticism [the yet unsolved mystery of the 'Western' text] does so under the almost ominous words of B. H. Streeter, who said that many a scholar '. . . has met his Waterloo in the attempt to account for, or explain away, the existence of the Bezan text'" (Epp, *Theological Tendency of Codex Bezae Cantabrigiensis*, 165). I have been unable to examine the source of the original Streeter quote, which Epp reports as occurring in "Codices 157, 1071 and the Caesarean Text," 150. Bruce Metzger offers a similar, albeit less poetic, view: "In the book of Acts the problems raised by the Western text become most acute, for the Western text of Acts is nearly ten percent longer than the form that is commonly regarded to be the original text of that book" (Metzger, *Textual Commentary*, 6*). However, a thorough examination of the Western and Alexandrian text types need not detain us here, since a case-by-case investigation will suffice. Regarding the variant in v. 25, the question is whether τόπον or κλῆρον is the correct reading. If κλῆρον is correct, the word recalls v. 17 (καὶ ἔλαχεν τὸν κλῆρον τῆς διακονίας ταύτης), where it is used to indicate that Judas had had a part in Jesus' ministry. No sense of ecclesiastical office or entitlement seems to be present in v. 17. If κλῆρον is used with the same connotations in v. 25, it seems likely that the apostolic replacement is to a ministerial task rather than to an office. Ecclesiastical function is in view, despite any language in v. 25 that might suggest ecclesiastical office. On the other hand, if the correct reading is τόπον, then it becomes more difficult to understand this phrase as being innocent of any official overtones. It becomes important, therefore, to establish the correct reading here. Both readings would fit naturally within the context: τόπον anticipates the τόπον later in the same verse, but κλῆρον recalls the earlier use of the same word in v. 17 and looks forward its use in v. 26. Moreover, both readings own a lengthy pedigree in the manuscripts and ancient translations. τόπον has the support of manuscripts deemed of the first order of importance in the Nestle-Aland text (p^{74}, A, B, C [original reading], D and Ψ). However, other important manuscripts support κλῆρον (ℵ, C [third corrector], E, 33, and 1739 [third corrector]). Similarly, τόπον is supported by the Latin translations (the Vulgate, as well as part of the Old Latin text type) and all the Coptic versions, while κλῆρον has the support of the Majority text (the majority of Greek texts, including the Koine text type) and the Syriac versions (except for a marginal reading in the Harklensis). The text critical axiom of *lectio difficilior probabilior* seems to be of little direct help in this instance, because whether τόπον or κλῆρον is deemed the more difficult reading depends on whether one believes Luke to have been providing an etiological account for the emergence of ecclesiastical office in his own time. If the Lukan community received this passage etiologically, then τόπον would have been the preferred choice, making κλῆρον the *lectio difficilior*. On the other hand, if ecclesiastical offices had not yet emerged in Luke's community, then τόπον would be the *lectio difficilior*. But this, then, begs the question. In the final analysis, three items favor τόπον: (1) the strength of the manuscripts p^{74}, A, B, C*, D and Ψ, (2) the fact that the original reading of C was τόπον and (3) the evidence that the earliest translation (Old Latin) supports τόπον. Therefore, we must agree with the reading of the Nestle-Aland text.

Judas.[18] However, it is instructive to consider the NT usage of the word ἀποστολή. This word occurs only three other times in the NT: Rom 1:5, 1 Cor 9:2, and Gal 2:8. In the first case, Paul applies ἀποστολή to himself.[19] First Corinthians 9:2 says that the Corinthians were the seal of Paul's own apostleship, while Gal 2:8 refers to Peter's apostleship to the circumcised. The Rom 1:5 occurrence is especially interesting because it combines the word χάριν with ἀποστολήν. As Bruce points out, the construction here is likely a hendiadys, which implies that apostleship is a divine gift.[20] It may be desirable in translation, therefore, to employ a word that more readily captures a sense of giftedness rather than a sense of entitlement, which is sometimes associated with official titles.[21] To that end, it may be possible to translate Acts 1:25 thus: "To receive the place of this ministry and commission from which Judas departed to go to his own place."

These observations regarding the role of the apostles in Acts 1 may be brought into focus by an examination through the lens of the models developed in ch. 2 above. It is helpful to recall, first, that there are four ideal types of authority: legal authority, traditional authority, charismatic authority, and professional authority. Despite the fact that it is anachronistic to speak of legal authority in the early church, there can be little doubt that Luke thought of the apostles in terms analogous to legal authority. This can be seen because Luke portrays the apostles as having been appointed by Jesus (Luke 6:13–16), because he views the abdication of Judas as creating a vacancy that needed to be filled (Acts 1:20–22), and because he indicates that, although at least two individuals met the qualifications, only one was chosen (Acts 1:23). These considerations indicate that a leadership "slot" had been created that had to be filled by some qualified individual. Like legal authority, therefore,

18. Cf. Haenchen, *Acts*, 162, n. 10.

19. It is possible that Paul applies ἀποστολή to all the believers in Roman, since he uses the first person plural: ἐλάβομεν χάριν καὶ ἀποστολὴν. However, the contrast between the first person plural here in v. 5 and the second person plural in v. 6, suggests that the first person plural does not include the recipients of the letter, despite the fact that Paul does not list any co-authors. Cf. Morris, *Epistle to the Romans*, 48; Murray, *Epistle to the Romans*, 1:12.

20. Bruce, *Letter of Paul to the Romans*, 70. Cf. Fitzmyer, *Romans*, 237.

21. Cf. Ernst Käsemann: "The long ecclesiastical tradition that has distinguished office and charisma has resulted in removing the apostolate in general from the charismata and even its opposition to them" (*Commentary on Romans*, 14).

the authority of the apostles in Acts 1 rested upon a formalized arrangement in which authoritative position precedes authoritative person.[22]

Further analysis of their role as portrayed in Acts 1 shows that the apostles are best classified under the manager-leader rubric, not innovator-leader. Although the limits of our source do not permit an exhaustive evaluation of all the points of the model with respect to the apostles' pre-Pentecost leadership, such evidence as we do have strongly aligns with the manager-leader model. We see, first, that the emphasis in the text is upon maintenance of status and exemplification of contentment (characteristics of the strong group/low grid component of the manager-leader model). This emphasis is evident in such comments as οὗτοι πάντες ἦσαν προσκαρτεροῦντες ὁμοθυμαδὸν τῇ προσευχῇ (v. 14). To be sure, devotion to prayer is not exclusive to practitioners of the manager-leader model. But in the present case, the prayer occurs in the upper room, where the eleven had gone in order to wait as instructed by Jesus, not in order to lead the group in innovative ways. There also seems to have developed already at this early stage the rudiments of a hierarchy, a development predicted by the patronage component of the manager-leader model. As indicated in v. 15, approximately one hundred twenty people were present in the upper room. Among these one hundred twenty, the eleven (together with Mary, the mother of Jesus) are mentioned by name, implying that they were somehow distinguished from the others. Among the eleven, Peter is singled out to hold a unique leadership position.

Thus, many of the elements of the manager-leader model hold true of the apostles as described in Acts 1. At the same time, characteristics of innovator-leadership are missing from the description. For example, there is no evidence of attempts to re-distribute wealth or to redefine "ultimate good," "honor," or "kinship." Nor is there a subversion of the patronage system or the elimination of brokers. As we shall see, these qualities of innovator-leaders are true of the apostles later in Acts. But

22. The fact that later vacancies among the Twelve are not filled (e.g., James) does not nullify the arguments for legal authority as a basis for Luke's understanding of the role of the Twelve in the pre-Pentecost community. There are two possible explanations for the later non-replacement: either the task for which the apostles were selected had been completed or a change in the church's understanding of the nature of leadership no longer demanded such vacancies to be filled. The latter explanation is attractive, since we will be arguing that the Twelve changed from manager-leaders to innovator-leaders. See pages 174–75.

in Acts 1, the apostles are best described as manager-leaders. We will be arguing, therefore, for a changing understanding of leadership in the early church as exemplified in Acts.

The Role of Peter

One of the more interesting aspects of Acts 1:15–26 as pertains to ecclesiastical authority is the role of Peter in the narrative. From a sociological perspective, it can be observed that Peter has the role of protecting the honor of the group. It will be recalled from our earlier discussion that the first-century society can be characterized as strong group/low grid (see pages 40–42). As a group within such a culture, the Jerusalem community would have been profoundly impacted by Jesus' death. The group would have been experiencing a loss of orientation at the death of their leader. Their convictions regarding the person of Jesus would have seemed contradicted by the course of events. To use the parlance of group/grid, the group was experiencing a drop in grid.

Such a drop in grid would be associated with group dishonor. Not only was the death of Jesus a personal blow to the disciples, it was also a challenge to the honor of each individual within the group. Within honor/shame societies, it is the responsibility of dominant individuals within the group to defend the group honor in relation to outsiders who might challenge that honor. From this point of view, it seems that Peter, more than taking on a leadership role within the community, is imaging the community to the outside world. The group's honor is embedded in him: if Peter failed to defend the honor of the group, Peter and his entire group would have been regarded as dishonorable. Conversely, by defending the group's honor, Peter demonstrated himself to be an honorable member of an honorable group. Therefore, Peter was compelled by honor/shame cultural scripts to defend his group's honor.[23] He accomplished this by reconstituting the Twelve, an act that represented a powerful riposte to the honor challenge faced by the group. If Peter had allowed the vacancy of Judas's spot to remain, it would have been an

---

23. Nelson P. Estrada also argues that Peter's actions constituted a defense of honor. However, Estrada views Peter's defense as part of a larger process of status transformation intended to validate the leadership of the apostles within the community—both the primitive community and Luke's community (Estrada, *Followers to Leaders*, 151–52). The view proposed in the present study is that Peter acts to mobilize the group in order for the group to defend its honor against outsiders.

enduring emblem of the shame of Judas's betrayal and of Jesus' death. His inaction would have been interpreted as an inability to defend his group's honor.[24]

Thus, Peter was defending the honor of Jesus and the Jesus group against the extreme challenge of Judas's betrayal and demise. Judas, although a well-placed member of the group, had rejected the group and its leader. Jesus had gathered an inner circle consisting of the Twelve, but one of the Twelve had shamed the group. The denigration of Judas in Peter's speech can be read as a counter-challenge aimed at disparaging the honor of Judas. The replacement of Judas, therefore, was a means of denying Judas an honorable place in the history of the Twelve, while at the same time defending Jesus' honor.

Although Peter is thus pictured as a dominant individual within the community, he does not have the characteristics of an administrator of that community in this passage. He stands up to address the group, he speaks words of exhortation, and he relates scripture. Therefore, he exhibits here the role of a teacher, not that of administrator. However, even the teacher role seems to be subordinated to that of guardian of honor, as we have just seen. The purpose of Peter's teaching is to motivate the group to undertake the actions necessary to restore the group's honor.

Moreover, the fact that Peter initiates the process for the replacement of Judas does not imply that he was functioning as an innovative leader. Rather, as we have seen, he was following the cultural scripts in defense of his group's honor. His act of leadership is not an instance of innovative leadership but an attempt to re-establish the status quo. In other words, Peter was working to maintain the group's status, to protect the image of the group among outsiders, to effectively play the honor "game," and to improve incrementally the situation of the group. In brief, Peter was a manager-leader. It seems likely, therefore, that Peter accepted this role, not because he had a visionary perspective for the group, but because his dyadic partners expected him to take a leadership role.

Thus, Peter and the Twelve were all functioning as manager-leaders in Acts 1:15–26. They were focused on maintaining group status, controlling internal group structure, and defending group honor. In short,

---

24. Cf. Malina, *New Testament World*, 35.

they were acting according to the culturally expected norms for group leaders in the first century. As we shall see, the situation is dramatically different in Acts 6.

Selection of the Seven (Acts 6:1–7)

Acts 6:1–7 contains the well-known account of a dispute within the primitive church and the solution to that dispute. According to this passage, the Hellenist believers complained against the Hebrew believers because the Hellenist widows were being overlooked in the daily διακονία.[25] The Twelve responded to the complaint by proposing that the community nominate seven individuals to oversee the distribution of the common funds in order to relieve the Twelve of table-service duties. The Twelve were to devote their time instead to the ministry of the word. Seven men, who are mentioned by name, were then selected for this leadership role.

Commentators are quick to note that the choice of seven leaders seems to reflect a Jewish paradigm of community leadership, where seven was a common number for leadership bodies.[26] It seems unlikely, however, that simply having the same number of members should be viewed as sufficient grounds for suggesting a similarity of form and function for the leadership bodies of the two. Indeed, as we shall see, it seems that the account portrays a type of leadership that is more counter-cultural than is usually appreciated.[27]

Acts 6:1–7 is also important for the study of ecclesiastical authority because of the repeated occurrence of the διάκον- word group. Students of the text have sometimes seen here an etiology for the ecclesial office of

---

25. For a discussion of how the early Christian distribution of food differed from Rabbinic and Essene practices, see Capper, "Palestinian Cultural Context," 350–53. Capper claims, "The dispute over economic arrangements in Acts 6:1–6 is thus a record of the point at which community of goods was programmed out of the social form of the developing wider church" (Capper, "Christian Community of Goods," 354). His view of a two-tiered system, with the Hebrews practicing community of goods and the Hellenists practicing occasional charity for the poor, seems to overreach the evidence from Acts 6.

26. Haenchen, *Acts*, 263.

27. Cf. Keener, *The IVP Bible Background Commentary*, 338: "Those with political power generally repressed complaining minorities; here the apostles hand the whole system over to the offended minority. This may thus be the first recorded instance of what we might today call 'affirmative action.'"

deacon, yet most commentators point out that the term διάκονος does not occur in this passage. For this reason, it is unlikely that this account was intended to describe the institution of the diaconate. Exegetes since F. C. Baur have found the mention of Hellenists and Hebrews to be of more interest, seeing in this episode an understated intimation of an ideological conflict between factions in the early church. According to Baur, the Hellenists were antinomian supporters of Pauline Christianity, while the Hebrews were law-abiding adherents to Petrine Christianity.[28] Recent researchers have rejected much of Baur's typology, but the supposed rift between Hellenists and Hebrews, together with a suspicion of underlying ideological conflict, continues to capture scholars' imaginations. Sociological studies of this passage have tended to focus on the identity and status of the Hellenists and Hebrews.[29] The present study, in contrast, will focus on the interactions of the characters in the story in light of the cultural scripts of the first century, rather than on trying to evaluate the sociological identity and strata of the groups involved.

From this perspective, a number of important observations can be made regarding the nature of ecclesiastical authority in the Jerusalem church. It should first be noted that, although the text explicitly states that the complaint was against the Hebrews (v. 1), the charge must surely be understood to have rested ultimately at the doorstep of the Twelve, who had charge of the distribution of the community's property (Acts 4:35). For this reason, the Acts 6 episode should be understood as a challenge to the honor of the Twelve. The contrast with the situation earlier in Acts can hardly be more pronounced. There (e.g., Acts 2:42–43 and 4:33), the Twelve were held in high esteem and could seemingly do no wrong. Here, the Hellenists complained against the Hebrews over a perceived preferentially motivated management of community resources. According to the leadership models developed above, first-century leaders were uniquely responsible for the honor of their group (see pages 52–58). The model aligns with the description in the present

---

28. Baur, *Paul*, 39. Baur also postulates a synthesis between the two types, which he characterizes as Johannine Christianity. He uses a Hegelian typology of thesis (Petrine-Jewish Christianity), antithesis (Pauline-Gentile Christianity), and synthesis (Johannine Christianity and early Catholicism) to date the books of the NT according to their *Tendenz*. Baur, in 1831, set out his method in the epoch-making article, "Die Christuspartei in der korinthischen Gemeinde."

29. See esp. Hill, *Hellenists and Hebrews*.

passage, since the Twelve—and not the Hebrews alone—respond to the honor challenge issued by the Hellenists. Thus, although the complaint was not directed specifically against them, it seems reasonable to conclude that the Twelve especially felt the weight of the charge.

The charge and its resolution may be compared to the incident in Exodus 18:13–27, where Moses likewise organized a system of helpers to handle the heavy load.[30] The two accounts, however, differ in at least two ways. First, the solution that Moses implemented was clearly hierarchical in nature. Legal disputes that were too heavy for lower-level judges to handle worked their way up the hierarchy until they could be resolved. Moses himself, being at the top of the hierarchy, judged only the most difficult cases. In contrast, the system implemented in Acts 6 involved a division of labor, where the two groups were responsible for different kinds of activities, not different degrees of difficulty within a single task. We shall have more to say regarding this observation below. A second difference relates to the nature of the problem addressed by the reorganizations. In Moses's case, his father-in-law raised the issue, not the constituents who felt they were being wronged. Moreover, Moses was not accused of any wrongdoing, merely of running the risk of becoming overwhelmed by the workload. The Hebrews in the present passage, however, were accused of favoritism in their handling of the community's resources.[31]

When viewed from the perspective of an honor challenge, therefore, it becomes evident that Luke is not masking a deeper, ideological issue. Little could be more serious than a challenge from within the community to the honor of its leaders. From this point of view, quests for the hidden, underlying rift behind this passage—such as the studies of F. C. Baur and his successors—seem ill advised.[32] Having missed the

---

30. Bruce, *Acts*, 182; Gaventa, *Acts*, 114. Acts 6:1–6 is often also compared with Numbers 27:15–23, since both passages mention the laying on of hands (Johnson, *Acts*, 107; Marshall, *Acts*, 127; Witherington, *Acts*, 251). Cf. Kilmartin, "Ministry and Ordination," 51.

31. Cf. Gaventa, *Acts*, 113: "Of special pertinence to Acts 6, Israel is also chastised sharply when its widows are neglected (e.g., Isa 10:1–2; Zech 7:10–12). That history makes the neglect of widows within this community a serious matter. To claim that this community, in which 'there was not a needy person' (4:34), neglects its widows is to offer a stinging indictment."

32. See note 28. More recently—and from a decidedly different but equally misguided perspective—see Marshall, *Acts*, 125: "These facts [regarding the Seven] have

gravity of the issue that is expressed, such investigators are forced to propose theological divisions between the Hebrews and Hellenists and to raise these supposed ideological distinctions to a level of intensity they did not have in the first century.

According to the cultural scripts of an honor/shame based society, there are a number of responses that can be made to an honor challenge such as this one (see pages 44–47). For instance, challenged individuals can meet the challenge directly by denial of the accusation or by retribution against the challenger. Alternatively, the challenged person might deflect the challenge. One might place the blame on someone else or offer an excuse. One could legitimize the behavior by offering examples from history or from Scripture for justification. Or, as demonstrated by Moses and Jethro, one could organize to fix the problem.[33]

The actual response of the Twelve shows some affinities with the expected response, but it exhibits radical departures, as well. The first thing the Twelve do is to call together the whole assembly (v. 2). This action is already an unexpected response, since it entails a public acknowledgement of the problem. Next, the Twelve deflect the challenge first by offering an excuse (v. 2). They say, in effect, that they are rightly focused on their primary task and that the oversight of the Hellenist widows is merely an unintended, albeit unfortunate consequence. More importantly, the Twelve deflect the challenge by adducing kinship language (v. 3). As discussed earlier, the agonistic interactions of challenge and riposte characteristic of an honor/shame society such as that of

---

suggested to many scholars that the complaint about the poor relief was but a symptom of a deeper problem, namely that the Aramaic-speaking Christians and the Greek-speaking Christians were dividing into two separate groups, the latter being more radical in its attitude to Judaism, and that what we really have in this incident is the appointment of a set of leaders for the Greek-speaking Christians. Some suggestion of this kind is inherently probable."

33. Cf. Malina, *New Testament World*, 35: "Any reaction on the part of the receiver of a challenge comprises his response. Such responses cover a range of reactions, from a 'positive' refusal to act, through acceptance of the message, to a 'negative' refusal to react. By this I mean that a person receiving the challenge message can refuse the challenge positively by a display of scorn, disdain or contempt. If he is inferior or equal to the challenger, that would require the challenger to take steps to obliterate the insulting response, since such a response locates the challenger as an inferior. On the other hand, the receiver can accept the challenge message and offer a counterchallenge, and the exchange between them will continue. Or finally, the receiver can react by offering nothing by way of response; he can fail or neglect to respond, and this would imply dishonor for the receiver."

the first century, are reserved for males outside one's own family (see page 45). By addressing the congregation as brothers (ἀδελφοί, v. 3), the Twelve transform the event from a power struggle into an internal family concern to be worked out amicably. This reaction permits an increase in honor, not of the Twelve at the expense of the Seven, but of the Twelve together with the Seven and the whole group (v. 7). In a culture where honor, like all good, is considered limited, such a demonstration of mutually increasing honor is remarkable indeed.

After this dramatic alteration of the tenor of the conflict through the use of kinship language, the Twelve propose an organizational change in order to fix the problem. The change seems to bear some affinities to the style of organization within the patterns of Greco-Roman religious authority, as noted above (see pages 100–103). In the Jerusalem church, as in many Greco-Roman religions, the structure is based on differentiation of tasks, not upon hierarchical subordination and supervision. In a strict hierarchy, such as the one proposed by Moses, superiors oversee the work of subordinates and can either affirm or overrule the decisions taken at the lower levels of the hierarchy. Here in Acts, the supposed subordinates (the Seven) receive responsibility over a mundane task, while the supposed superiors (the Twelve) restrict themselves to the spiritual tasks of the community. The language of v. 4 implies that the Twelve retain no control over the work assigned to the Seven; they say ἡμεῖς δὲ τῇ προσευχῇ καὶ τῇ διακονίᾳ τοῦ λόγου προσκαρτερήσομεν while insisting that they not be distracted from this primary task by waiting tables. Thus, a hierarchy existed only in the sense that there were higher and lower tasks assigned to the two groups, not in the sense that higher-ranking officers had authority over lower ones.[34]

From the preceding discussion, it is clear that the response of the Twelve to the honor challenge from the Hellenists followed some of the expected patterns of culturally appropriate response (offering an excuse for the problem, proposing an organizational change, differentiating tasks for different groups), while also differing in some respects (publicly acknowledging the problem, using fictive kinship language, imple-

---

34. Cf. Öhler, "Die Jerusalemer Urgemeinde," 410–11. Öhler argues that the primitive Jerusalem community incorporated a hierarchical structure, which he compares to that of Greco-Roman associations. He also argues for an egalitarian principle in the primitive community. He writes, "Egalität und Hierarchie schließen sich nicht aus" (411).

menting a modified hierarchy). Several other features of the response, however, demonstrate a radical departure from the norm. For example, it should be noted that the honor of the Twelve is not diminished as a result of this episode. They retain honor, in the first place, by initiating the process recorded in Acts 6:2–7. The Twelve are the ones who summoned the congregation; it was at their behest that the matter was brought to the fore and a solution sought. Second, the Twelve retained honor by noting the importance of their function, namely, prayer and the ministry of the Word. Thus, although their workload was reduced, the significance of the work they did was high relative to that of the average member of the church. Moreover, the Twelve addressed the problem. By fixing the problem in a way that was amenable to all, their favor in the eyes of the people was salvaged. Finally, we may deduce that their honor was not reduced because members of the group—especially Peter, but also James (12:2) and John (8:14, 12:2)—continue to figure prominently in the narrative of Acts.

The Role of the Congregation

Although the Seven and the Twelve get most of the attention in terms of ecclesiastical authority as indicated in Acts 6:1–7, the congregation itself performs functions usually associated with leadership. In v. 3,[35]

---

35. A number of textual variants obscure the text at the beginning of v. 3. The first variant involves a substantially different construction of the first six words of the verse (as counted by the chosen text in Nestle-Aland). Where Nestle-Aland has ἐπισκέψασθε δέ, ἀδελφοί, ἄνδρας ἐξ ὑμῶν, some manuscripts have τί οὖν ἐστιν, ἀδελφοί· ἐπισκέψασθε ἐξ ὑμῶν αὐτῶν ἄνδρας. This variant is found in the fifth century Greek manuscript, codex Bezae (D), the fifth and twelfth century Old Latin manuscripts, h and p, and the Middle Egyptian tradition. It adds a phrase (τί οὖν ἐστιν), inserts a word (αὐτῶν), and rearranges the order. The added phrase adds nothing to the essential meaning of the passage; it merely lends a more conversational tone. (Cf. Metzger, *Textual Commentary*, 294: "τί οὖν ἐστιν, ἀδελφοί . . . lends a colloquial touch to the narrative.") The addition of the word αὐτῶν, however, is especially interesting in light of the fact that the referent of ὑμῶν can be debated. The αὐτῶν functions as an intensifier ("you *yourselves*"), and therefore adds emphasis but no essential change in meaning. The second textual variant in v. 3 involves the word δέ. δέ is replaced by δή (adduced by A, a fifth century Greek manuscript), by οὖν (represented by C, E, Ψ, 33, and 1739, fifth, sixth, ninth and tenth century Greek manuscripts; also by the Koine text type and the Latin and Syriac translations), and by δὲ οὖν (found in 1175, a tenth century manuscript). δέ is omitted by p^{74} (a seventh century manuscript), but is supported by ℵ and B (fourth century manuscripts). The reading of the Nestle-Aland text is to be accepted because it is the one variation that can give rise to all the others. There is one additional variant in this

the Twelve tell the congregation to select (ἐπισκέψασθε) capable men.[36] The use of ἐπισκέψασθε here is especially interesting because, although the word has semantic links to ecclesiastical authority, it is used in this case to describe a task of the community. Seven of the eleven NT occurrences of ἐπισκέπτομαι are found in Luke-Acts. Here it is used as an imperative that the apostles issue to the congregation in response to the complaint regarding the overlooked widows. Since it is a grammatical imperative issued by the apostles, the construction could imply that the apostles had authority over the congregation. It should be noted, however, that the use of an imperatival construction does not necessarily imply a position of power by the speaker(s) over the hearer(s). The fact that the NT sometimes uses the imperative mood to address God makes this abundantly clear.

According to BDAG, ἐπισκέπτομαι has three central uses: "to make a careful inspection, to look at, examine, inspect; to go to see a person with helpful intent, visit someone; to exercise oversight in behalf of, look after, make an appearance to help, of divine oversight."[37] The usage in Acts 6:3 is classified as following the first meaning. This classification, however, is not particularly helpful for understanding the precise nature of what the apostles are asking the congregation to do. It is necessary, therefore, to examine the NT uses of ἐπισκέπτομαι in context. Outside Luke-Acts, the sense of ἐπισκέπτομαι seems to be, "to visit for the purpose of relieving suffering." The first two instances of ἐπισκέπτομαι come in the Matthean account of the last judgment. The word is used to describe the action of the sheep when they see Jesus

---

verse. Some manuscripts add ἁγίου after πνεύματος. In this case, the presence of ἁγίου seems merely to make explicit that which is understood by the word πνεύματος in this context. Both readings have extensive manuscript support.

36. It is true, of course, that the congregation seems to play a role in the selection of Matthias as recorded in Acts 1. It seems doubtful that the plural verbs in that passage refer only to the eleven and not the whole community. Yet the two instances seem to differ in degree, marked especially by the key word ἐπισκέψασθε. In Acts 1, the congregation merely nominates (ἔστησαν) two candidates, whom God chooses, whereas the community in Acts 6 seems to have a more vital role. Contrast the ἔστησαν of Acts 1:23 with the ἐξελέξαντο of Acts 6:5. It should be noted, too, that codex Vaticanus (B) reads ἐπισκεψώμεθα for ἐπισκέψασθε. According to James Hardy Ropes, the change to ἐπισκεψώμεθα "seems to be due to the desire not to exclude the apostles from a share in the selection of the Seven. It is clearly inconsistent with vs. 6 in the usual text" (Ropes, *Text of Acts*, 56).

37. BDAG, "ἐπισκέπτομαι," 378.

sick (Matt 25:36) and the inaction of the goats when they see Jesus sick and in prison (Matt 25:43). We should not imagine that the word in these verses describes a mere visitation without any effort to minister to Jesus' needs. Similarly, in Jas 1:27, ἐπισκέπτομαι is used to describe the action associated with θρησκεία καθαρὰ καὶ ἀμίαντος pertaining to ὀρφανοὺς καὶ χήρας. Given the larger context of James, which denounces faith without deeds (Jas 2:14–26), ἐπισκέπτομαι cannot here mean other than to take care of orphans and widows, that is, to visit them for the purpose of relieving their suffering. The final NT occurrence outside Luke-Acts is in Heb 2:6, where it occurs in a quotation from Ps 8:5–7 (LXX). Within the context of Heb 2, the quotation is given a Christological interpretation, and the word ἐπισκέπτομαι indicates God's care for the υἱὸς ἀνθρώπου.

When we come to ἐπισκέπτομαι in Luke-Acts, there is a broader range of meaning. The three occurrences in Luke bear greatest affinity to Heb 2:6 because they indicate God's provision for people. Luke 1:68 pairs ἐπισκέπτομαι with ἐποίησεν λύτρωσιν τῷ λαῷ αὐτοῦ: "He made redemption for his people." In Luke 1:78, the subject of ἐπισκέπτομαι is ἀνατολὴ ἐξ ὕψους. It is clear from the context, however, that the referent is God, since this visitation brings σπλάγχνα ἐλέους θεοῦ ἡμῶν. Luke 7:16 uses ἐπισκέπτομαι, where the immediate context links God's visitation with the rising of a prophet. It is not apparent from this juxtaposition alone that the use of ἐπισκέπτομαι here involves provision for God's people, but the wider context demonstrates that the recognition of the rising of a prophet and the declaration that God has visited his people both stem from Jesus' raising of the Nain widow's dead son.

Most of the occurrences of ἐπισκέπτομαι in Acts follow the pattern we have seen in Luke and the rest of the NT. Acts 7:23, for instance, uses ἐπισκέπτομαι to describe Moses's intention toward his fellow Israelites. The next verse describes the result of this intention: he noted the mistreatment of an Israelite at the hands of an Egyptian and delivered the former by killing the latter. In Acts 15:14, ἐπισκέπτομαι describes God's activity in taking a people for himself from the Gentiles. The phrase reads, ὁ θεὸς ἐπεσκέψατο λαβεῖν ἐξ ἐθνῶν λαὸν τῷ ὀνόματι αὐτοῦ. As in the other uses of ἐπισκέπτομαι, the visitation has a purpose, in this case to take a people for his name. In light of the use elsewhere, we may presume that this activity results in the alleviation of suffering on the part of the selected people. In Acts 15:36, Paul, using ἐπισκέπτομαι as a hortatory subjunctive, suggests to Barnabas that they should visit the new believers in the cities where they had preached. Again, it seems likely that the purpose of the visit would be for the encouragement— and thus the easing of any suffering they might be experiencing—of the new believers.

But the usage in Acts 6:3 seems to be of a different sort. As noted above, BDAG lists this usage under the heading, "to make a careful inspection, look at, examine, inspect." BDAG further distinguishes the use here, listing "look for, with interest in selection, select" as the meaning. It seems, therefore, that "select" or "choose" is the best translation of ἐπισκέπτομαι in Acts 6:3. Nevertheless, it seems likely that a component of alleviation of suffering is present in the connotation of the word in the present context. This is true because the purpose of selecting the Seven is to correct the injustice to the Hellenist widows.

In addition to their role in the selection of the Seven, the congregation also may have laid hands on the Seven (v. 6).[38] The phrase ἐπέθηκαν αὐτοῖς τὰς χεῖρας in v. 6 evokes the image of diaconal ordination.[39] With millennia of ecclesiastical history coloring our view, it is

38. Jacob Jervell takes the view that the whole congregation places hands on the Seven: "Durch die Handauflegung und das Gebet werden sie von der Urgemeinde und den Leitern des Volkes beglaubigt" (Jervell, *Die Apostelgeschichte*, 220). Commentators taking the opposing view—that only the apostles placed hands on the Seven—include Ben Witherington (*Acts*, 251) and F. F. Bruce (*Acts*, 184-85). Beverly R. Gaventa expresses a more cautious view: "The commissioning of these seven men involves not the apostles alone but the entire gathering of believers. . . . And, despite the NRSV's rendering of v. 6, it is not necessarily the apostles alone who pray and lay hands on the seven. The Greek is ambiguous. It may mean that 'they [i.e., the apostles]' or that 'they [i.e., the group addressed in v. 3] prayed and laid hands on them.' Luke's very ambiguity at this point suggests his lack of interest in lines of human authority" (Gaventa, *Acts*, 115).

39. Vigorous debate surrounds the precise meaning of the phrase. Important contributions to the discussion include Coppens, "L'imposition des mains"; Ferguson, "Laying on of Hands"; and Kilmartin, "Ministry and Ordination." Coppens argues for three different types of imposition of hands in the NT: for rites of healing, of ordination, and of impartation of the Spirit after baptism. He identifies the use in Acts 6:6 as qualifying the recipients for service of the community (Coppens, "L'imposition des mains," 420-21). In contrast, Ferguson argues that the Christian use of ἐπιτίθημι (τὰς χεῖρας) derives from the Hebrew *śim*, not *samakh*, thus indicating a blessing, rather than an ordination (Ferguson, "Laying on of Hands," 1-2). He adds, "Blessing, of course, in ancient thought was more than a kindly wish; it was thought of as imparting something very definite" (Ferguson, "Laying on of Hands," 2). Kilmartin, however, remains unconvinced by Ferguson's argument (Kilmartin, "Ministry and Ordination," 43). He says, "But it is not certain that Lk intends Acts 6:1-6 to serve as model for what is being

tempting to picture the apostles gathering around each of the Seven, placing their hands on them, and ordaining them into the ministry of deacon. This view, however, depends in part on the identification of the subject of the verb ἐπιτίθημι. The ambiguity in this regard stems from the fact that the nearest plural noun is τῶν ἀποστόλων while the subject of the preceding third person plural verb (ἔστησαν) is either ἀδελφοί (v. 3) or πᾶν τὸ πλῆθος (v. 5, now understood as a plurality, as demonstrated by the plural verb, ἐξελέξαντο). In other words, the question is whether we are to understand a change in subject from the first half of v. 6 to the second half when there is no explicit nominative in either case. The matter cannot be resolved on the basis of grammar alone, since there is no nominative plural noun in the entire sentence. If we grant that ἀδελφοί and πᾶν τὸ πλῆθος refer to the same group of individuals, then it becomes clear that the first two plural verbs in the sentence have the same subject; the whole group of believers does the choosing (ἐξελέξαντο) as well as the presenting (ἔστησαν) of the men before the apostles.[40] It seems likely, therefore, that the third plural verb has the same subject. To be sure, the nearest possible antecedent for the subject of the third verb is τῶν ἀποστόλων, yet Luke does not normally switch subjects without expressing the subject in the nominative. A computer search for the construction found here—plural indicative verb, plural non-nominative noun, plural indicative verb—returns twenty-nine instances in Luke-Acts in addition to the one in Acts 6:6.[41] Of the twenty-

---

done or should be done in commissioning rites of the various churches.... The meaning of the [laying on of hands] and prayer in Acts is not immediately evident. It may represent another example of the popularity of the gesture for the conferral of blessings among Christians in contrast to Jews. But this rite can be considered a forerunner of the ordination rite of the Pastorals" (Kilmartin, "Ministry and Ordination," 48).

40. Cf. Nagel, "Twelve and the Seven,"119. Nagel correctly states that the whole body of believers selects the Seven, but he anachronistically describes the selection as "an election (ἐξελέξαντο) of the seven by the deliberative body of the disciples (πλῆθος)."

41. The specific search sequence, using Accordance 6.9, was as follows: third person plural indicative verb, no nominative noun, a non-nominative plural noun, no nominative noun, third person plural indicative verb, all within ten words of each other. The "hits" were Luke 4:40, 5:33, 6:44, 9:36, 19:44, 20:31, 20:47, 21:12, 23:23, 23:34, 23:56, 24:23; Acts 4:3, 5:18, 6:6, 7:41, 7:54, 7:57, 8:17, 8:25, 13:5, 15:4, 15:32, 16:4, 16:40, 19:6, 19:19, 27:28, 28:27. Acts 2:17 provided a thirtieth "hit," but it is clearly anomalous, since a nominative noun intervenes between the two verbs. The reason for the anomaly seems to be that the underlying tagged text parses πρεσβύτεροι as a comparative adjective rather than a nominative noun.

nine, only two (Luke 24:23 and Acts 8:17) exhibit a change in subject from the first to the second verb. In Luke 24:23, the antecedent of the changed subject is indeed the intervening noun, but the subject of the second verb is an explicitly stated relative pronoun in the nominative case. In Acts 8:17, the subject of the second verb refers, not to the intervening noun, but to an intervening pronoun in the genitive case. Thus, unless Acts 6:6 is the lone example, Luke never changes the subject of a second verb to an intervening noun without the use of a pronoun. Therefore, the possibility must be conceded that the whole group of disciples, and not just the apostles, placed their hands on the Seven.

The congregation of the primitive church, it may be concluded, participated in certain important functions that later came under the exclusive purview of the ordained clergy. However, we should not imagine the early church as an egalitarian society. Although the congregation performed functions later associated with leadership, the congregants were commanded to perform at least one of these functions (ἐπισκέψασθε) by the Twelve. Thus, the primitive church rejected a patriarchal authority structure while maintaining distinctions within its ranks. We may concur, therefore, with S. Scott Bartchy, who has argued that anti-patriarchy and egalitarianism are not synonymous.[42]

---

42. S. Scott Bartchy, "Divine Power," 97: "In light of ongoing discussions among scholars and social analysts about patriarchy and egalitarian practice as opposing ends of the same power spectrum, it is important to argue here that it was not Luke's intent to present these Jesus communities as living in an egalitarian social structure. Rather, I am persuaded that Luke thought in antipatriarchal terms while not being egalitarian. How could this be? Three points, in particular, need to be noted: (1) that in the Greco-Roman world, two institutions provided the primary metaphors for all human relationships: kinship and politics; (2) that the term 'patriarchy' belongs to the semantic field of kinship, whereas the term 'egalitarian' belongs to the semantic field of politics and so refers to such things as equal access to the vote, positions of public leadership, and the ownership of property; (3) that, therefore, the opposite of patriarchy is not egalitarianism but something else—something else for which we may not have a better term than simply 'non-patriarchy'—while the opposite of egalitarianism is not patriarchy but monarchy, oligarchy, or despotism." Cf. Rowe, "Authority and Community," 106–7: ". . . commitments to anthropological equality and to the appointment of certain persons to positions of leadership stand in conflict with each other only if we accept the (modern) premise . . . that authority is of necessity fundamentally detrimental to human beings. Acts, however, cannot be read profitably in these terms and this premise must be rejected. In marked contrast to much modern anthropology, for Luke the elevation of Paul and the apostles serves to underwrite human equality."

Authority of the Seven

As noted earlier, the Seven chosen in this passage are sometimes seen as the first deacons of the Christian church. While we have argued that such a view is unwarranted, it must still be acknowledged that the Seven serve a leadership role in the book of Acts. Yet the structure of that leadership comes as a surprise in light of first-century religious leadership patterns. In Jewish religion, of course, eligibility for religious leadership was restricted along racial lines. The requirement that priests be Jews by birth is a logical corollary of the hereditary nature of the priesthood, and the same qualification was likely expected of leaders in the synagogues of the diaspora. Leadership within the early church as represented by the Seven, however, was not ethnically homogeneous. Not only were there non-Hebrew speakers among the Seven, one of them is explicitly described as a proselyte from Antioch!

If the form of leadership for the Seven is surprising, their functions are even more counter-cultural. The task for which they are explicitly chosen is διακονεῖν τραπέζαις (v. 2). It should be clear from the context, however, that something more than the simple serving of food is in view.[43] At the minimum, the Seven are charged with the equitable distribution of physical benefits. Otherwise, the proposed solution would have left the instigating issue unresolved. The spiritual requirements listed for the potential candidates, however, seem to be disproportionate to the mundane task explicitly required of the Seven. These qualifications anticipate the larger role the Seven will play in the church. Thus, we may surmise that the Twelve anticipated—and embraced the idea—that the Seven would take on spiritual leadership tasks.[44]

With some irony, it should be noted that the Seven are never characterized as actually performing the administrative task for which they were selected. Instead, the next scenes describe Stephen's miracle working and his speech before the Sanhedrin—activities more akin to τῇ προσευχῇ καὶ τῇ διακονίᾳ τοῦ λόγου of the Apostles than the

---

43. See, for example, Gaventa, *Acts*, 112; Witherington, *Acts*, 248.

44. Perry L. Stepp views the spiritual activity of Stephen as evidence that succession from the Twelve to the Seven has taken place. He says, "Note also the confirmation that succession has taken place—Stephen, successor to the apostles in one aspect of their ministry, begins to succeed them in other aspects (i.e. preaching and performing miracles.)" (Stepp, *Leadership Succession*, 95).

διακονεῖν τραπέζαις expected of the Seven.[45] Immediately after the description of Stephen's martyrdom and the ensuing persecution, Luke reports the ministry of Philip, another of the Seven. Philip also performs miracles, as well as preaching Christ (8:5), interpreting Scripture (8:35), and baptizing (8:38). The only thing the Twelve do that Philip is not said to do is give the Holy Spirit through the laying on of hands. Yet even bestowing the Holy Spirit is not the exclusive purview of the Twelve. Not only is the Spirit given apart from the participation of the Twelve (13:52), the Spirit is also given upon the laying on of the hands of Ananias (9:17–18) and of Paul (19:6).

Unlimited Honor

As we have seen, a perception existed in the first century that there was a limit to the amount of anything deemed desirable, including honor. In order for one person to gain honor, another had to lose honor. Remarkably, the episode recorded in Acts 6:1–7 demonstrates that honor did not follow this pattern in the early church; instead, honor was unlimited. Within the group, honor increased among all the constituent subgroups. The Twelve, as we have seen, retained their honor by focusing attention on the significance of the tasks they chose to perform. But the congregation also played an honorable role. When the Twelve enlisted the larger congregation for the solution of the problem, they demonstrated that an honor challenge could be met in a way that allowed the challenged individuals (the Twelve) to retain honor while simultaneously increasing the honor of the challengers (the congregation) instead of stripping them of honor. In the same way, the Seven clearly gained in honor.

It could be argued that the Twelve lost honor and authority to the Seven through this episode, but we have demonstrated above that the Twelve actually retained their honor. Although it is true that Peter, for example, seems to have less authority within the Jerusalem church later in the narrative (see, for example, Acts 15, where Peter speaks, but James

---

45. Cf. Stepp's perspective: "In a sense, here the successor is the predecessor's delegate, given some of the predecessor's authority to accomplish certain tasks—in this case, a list which the Holy Spirit quickly expands, so that the delegate becomes more and more a successor." Stepp considers Acts 6 to be an example of weak succession, where the successor does not replace the predecessor. He finds parallels to this situation in the LXX and Lysias, *Pension* 6 (Stepp, *Leadership Succession*, 95).

has the final word), that reduction does not stem from the episode with the Seven. If that had been the case, then the narrative would have reflected an on-going interest in the Seven after the disappearance of the Twelve. Instead, Peter comes under the authority of the elders, not of the Seven, who were scattered after the persecution stemming from the martyrdom of Stephen. While it is possible that an unrecorded incident led to an increase in the authority of James and the unnamed elders at the expense of Peter's authority, in light of the account in Acts 6, it seems more likely that Peter had voluntarily limited his own authority.[46] Whether this self-limitation was undertaken in order to free himself for ministry in the Diaspora or in order to give others an opportunity to lead, the result was the increase of the honor for the group as a whole.

Similarly, it is clear in Acts 6:7 that the honor of the Jerusalem church, once threatened by internal conflict, increased as a result of the actions of the Twelve in response to the threat. Luke reports here that the word of God spread, that the number of believers increased, and many priests became obedient to the faith. Therefore, the Twelve demonstrated the paradox that honor is increased when it is shared, not grasped. It is no coincidence that Luke mentions the conversion of the priests in this context. As we have seen, a gulf separated the chief priests and the regular priests in Second Temple Judaism. The contrast between the behavior of the chief priests (the leaders of Temple religion) and the Twelve (the leaders of the Jerusalem church) is marked. Whereas the chief priests seem to have maintained a broad gap between themselves and the common priests in terms of honor, authority and wealth, the Twelve in Acts 6 work to diminish the honor and authority gap between themselves and the next-level authorities and the general congregation.

Comparing Authority Structures

The authority structures pictured in Acts 6:1–7 have little in common with the structures of the Jewish or Greco-Roman religions studied earlier. As we have just seen, the authority portrayed in this passage leads to shared honor. Such a perspective differs, for example, from the attitude toward authority exhibited by Augustus, who boasted of gathering more

---

46. For a discussion of Peter's changing role in the context of his later imprisonment at the hands of Herod, see pages 167–79.

and more religious titles—and therefore honor—for himself. Similarly, priesthoods in the Greek religions were sought after as a means of gaining honor. Yet in the Acts 6 episode, the Twelve did not insist on exclusive leadership rights.[47] Instead, they offered positions of authority to others. This approach to leadership contrasts also with the behavior of leaders within Second Temple Judaism. We have already seen that the chief priests did not extend their honor to the common priests. To be sure, the Pharisees seem to have garnered honor within Second Temple Judaism apart from the honor of the chief priests. But this seems to be a case of the exception that proves the rule: the honor of the Pharisees came at the expense of other groups, as indicated by such agonistic encounters as recorded in Josephus, *Ant.* 13.288-96. An exception to this pattern may be found in the multiplication of offices in the diaspora synagogues, but, as we have already seen (see pages 120-23), the abundance of official titles dates from a period after the formation of the early church. Thus, we may conclude that the sharing of honor within the leadership of a religious group was unique to the early church.

The diffusion of authority throughout the congregation was also unique within the early church. To generalize from our earlier observations regarding both Greco-Roman and Jewish religions, there was a wide disparity between the authority of the religious functionaries and that of the general worshippers. Even in the mysteries where congregants had some ability to move upward in the authority levels of the cults, authority rested ultimately with the upper echelon. For example, even as Lucius undertook successive initiations in the Isis cult, he remained under the pervasive, albeit benevolent authority of his superior (see pages 94-96). A similar situation holds even in Qumran, to take an example from Jewish religion. Despite frequent reference to "the Many" in the Rule of the Community, lower members of the hierarchy did not share authority. Indeed, each member had less authority than the person immediately higher in the hierarchy, since he had to obey his superior. Moreover, placement within the hierarchy does not seem to have been

47. Cf. González, "Reading from My Bicultural Place," 145: "The twelve decide that they will give to these seven the administrative tasks and that they will reserve for themselves the ministry of the word. But even this is not enough for the Spirit, who has other ideas. Were we to continue reading the book of Acts, we would find that immediately after the passage read, we are told that Stephen, one of the seven elected to manage the financial resources of the church and not to preach, is giving witness, first with his speech, and then with his life."

subject to the unqualified control of the Many but relied on seniority and the annual review of conduct. Although not explicitly stated, it seems that the most senior members of the community, not the majority, conducted this review. Therefore, to return to Acts 6, we may conclude that the degree of authority granted to the community by the Twelve was remarkable among religious communities in the first century.

Even more notable is the conclusion that in the early church, authority was no longer considered something to be grasped. As we have seen, the Twelve willingly ceded authority to the community and the Seven for the paradoxical purpose of increasing the honor of the entire community and all subgroups. We have already recalled the opposite approach exemplified by Augustus's appetite for obtaining more religious offices. We may further recall the penchant for purchasing priesthoods among the Greeks as a means of increasing honor. The contrast between the Greco-Roman approach and that of the Twelve is marked indeed. Whereas functionaries of Greco-Roman religions pursued authority as a means of gaining honor, the Twelve gained honor by eschewing the retention of authority they already possessed. This voluntary self-limitation is consonant with Paul's exhortations regarding attitudes toward personal rights. Perhaps the most memorable example is the Christ-hymn of Phil 2, where Paul declares that Jesus οὐχ ἁρπαγμὸν ἡγήσατο τὸ εἶναι ἴσα θεῷ. It should be noted, therefore, that the changing attitude toward authority in the early church—from manager-leadership in Acts 1 to innovator-leadership in Acts 6—corresponded to deepening understanding of the nature of God as revealed in Christ.[48]

Peter's Imprisonment and Release (Acts 12:1–25)

At first glance, Acts 12 seems to have very little to do with ecclesiastical authority in the early church. The chapter relates the martyrdom of James the Apostle, the subsequent imprisonment of Peter during Passover at the hands of Herod, an angel's appearance to Peter, Peter's escape from the barricaded and well guarded prison, his appearance at the house of John Mark's mother, the greeting by Rhoda, the disbelief of the gathered believers, Peter's instructions to report his prison escape to James and the brothers,[49] his departure to "another place," the death

---

48. Bartchy, "Divine Power," 89–90.

49. According to Bradley Blue, "Peter's own instructions to the group assembled in

168   THE DIFFUSION OF ECCLESIASTICAL AUTHORITY

of Herod under supernatural circumstances, and the continued growth of the church as a result of all these events. Aside from the mention of three church leaders by name (James the Apostle, Peter, and James the brother of Jesus), the chapter seems to offer little insight into ecclesiastical authority.

Yet some scholars have argued that Acts 12 represents the transition of leadership from the first-generation apostolic leadership to the second-generation leadership of James and the elders.[50] It is easy to see why scholars might think this way when ch. 12 is placed within the larger context of Acts. Whereas the apostles loom large in the narrative of the first part of Acts, the apostles virtually disappear after ch. 12. Peter is one of the main characters in Acts 1–12, but he is mentioned by name only once thereafter. One of the most vigorous statements of the view that Acts 12:1–17 is pivotal in the development of ecclesiastical authority as expressed in Acts is an article by Robert W. Wall:

> Our thesis is that Acts 12 constitutes Luke's response to that very question [What is the relationship between Peter and the Twelve, and those who bear witness to the risen Christ after them, James and Paul?]. More than simply narrating those events which bridge the 'apostolic' and 'postapostolic' periods, Luke's handling of the traditions of Peter's miraculous escape from Herod's prison intends to convince his audience that a legitimate succession took place and the effects of Jesus' messianic mission continue into the 'postapostolic' period in which they now live.[51]

Wall bases his position upon parallels between the story of Jesus' arrest, entombment, resurrection, and ascension, on the one hand; and the Acts account of Peter's arrest, imprisonment, release, and departure, on the other.[52] The specifics of the parallels are illustrated in Table 5.1.

Mary's house to tell of his release to James and the brethren (12:17), who were presumably meeting elsewhere, points to the meeting places but should not be interpreted as a reference to a schism (latent or otherwise) in the early church in Jerusalem; rather, it confirms the obvious: it was impossible to assemble all the believers (even a majority) under one roof" (Blue, "Acts and the House Church," 136).

50. See esp. Wall, "Successors." See also Barrett, *Acts I–XIV*, 570; Bauckham, "James and the Jerusalem Church," 432–40; Fitzmyer, *Acts*, 485; Haenchen, *Acts*, 391; Johnson, *Acts*, 217; Morton, "Acts 12:1–19," 69; Spencer, "Out of Mind," 145–46.

51. Wall, "Successors," 631.

52. This is an oversimplification of Wall's argument. It should be noted that Wall's basis for identifying the parallels between Jesus and Peter stems from the recognition

Table 5.1: Typological Parallels between Jesus and Peter[53]

Jesus	Peter
Arrested in Jerusalem	Arrested in Jerusalem
Arrested during Passover	Arrested during Passover
Arrested by Herod	Arrested by Herod Agrippa I
Peter says he will go to prison for Jesus	Peter is in prison for Jesus
Jesus predicts transfer of leadership to Peter (Luke 22:32)	
Jesus prays for Peter's restoration	Community prays for Peter's release
Tomb blocked by stone[54]	Prison fortified by iron
Tomb guarded by soldiers[55]	Tomb guarded by soldiers
Disciples' incredulity at Jesus' appearance	Rhoda's incredulity
Disciples disbelieve women's testimony	Disciples disbelieve Rhoda[56]

of Luke's underlying hermeneutic of interpreting events in light of the significance of Jesus' death and resurrection (Wall, "Successors," 633). Cf. Garrett, "Exodus from Bondage," 660–75. In other words, the similarities found in Acts 12 are actually a part of Luke's larger program of presenting his material within a Christological and soteriological framework. In this respect, Wall's argument is superior to a similarly shaped argument presented in MacDonald, "Luke's Emulation of Homer." See pages 170–73.

53. Compiled from Wall, "Successors," 634–42.

54. Here Wall acknowledges that the parallel account comes from Matthew and not Luke. However, he considers the juxtaposition valid because Luke would have known the passage in Matthew, which comes from the traditional Passion material Luke also drew upon. Moreover, Wall argues that typological thinking, which recognized the same parallels between Jesus and Peter that Luke himself wished to highlight, may already have shaped his sources. He says, "Sharply put, we find here a remnant of pre-Lucan Petrine tradition, which echoes elements of Matthew's gospel tradition, that has been recycled in Luke's narrative according to his typological thinking and theological intentions" (Wall, "Successors," 637).

55. See note 54.

56. Cf. the analysis of J. Albert Harrill as an example of the *serva currens* stock character in Greco-Roman comedy. He says, "Far from being a realistic representation that indicates Luke's use of some historical source, Rhoda is a running cliché of Greco-Roman situation comedy. Her function is to intensify the anticipation of the reader, to develop irony (inasmuch as the reader has more knowledge of the situation than do the characters), and to provide comic relief at a critical juncture in the narrative when all seems lost. Luke creates an artificial character Rhoda to heighten the audience's desire for a more realistic effect in the scene that follows, the appearance of Peter before the apostles" (Harrill, "Dramatic Function," 151). He concludes, "The sequence is a piece of escapist comedy that siphons implausibility from the scene, by which the subsequent action could be made to seem more real" (Harrill, "Dramatic Function," 157). Cf. Morton, "Acts 12:1–19," 67–69. For Morton, Luke's humor serves a deeper purpose (e.g., to highlight God's reversal of power structures).

Jesus	Peter
Gradual growth of disciples' faith	Gradual growth of disciples' faith
Εἶπεν δὲ πρὸς αὐτούς introducing Jesus' summary statement	εἶπέν τε introducing Peter's statement
Commands disciples to be witnesses	Commands disciples to tell James and brothers[57]
Ascension into heaven	Departure to another place

Although not convincing in every detail, the cumulative effect of Wall's argument seems persuasive.[58] We shall presently offer a friendly amendment to his proposal. First, however, it is necessary to address several perennial questions relating to Acts 12.

Historicity of Acts 12:1–17

Acts 12:1–17 has long caused scholars to inquire regarding its historicity, not least because of its miraculous content. A recent article by Dennis R. MacDonald challenges the historicity of Acts 12:1–17 on different, but not entirely new grounds:

> If my exegesis is correct, the Acts of the Apostles is self-conscious fiction. Its author expected the reader to recognize it as such and to compare his tales with similar tales in Greek poetry. The historical stratum, if any, is extremely thin and from my perspective quite uninteresting. The only historical information in Acts 12:1–17 may be that James the brother of John was martyred by Herod Agrippa and that, perhaps, Peter was imprisoned in Judea. The prison break is a fiction, the angel is a fiction, Rhoda is a fiction. Furthermore, it is as fiction that Luke intended his readers to appreciate the tale.[59]

---

57. Wall does not consider the possibility that Peter's command could parallel another command from elsewhere in the Passion narrative, namely, the command of the νεανίσκον for the women to report to Peter and the disciples that Jesus would precede them into Galilee where they would see him (Mk 16:7). If this parallel were deemed genuine, we could speculate that the singling out of Peter in the Gospel narrative and of James in Acts both relate to the restoration of someone who had earlier denied Jesus. The Fourth Gospel reports that Jesus' brothers did not believe in him (Jn 7:5).

58. Wall's article has not found universal acceptance. See, for example, Gaventa and Witherington, who explicitly reject the notion that Acts 12 represents a leadership change (Gaventa, *Acts*, 188; Witherington, *Acts*, 388).

59. MacDonald, "Luke's Emulation of Homer," 197.

Authority in the Jerusalem Church 171

Remarkably, the shape of MacDonald's argument is similar to Wall's. Like Wall, MacDonald also sees a series of parallels between Acts 12 and another piece of literature. In MacDonald's case, the paralleled literature is Iliad 24. MacDonald's parallels are reproduced in Table 5.2.

Table 5.2: Parallels between Iliad 24 and Acts 12:1–17[60]

Iliad 24	Acts 12:1–17
Achilles had slain many Trojans, including Hector.	Herod had "laid violent hands" on many believers and killed James.
The Greeks protected their ships with (φυλακτῆρες) and barred gates (πύλαι).	"Peter was placed in a prison with "four tetrads of soldiers to guard (φυλάσσειν) him."
Priam prayed to Zeus.	Believers prayed to God.
Priam and others slept (κοιμήσαντο). Hermes had put the guards (φυλακῆρες) to sleep.	"Peter was sleeping (κοιμώμενος) between two soldiers, while guards (φύλακες) in front of the door kept watch.
Hermes "stood (στῆ)" above Priam's head and waked him.	An angel "stood there (ἐπέστη)" and waked Peter.
Hermes yoked the horses and mules.	The angel told Peter to get dressed.
Priam left unnoticed by the sleeping guards.	Peter left unnoticed by the sleeping guards.
Hermes opened the barred gates and bolted door and promptly left.	The angel opened the iron gate leading to the city and promptly left.
Hermes revealed that he was a god.	Peter understood he had been rescued by an angel.
Priam proceeded to Troy.	Peter proceeded to the home of Mary.
Cassandra saw Priam approaching and went to tell the others.	Rhoda heard Peter knocking at the door, recognized the voice, and went to tell the others.
Cassandra was often considered mad.	Those inside thought Rhoda mad.
Priam had to wait outside the gate.	Peter had to wait outside the gate.
Finally, Priam entered and the Trojans continued their wailing and prepared for the funeral.	Finally, Peter entered and told them what wonderful things "the Lord" had done.

As with all comparisons, the items compared are identified as members of a broader class. The difficulty arises when the classification is too

60. The table is taken from Dennis R. MacDonald, "Luke's Emulation of Homer," *Forum* 3 (2000), 197–205. Used by permission of Polebridge Press.

broad to warrant a meaningful comparison. Such sometimes seems to be the case with MacDonald's parallels; the level of abstraction necessary to maintain the supposed parallels occasionally stretches credulity. Moreover, they often seem less convincing than those noted by Wall.

MacDonald's article is an example of a larger discussion, which addresses the question of the historicity of Acts 12.[61] Although many scholars maintain that Acts 12 relies on traditional material and therefore has at least an historical kernel, others argue that the miraculous nature of the narrative, coupled with the existence of similar miraculous escape stories in ancient literature, indicate that Acts 12 is a complete fabrication by Luke. Skeptics reject the account out of hand, preferring instead to conjecture some sort of rescue by the believers with a convenient cover story concocted to deflect charges of subversive activity against the government. Yet even less skeptical scholars must wrestle with the fact that such stories are not uncommon in classical literature. In addition to the Iliad parallels already mentioned, two additional instances are especially pertinent to the present discussion: Euripides, *Bacch.* 447–48 and Ovid, *Metam.* 3.699–700.[62] In Euripides's drama, the attendant says that the bonds (δεσμά) that held the Bacchantes were loosed (διελύθη) of their own accord (αὐτόματα) and the doors (θύρετρ') opened (ἀνῆκαν) without mortal hands (ἄνευ θνητῆς χερός). The language bears striking resemblance to the text of Acts 12. In v. 7, the chains fell from Peter's hands (ἐξέπεσαν αὐτοῦ αἱ ἁλύσεις ἐκ τῶν χειρῶν), and v. 10 describes the iron gate (τὴν πύλην τὴν σιδηρᾶν) that opened of its own accord (ἥτις αὐτομάτη ἠνοίγη). Aside from the word αὐτόματος, different language is used in the two stories. It should be noted that in *Bacchae* the bonds were loosed automatically, while in Acts it is the doors that were opened automatically. Nevertheless, the parallels are remarkable. Although Ovid wrote in Latin, the description in *Metam.* 3.699–700 also bears striking resemblance to the account in Acts 12. In *Metamorphoses*, the chains binding Acoetes were loosed

---

61. The discussion of the historicity of Acts 12 is itself a part of a larger discussion of the relationship of Acts to Greco-Roman literature. Contributions to the discussion include Harrill, "Dramatic Function"; MacDonald, "Luke's Emulation of Homer"; MacDonald, *Does the New Testament Imitate Homer?*; and Praeder, "Luke-Acts and the Ancient Novel."

62. See also Philostratus, *Vit. Apoll.* 7.34, 38; and 8.30.

and fell off without aid (*sponte*), and the doors opened of their own accord (*sponte*).

Given the close parallels between Acts and these accounts which predate it, it seems likely that Luke was familiar with at least one of them. This does not imply, however, that Luke fabricated the story.[63] Rather, Luke likely borrowed an extant conceptual framework and some of its language in order to describe an otherwise incredible event. Two observations support the claim of an historical kernel for this story. First, Luke's account describes a key figure the others lack, namely, the angel. On its own, the introduction of an angel might seem unhistorical, but where one story is thought to depend on another source, the introduction of unique material demonstrates that any dependency is governed by principles other than mere slavish reliance. Second, the details offered regarding Peter's initial perception have the ring of genuine reminiscence, not of historical fabrication. If Luke were to invent a story about an early leader of the Christian movement, surely he could have supplied a more complimentary version of Peter's thoughts! In the final analysis, the validity of the present study does not rely on the historicity of the Acts 12 miraculous deliverance. It suffices to note that Luke believed it happened and to deduce from his descriptions the nature of ecclesiastical authority as reflected in the account.

---

63. Cf. the analysis of Luke-Acts as an ancient novel by Susan Marie Praeder. She says, "It is not the case, as is often supposed, that the events and existents of ancient novels are entirely fictional and that their fictionality at once separates them from the ancient histories and biographies with their historically-true narrative worlds" (Praeder, "Luke-Acts and the Ancient Novel," 278). She goes on to assert, "Previous comparison of Luke-Acts to the ancient novels has been impeded by certain preconceptions about Luke-Acts or the ancient novels and too narrow an understanding of genre and generic criteria. There is a certain reluctance, even among critical scholars, to compare Luke-Acts to the ancient novels for fear, it seems, that if resemblances between the two are discovered, Luke-Acts will have to be declared fictional and Christianity's claims false .... There are no grounds for such a fear" (Praeder, "Luke-Acts and the Ancient Novel," 283). Cf. also Garrett, "Exodus from Bondage," 678: "The appropriation by biblical writers of mythic structures sometimes functions to *undergird* a historical conception of existence . . . For Luke, historical events are the window through which one can discern the transhistorical plan of God (Acts 2:23; 4:27–28). . . . The first exodus under Moses and the second exodus under Jesus were the historical events through which God initiated this transhistorical plan, they in turn provide the archetypal pattern for God's subsequent acts of intervention in Christian history" (emphasis original). Cf. also Heimerdinger, "Seven Steps," 310.

The Non-Replacement of James

Many commentators have noted the curious fact that a new Apostle was chosen to replace Judas whereas the death of James leads to no similar replacement.[64] One possible explanation for this observation is the proposal that Luke passed quickly over the account of James's death in order to focus attention on James, the brother of Jesus, who would soon gain greater prominence in the narrative.[65] Another explanation is that the non-replacement of James reflects the waning authority of the Twelve relative to other leaders within the Jerusalem community: since the Twelve no longer held the degree of authority they had immediately after the death of Jesus, the community felt no need to replace James.[66] Another possible explanation is that the Twelve retained their position as representatives of the twelve tribes of Israel even after death. Only Judas had to be replaced because he had disqualified himself from such representation by willfully choosing to betray Jesus. James did not vacate his place and therefore retained his apostleship.[67]

Although these proposals have some merit, perhaps an alternative explanation might prove helpful to the present discussion of ecclesiastical authority. I would posit that the replacement of Judas resulted from sociological pressure that was absent in the circumstances surrounding the death of James. As observed above, the honor of the group was threatened by the execution of Jesus, the betrayal of Judas, and Judas's demise. Peter's motivation for replacing Judas was the desire to exonerate the group and restore its honor in the eyes of the surrounding population. Since that episode, however, Peter and the church had learned that honor depends neither upon the vigorous defense of honor challenges nor upon the ability to maintain the group's leadership structure in the face of cultural expectations. Instead, honor is increased for all when authority is shared. Thus, the pressure to fill a leadership vacancy as a means of restoring group honor would have been obviated within the Jerusalem church by the realization that honor could be increased through other means.

---

64. See, for example, Barrett, *Acts I–XIV*, 569; Fitzmyer, *Acts*, 486; Spencer, *Journeying*, 138.

65. Johnson, *Acts*, 217.

66. Wall, "Successors," 636. Cf. Fitzmyer, *Acts*, 486.

67. Cf. Bruce, *Acts*, 109.

It seems likely, therefore, that Luke accurately represents the early believers' growing understanding of leadership in this new movement. As we have seen earlier, Peter seems not to have fully understood Jesus' vision that leadership in the new covenant involved laying down one's life, not lording over subordinates, and that there should be none called Father. If Peter and the others were growing in their understanding, then we should expect that certain actions taken early in the movement's history (e.g., replacing Judas) would not be repeated at a later time (thus explaining why James was not replaced). For this reason, the attention of the community was no longer focused on the replacement of James as it had been on Judas, but upon spreading the Word of the Lord. This is exactly what Luke reports happened in v. 24: Ὁ δὲ λόγος τοῦ θεοῦ ηὔξανεν καὶ ἐπληθύνετο.[68]

Peter's ἕτερον τόπον

The clause καὶ ἐξελθὼν ἐπορεύθη εἰς ἕτερον τόπον (v. 17) is an enigmatic statement the interpretation of which is open to debate. Where did Peter go, and why did he himself not go to James?[69] Why is the ἕτερος τόπος not specified? The text does not explicitly supply the answers to these questions. Any answers, therefore, must rely on speculation and

68. According to H. Alan Brehm, this clause forms an important part of the summary statements in Acts. He writes, "Through the repetition of the almost stereotypical phrase 'and the word grew' Luke uses the summary statements to support the theme of the spread of the gospel and the growth of the churches. He placed these statements at important points of transition in Acts as subtle reminders of his intention to show how the word grew from Jerusalem, through Samaria and Syria to Asia Minor, and eventually past Greece to Rome, thus 'to the ends of the earth'" (Brehm, "Significance of the Summaries," 40). Thus, this clause in Acts 12:24 lends further support to the notion that this chapter represents an important transition of leadership.

69. In v. 17, Peter instructs the disciples gathered at the home of Mary mother of John Mark to report his miraculous deliverance to James and the brothers. The implication is that James and the brothers are somehow leaders who would need to know the news. It would be desirable, therefore, to establish the identity of these brothers in order to gain a fuller picture of the leadership structures of the primitive Jerusalem church. However, two factors militate against this possibility. First, there seems to be nothing in the context to positively identify the brothers. Nothing more is said about them. Second, it is probable that the use of ἀδελφοί here does not indicate a group of leaders over whom James presides, but rather it is used simply to indicate those believers who were not present at Mary's home when Peter appeared there. On this view, James is still singled out as a leader among the brothers. It would seem, therefore, that this passage reflects the growing importance of James within the Jerusalem church.

must remain tentative, based as they are on the silence of the text. That silence is remarkable since, as already noted, Peter is a main character in Acts 1–12 (being mentioned by name fifty-five times) but drops from the narrative after this incident except for a brief appearance in ch. 15. Scholars have proposed a variety of explanations for Peter's ἕτερον τόπον. For example, some suggest that the phrase is a euphemism for the execution of Peter,[70] that Peter departed at this time for Antioch (cf. Gal 2:11),[71] or that Peter's destination had been deliberately obscured in the

70. Mentioned but rejected by Johnson, *Acts*, 214. This view is dependent upon interpreting Peter's deliverance as ahistorical. Moreover, it requires an explanation for the appearance of Peter in Acts 15. One possibility would be to argue that Luke has rearranged the historical chronology and that Acts 15 actually took place before Peter's imprisonment and supposed execution.

71. Cf. Haenchen, *Acts*, 386. It is interesting to consider in this connection that the entirety of Acts 12 is demarcated by an inclusio from Acts 11:30 to Acts 12:25. In the former verse, Barnabas and Saul are sent from Antioch to the Jerusalem elders with a monetary gift for the mitigation of a prophesied famine; in the latter Barnabas and Saul return from Jerusalem having completed their objective (πληρώσαντες τὴν διακονίαν). This is the logic of the inclusio; textual variants put this into question. Some manuscripts read ἐξ Ἰερουσαλήμ; others ἀπό Ἰερουσαλήμ; and still others εἰς Ἰερουσαλήμ. Many of the manuscripts that have ἐξ Ἰερουσαλήμ or ἀπό Ἰερουσαλήμ also insert εἰς Ἀντιόχειαν. In this case, it seems that the best reading is that of the Nestle-Aland text, namely, εἰς Ἰερουσαλήμ. Given the logic of the inclusio explained above, εἰς Ἰερουσαλήμ is clearly the *lectio difficilior*. Moreover, εἰς Ἰερουσαλήμ is the reading that most readily explains all the other readings, which may all be viewed as alternative ways of attempting to correct an apparent mistake in the manuscript. Interestingly, despite having access to the correct text, many modern translations make similar emendations. For example, NASB, KJV, and NIV all read "from Jerusalem." NRSV correctly reads, "to Jerusalem."

What, then, does it mean to say that Barnabas and Saul returned to Jerusalem? The implication is that the two must have gone to Jerusalem with the gift (Acts 11:30), departed Jerusalem (not narrated in the text), and returned to Jerusalem having completed the unspecified task (Acts 12:25). Given the fact that the text expressly states that the house Peter came to belonged to the mother of John Mark (12:12) and that Barnabas and Saul took John Mark with them when they returned to Jerusalem, it is conceivable that Luke intends us to imagine that Barnabas and Saul had left Jerusalem in order to find John Mark and bring him with them to Jerusalem. A more likely solution is that Acts 11:30 and 12:25 do not form an inclusio of the normal type. Rather, Acts 12:1–24 forms an extended aside and 12:25 picks up where 11:30 left off. In Acts 11:30, Barnabas and Saul are sent to Jerusalem; in 12:25 they arrive. They are said to return (ὑπέστρεψαν) to Jerusalem because they had been there at earlier points in the narrative. The use of ὑπέστρεψαν, then, is wrongly thought to refer to the return of the two to Antioch at the completion of their Jerusalem mission. The mention of John Mark then forms the connection between the inserted story of Peter and Acts 12:25.

received tradition in order to conceal his location from Herod.[72] Jenny Heimerdinger suggests a particularly intriguing possibility. She sees a theological connection with the exile motif of Ezekiel: both Ezekiel and Peter go εἰς ἕτερον τόπον (Ez 12:3 and Acts 12:17) as a prophetic enactment of an exile, which results from Jewish unbelief.[73]

Another possibility seems reasonable in light of the present discussion of ecclesiastical authority. The ἐξελθὼν ἐπορεύθη εἰς ἕτερον τόπον of 12:17 could have been a deliberate contrast to the πορευθῆναι εἰς τὸν τόπον τὸν ἴδιον of 1:25. The construction πορεύομαι plus εἰς plus modified τόπον occurs only three times in the NT, all in Luke-Acts. The first occurrence is in Luke 4:42, where Jesus is said to have gone to an ἔρημον τόπον. Although one could argue that πορεύομαι plus εἰς plus modified τόπον is a Lukan idiom, it does not seem likely that only three occurrences constitutes the utilization of a stock phrase. On the other hand, it seems likely that a Greek reader of Acts could have been expected to hear a verbal echo of 1:25 in 12:17. When we consider that both Acts 1 and Acts 12 likely narrate changes in leadership within the Jerusalem church, the probability increases that Luke intended a contrast between Judas going to his own place and Peter going to another place.

This interpretation of Peter's ἕτερον τόπον has interesting implications for ecclesiastical authority. Whereas Judas vacated his leadership (1:25) to go to his own place, Peter retained his authority in the church. Judas's ὁ τόπος ὁ ἴδιος, barren of any connection to the primitive church, contrasts with Peter's ἕτερον τόπον, fertile with opportunities for continued ministry and leadership. Thus, although Judas's departure from Jerusalem entailed a loss of authority in the church, Peter's departure resulted in further contributions to the growth of the church (12:24). Luke had already narrated Peter's ministry in Lydda, Joppa, and Caesarea (9:32—10:48); his new ministry likely resembled that episode in both scope and method. In this respect, the ἕτερον τόπον of 12:17 represents a further expansion of the church into a new, albeit unnamed area. Peter's departure from Jerusalem, then, represented a geographical extension of the ecclesiastical authority of the early church.

---

72. Cf. Barrett, *Acts I–XIV*, 587; Witherington, *Acts*, 389.
73. Heimerdinger, "Seven Steps," 307–8.

Peter Authorizes Additional Leadership

As we have seen, Wall asserts that Peter authorizes the transfer of leadership from the first generation to the second generation, namely, James and the elders. For Wall, this transition was not just a literary device to indicate the switch in the narrative, but a deliberate, theologically motivated discourse. It was Luke's answer to the question of whether second generation leadership was a legitimate heir to the leadership of the first generation. This is an important observation, but the present study suggests a modification: Peter did not authorize an outright replacement to his leadership but rather initiated a process that began with shared leadership and culminated in an eventual transfer of authority.

In the first place, Peter's departure was not into a first-century equivalent of retirement but, as we have argued above, into continued ministry and further leadership. Although he may have relinquished direct oversight of the Jerusalem church, which he seems to have already done earlier in the Acts narrative by virtue of his presence elsewhere, he did not renounce his place of leadership in the larger movement of the church. Rather, the locus of his authority was displaced to another location.

The notion that Peter could move to another place without losing his authority within the church had precedent in Acts 6. As we have seen, the Twelve had demonstrated in the episode recorded there that shared authority leads to increased honor for the group and each of its component constituencies. Thus, Peter had already learned that authority is not to be hoarded but shared. Acts 12, then, represents an additional demonstration that the original leaders of the church remained ready to share their authority with others without necessitating a loss of stature.

It will be recalled, furthermore, that Peter plays a role in the Jerusalem council in Acts 15. Thus, Peter clearly retained a certain degree of influence in the early church. One of the strengths of Wall's argument is that it accounts for the dramatic decrease in the importance of Peter to the remainder of the Acts narrative after Acts 12. Yet it fails to adequately account for Peter's role in Acts 15. It might be argued that Acts 15 demonstrates a reduced role for Peter relative to James. Yet this reduction should be viewed as a later stage in the process of transferring leadership.

Finally, Wall's argument depends on a parallelism between Jesus and Peter. Yet Jesus did not vacate his place of leadership in favor of the subsequent leadership of the Twelve. Acts has many instances where Jesus continues to shape events (e.g., 2:33; 9:3–6, 34; and 16:7). Since Jesus himself retained his authority even after his ascension and transfer of authority to the Twelve, Peter likewise would have retained his position even after authorizing the leadership of James and the brothers. We may conclude, therefore, that Acts 12 represents an extension of the principle demonstrated in Acts 6. Not only is authority extensible across ethnicities, it can also be shared across geographic and chronologic lines.

Diffusion of Authority in the Jerusalem Church

Looking back over the three primary passages that have formed the central focus of the present chapter, there emerges a remarkable picture of the evolution of the understanding of authority in the early church. There was an increasing diffusion of authority at each stage of development. In Acts 1, a modest extension of authority was undertaken through the addition of an individual to the ranks of the Twelve. This, of course, did not entail any structural changes to the form of ecclesiastical authority in the early church. Indeed, we have argued that this action depended more upon the extant cultural perspectives on authority and honor than on the new, Christ-like viewpoint exhibited later. Acts 6 records a more radical transformation of authority. Here, the early church departs from the cultural norms regarding authority when the Twelve voluntarily shared their leadership with the subgroup that had challenged them. Not only was the congregation included in the decision-making process, an entirely new body was vested with authority. Moreover, as we have seen, that authority extended to include the same kinds of activities the Twelve themselves conducted. Acts 12 records the inception of a process whereby Peter (and, presumably, the Twelve) shared authority with James and the brothers.

With this progression in view, it becomes clear that Luke narrated a growing consciousness within the early church that authority is something to be shared for the advancement of the Kingdom and for greater honor for all. We have shown that Peter, together with the Twelve, used his authority before Pentecost to defend his honor and that of the group in face of extreme threats. They sought to save face by restoring the Apostles to the full number, thus defending the authority of the Twelve over against any challengers. After Pentecost, however, the Twelve no longer adhered to the common conception of authority. In Acts 6, a crisis resulted in the sharing of authority as a means of increasing group honor. By Acts 12, the sharing of authority was routine, allowing a subtle intimation of a momentous shift in the shape of ecclesiastical authority rather than requiring a formal procedure as narrated in Acts 6. To use the language employed in Chapter Two above, the apostles exhibited in the pre-Pentecost period an understanding of power as "power over," but they concentrated upon "power to" after Pentecost. By allowing others to share in their authority, they empowered increasing numbers of the group to participate in the spread of the Gospel. Thus, the diffusion of ecclesiastical authority portrayed in Acts 1–12 is driven by the conscious and selfless extension of power by the Twelve for the benefit of church growth.

6

Authority in the Diaspora Church

IN THE LAST CHAPTER, WE INVESTIGATED ECCLESIASTICAL AUTHORITY in the primitive, Jerusalem church as portrayed in Acts 1–12. We demonstrated that the church's conception of authority differed from that of the wider culture in remarkable ways. Instead of clinging to their rights, the Twelve increasingly shared power with more members of the church. Peter's pre-Pentecost speech closely follows the usual cultural scripts relating to defense of group honor, while the post-Pentecost episodes reveal leaders who eschew personal power for the sake of advancing the cause of the church. The paradoxical result is that both the original leaders and the new leaders gained greater authority.

We now turn our attention to Acts 13–28, where the narrative focuses more intently on the church outside Palestine. In contrast to ch. 5, the present chapter will explore the representation of ecclesiastical authority in the diaspora church. The first two passages that demand our attention (Acts 13:1–3 and 20:17–38) focus on interactions within the leadership circles of the Antioch and Ephesian churches, respectively. As we shall see, the leaders of these churches enjoyed a high degree of autonomy, while maintaining bonds with their counterparts elsewhere. The final two passages (Acts 15:1–35 and 21:17–26) describe interactions between the diaspora church and the Jerusalem church. Whereas Acts 15 relates to formal interactions on behalf of the respective local churches, Acts 21 describes the interactions between individual leaders on a personal level. In both cases, it will be seen that Jerusalem leaders and diaspora leaders relate to one another out of deference as well as mutual concern for the common cause of the growth of the church.

The Commissioning of Paul and Barnabas (Acts 13:1–3)

Acts 13 marks a significant transition in the narrative flow of Acts. As we saw in the previous chapter, Acts 12 narrates the imprisonment and release of Peter, together with the demise of Herod, his imprisoner. In the first verses of Acts 13, the reader is introduced to a scene where prophets and teachers from the Antioch church are gathered together praying. During the prayer, the Holy Spirit instructs the leaders to consecrate two of their members for another ministry. This ministry forms the basis for much of the narrative in the remainder of Acts.

Acts 13 affords for the first time in Acts a look into the leadership of a church in the diaspora. Here we find, as it were, an invitation into a leadership meeting. We learn that five prophets and teachers are present. They obey the Holy Spirit and commission Barnabas and Saul with fasting, prayer, and the laying on of hands. As we shall see, this episode yields interesting information regarding leadership in the early church.

Who Are the Teachers and Prophets?

Prophets and teachers are linked in Acts 13 as a group of leaders within the Antioch church. Neither group is prominent in the leadership structures intimated elsewhere in Acts; indeed, this is the only occurrence of the word διδάσκαλος in Acts. Moreover, the usual use of προφήτης in Acts is in reference to the prophetic writers of the OT. Including this instance in Acts 13, προφήτης is used only four times in Acts to refer to contemporary prophets. Acts 11:27–28 and 21:10 both refer to a prophet named Agabus, although Acts 11:27 refers also to a group of prophets. Aside from the prophets mentioned in Acts 13, Judas and Silas (Acts 15:32) are the only other prophets mentioned by name. It is unclear from the wording in Acts 13, however, whether all the individuals listed were both teachers and prophets, or whether some were teachers while others were prophets.

The text leaves the exact make-up of the Antioch leadership ambiguous.[1] It is unclear from the text whether the five individuals listed were the entirety of the leadership body, whether there were additional teachers and prophets in Antioch, or whether there were other kinds of leaders in the church besides the teachers and prophets. The situation

---

1. This is yet another example of Luke demonstrating a lack of interest in the form of ecclesiastical authority. See pages 187–90.

is complicated all the more by the presence of textual variants in v. 1, especially the addition of τινες after the first two words. According to Metzger, "The later text (E H L P 33 *al* syr^h arm and Textus Receptus) interpolates τινες after ἦσαν δέ in order to imply that the six [sic] persons about to be mentioned were not the only prophets and teachers in the church at Antioch."[2] The possibility of this meaning is further indicated by the existence of a second textual variant in the verse, in which ὅ τε is replaced by ἐν οἷς, "among whom."[3] Both of these variants, therefore, are properly viewed as attempts to remove the ambiguity of the original text in favor of an explicit statement that the list of five was a partial list of teachers and prophets who were active in the primitive Antioch church. It is entirely possible that these variants reflected the true situation in Antioch, but we must concede that the original text does not demand such an interpretation. For this reason, any evaluation of the precise constitution of the Antioch church leadership must remain speculative.

However, even if there were other leaders in the Antioch church, it is clear that the named individuals played an especially important leadership role in the Antioch church.[4] The fact that the five are listed by name indicates their renown—and therefore their importance—in the early church.[5] Most commentators agree that the list of leaders in v.

2. Metzger, *Textual Commentary*, 353.

3. Codex Bezae and the Vulgate. See Metzger, *Textual Commentary*, 353.

4. Surprisingly, very little attention is paid in the commentaries to the question of whether the Antioch church had additional leaders. The commentators seem to be far more interested in the identity of the named individuals. For example, Bruce, Witherington, Johnson, Gaventa, and Haenchen all offer speculation on the identities of Simeon, Lucius, and Manaen but say nothing about the textual variants discussed above and their implications for the constitution of the leadership of the Antioch church (Bruce, *Acts*, 292–93; Gaventa, *Acts*, 189–90; Haenchen, *Acts*, 394–95; Johnson, *Acts*, 220–21; Witherington, *Acts*, 392–93).

5. Four of the five names are clearly of Jewish origin: Barnabas, Simeon, Manaen, and Saul. But Lucius seems to be a Gentile name. Although some Jewish children were given Gentile names by Hellenizing Jews, most practicing Jews had recognizably Jewish names. (For discussions about the diversity implied by the five names, see, for example, Spencer, *Journeying*, 147.) Therefore, it seems likely that Lucius was a Gentile. If not a Gentile, then he most likely was born into a family that had been dissociating itself from its Jewish heritage. We may conclude, then, that the church in Antioch from this primitive period, counted non-Jews as highly placed members. Although this observation does not have direct bearing on the question of form and function of ecclesiastical authority, it does indicate the degree to which the inclusive message of the Gospel had

1 is a traditional one, implying that the five were important to the early church.[6] Yet it is not immediately clear what the role of the five might have been. Although they are identified as teachers and prophets, they are said to be serving (λειτουργούντων). What is the nature of this service? Λειτουργέω and its cognate nouns λειτουργία, λειτουργικός, and λειτουργός occur in the NT only fifteen times, including once in Luke and once in Acts. The basic meaning of the word group is related to service. BDAG offers "perform a public service" and "serve in a public office" as interpretations but notes that in the early Christian literature it almost always relates to religious and ritualistic activity of one type or another.[7] Still, it should be noted that the λειτουργέω word-group is often connected in the NT with ministry to physical needs. Romans 13:6 refers to earthly rulers as λειτουργοί of God. Romans 15:27 says εἰ γὰρ τοῖς πνευματικοῖς αὐτῶν ἐκοινώνησαν τὰ ἔθνη, ὀφείλουσιν καὶ ἐν τοῖς σαρκικοῖς λειτουργῆσαι αὐτοῖς, which clearly connects λειτουργέω with fleshly needs. Similarly, in 2 Cor 9:12, λειτουργία refers to supplying the needs (ὑστερήματα) of the saints. Philippians 2:25 and 30 refer to serving Paul's needs (τῆς χρείας μου).

The one occurrence in Luke's gospel pertains to priestly service in the Jerusalem Temple (cf. Phil 2:17, Heb 8:2, 9:21, and 10:11, which also allude to cultic service). Luke 1:23 says, καὶ ἐγένετο ὡς ἐπλήσθησαν αἱ ἡμέραι τῆς λειτουργίας αὐτοῦ, ἀπῆλθεν εἰς τὸν οἶκον αὐτοῦ. The reference is to Zacharias's rotation in the Levitical courses in the Temple. This ministry would have involved heavy manual labor, such as a great deal of lifting, shifting, and manipulation of sacrificial carcasses and wood (*Let. Aris.* 92–93). Moreover, the slaughter of animals at the Temple provided an important component of the diet of ordinary Jews, since they partook of a share of the sacrificial animal. Therefore, although λειτουργία primarily relates to ritual performance, there remains a heavy emphasis here on physical exertion as well as an element of service of providing for the sustenance of individuals.

---

penetrated the practice of the early church. That a Gentile could share a position of leadership co-equal with Jews demonstrates that the church in Antioch had actualized its convictions. This lived conviction, of course, makes the so-called Jerusalem council all the more poignant, as we shall see.

6. See, for example, Conzelmann, *Acts*, 99; Haenchen, *Acts*, 394; Jervell, *Apostelgeschichte*, 340.

7. BDAG, "λειτουργέω," 590–91.

In Acts 13:2, it is interesting to note that the verb is followed by the dative τῷ κυρίῳ. Here, then, the emphasis is more strongly on the spiritual aspect of λειτουργέω. One might compare the usage here (Λειτουργούντων δὲ αὐτῶν τῷ κυρίῳ καὶ νηστευόντων εἶπεν τὸ πνεῦμα τὸ ἅγιον) with that in *Herm. Mand.* 5.1.2, which uses λειτουργήσει with the dative τῷ θεῷ. Also instructive is *Did.* 15:1, which reads ὑμῖν γὰρ λειτουργοῦσι καὶ αὐτοὶ τὴν λειτουργίαν τῶν προφητῶν καὶ διδασκάλων. It is remarkable that the same two groups of individuals, the prophets and teachers, are mentioned in both Acts 13 and *Did.* 15:1. The conjunction of λειτουργέω and prophets and teachers in both passages leads one to postulate a common ecclesiastical environment for both. The connection is strengthened further by the fact that both passages are related to the church in Antioch: Acts 13:1–3 narrates an event which took place in Antioch, and the Didache may have been written in Antioch.[8] Therefore, it is all the more important to note that *Did.* 15:1 explicitly applies to bishops and deacons: the bishops and deacons perform (λειτουργέω) the ministry (λειτουργία) of prophets and teachers. For this reason, it is possible that the prophets and teachers listed in Acts 13 in fact were the officers of the congregation. However, it seems more likely that the Didache reflects a later, more developed point in the history of the Antioch church. Prophets and teachers are characterized by their function, whereas bishops and deacons are distinguished by their position. This distinction explains the force of the genitives in *Did.* 15:1; the way that bishops and deacons serve is by doing what prophets and teachers do, namely prophesying and teaching. If, then, the leadership of the individuals mentioned in Acts 13:1 was characterized by their prophesying and teaching, the question remains: what is the nature of their λειτουργία in this passage? According to Haenchen, the construction used here, λειτουργούντων . . . τῷ κυρίῳ, is a Septuagint expression meaning to pray.[9] This interpretation makes the most sense

---

8. Slee, *Church in Antioch*, 55–57. Slee also argues for a date "possibly as early as the mid-first century CE" (76). Cf. Aaron Milavec, who argues for the unity of the *Didache* and the independence of the *Didache* from the Canonical Gospels, thus allowing a date between 50–70 CE (Milavec, *The Didache*, xii–xiii and 739).

9. Haenchen, *Acts*, 395. Haenchen notes the usage of λειτουργεῖν in 2 Chr 5:14, 13:10, 35:3; Jdt 4:14; Joel 1:13, 2:17; Ezek 40:46, 44:16, 45:4; and Dan Θ 7:10. He also cites H. Strathmann's article on λειτουργέω in the TDNT in support of this interpretation. However, according to Strathmann, "The reference [in Acts 13:2] is obviously to a fellowship of prayer on the part of the five. . . though Lk.'s use of the term in Ac. 13:2

of the present passage, since the λειτουργία is directed toward the Lord, not the congregation, as we should expect if the five were teaching or prophesying. Indeed, despite claims to the contrary,[10] there is no indication in the passage to suggest that the congregation was present.[11]

Another aspect of the discussion regarding the teachers and prophets in this passage is the significance of the laying on of hands reported in v. 3. If we may be permitted to take Bede's eighth century commentary as reflective of the traditional view on the matter, the laying on of hands here indicates the ordination of Barnabas and Saul to the office of apostle. According to Bede,

> According to the historical order of events, it seems that it was in the thirteenth year after the Lord's passion that Saul received, with Barnabas, the office of apostle, and the name Paul. In the fourteenth year, in accord with the agreement of James, Cephas, and John, he [Paul] advanced to the office of teacher of the gentiles. *The History of the Church* is not inconsistent, since it says

---

stands in contrast to the LXX, Jewish Christian circles of the time would not regard it as unprecedented or strange" (H. Strathmann, "λειτουργέω, λειτουργία, λειτρουγός, λειτουργικός," *TDNT* 4:226). Even more surprisingly, Strathmann seems to contradict himself. He writes, "On the other hand, the terms are never used for the services or offices of leading personalities in the new community such as apostles, teachers, prophets, presbyters, bishops, etc. Such a use could not develop in the soil of primitive Christian thought. For the tasks of Christian office-bearers were not comparable with those of the priestly sacrificial cultus." Apparently, Strathmann is bracketing Acts 13:2 from consideration for usage as "services or offices," for he says, "Movement towards a new Christian terminology is to be found only in the one verse Ac. 13:2, where λειτουργεῖν is used for a fellowship of prayer, which hereby is indirectly described as a spiritualized priestly ministry" (Strathmann, "λειτουργέω, κτλ.," 228). This, however, begs the question. If in Acts 13:2 λειτουργέω should be taken to mean priestly service, then it clearly was used at least here for the "services or offices" of teachers and prophets.

10. Bruce, *Acts*, 294; Gaventa, *Acts*, 190–1; Haenchen, *Acts*, 395; Spencer, *Journeying*, 147. Bruce adduces for evidence the addition of πάντες in codex Bezae, which Metzger calls, "a typical Western expansion" (Metzger, *Textual Commentary*, 353). It should be noted, however, that the most natural antecedent for πάντες is the three leaders (Simeon, Lucius, and Manaen) mentioned in v. 1, not the congregants, who are not mentioned at all. Gaventa offers a somewhat more compelling rationale. She says, ". . . other Lukan descriptions of the common life of believers suggest that the setting here is the church's worship rather than official duties of the few (2:46–47; 4:23–31)" (Gaventa, *Acts*, 190).

11. Barrett, *Acts I–XIV*, 604; Witherington, *Acts*, 393.

that he was commanded by the apostles to preach in Judaea for twelve years.[12]

A similar view continues to find adherents. According to J. Coppens, for example, the view that the account represents the ordination of Barnabas and Saul to the office of apostle is supported by the solemnity of the liturgical scene and by the fact that just after this episode Barnabas and Paul receive the title ἀπόστολος for the first time in Acts (14:4, 14).[13] With good reason, few modern commentators have followed Coppens in embracing the traditional view. In the first place, the view seems to require a separation of scenes between v. 2 and v. 3 in order to allow for a different set of leaders present for the ordination.[14] Otherwise, Barnabas and Paul would have been ordained to the office of apostle by their peers, who had not yet attained that office. Second, the idea that the solemnity of the occasion implies an ordination ceremony merely begs the question; a commissional blessing may have fostered an equally solemn mood. Finally, the distance between the present passage and the mention of Barnabas and Paul as apostles seems too great to suggest that Luke was thinking back to a supposed ordination in 13:3 when he used the title in 14:4 and 14. Luke's use of different sources seems a more likely explanation for the occurrence of the title.

The Holy Spirit as Leader

As interesting as it is to examine the leadership structures as exhibited by the prophets and teachers in Acts 13, the thrust of the text itself resists such a reading to a certain extent. The text portrays the Holy Spirit as the true leader. According to Witherington,

> V. 4 makes abundantly clear that though the leaders in Antioch endorsed and prayed for these two men and their work, it was in fact the Holy Spirit who had both commanded the church to act and now sends these two men on their way.[15]

12. Bede, *Venerable Bede*, 117.
13. Coppens, "L'imposition des mains," 419–20.
14. This seems to be the reason for Coppens's suggestion for the scene change (Coppens, "L'imposition des mains," 418). Other scholars have suggested a scene change (e.g., Haenchen, *Acts*, 395. See also note 10). However, the purpose of arguing for a scene change is usually to indicate that the whole congregation commissioned the two, not to suggest that other leaders were there.
15. Witherington, *Acts*, 394.

A simple examination of the verbs in Acts 13:1–3 indicates the role of the Holy Spirit as the initiator. In v. 1, all the verb forms (ἦσαν, οὖσαν, and καλούμενος) are stative; they are used merely to describe the people present, not to narrate any activity. Similarly, the first two verbs in v. 2 (λειτουργούντων and νηστευόντων) are participles used to set the scene. They describe the concurrent activity of the human participants at the time when the Holy Spirit initiates the action described in the following verses. Moreover, the semantic domain of νηστεύω is associated with submission. Fasting is generally undertaken, not when confident of one's own self-sufficiency, but when imploring the aid of someone more powerful.[16] In contrast to the dependent posture of the prophets and teachers, the Holy Spirit initiates activity. Not only is τὸ πνεῦμα τὸ ἅγιον the subject of an active verb, the subsequent actions are the result of the command issued by the Holy Spirit.

The assertion that Luke portrays the Holy Spirit as leader in this passage is further strengthened by an examination of the verbs used to describe the "sending" of Paul and Barnabas. Although it is difficult to capture in translation, there are actually two different words used in the Greek for the sending by the prophets and teachers in v. 3 and by the Holy Spirit in v. 4.[17] Whereas the verb ἀπολύω is used to describe the action of the prophets and teachers, ἐκπέμπω describes the action of the Holy Spirit. ἀπολύω occurs fifteen times in Acts (Acts 3:13; 4:21, 23; 5:40; 13:3; 15:30, 33; 16:35, 36; 17:9; 19:40; 23:22; 26:32; 28:18, 25). In every instance, the word can be translated as "release" or "dismiss," not as "send out."[18] Nine instances (3:13; 4:21, 23; 5:40; 16:35, 36; 17:9;

---

16. Cf. Mitchell, "Practice of Fasting," 465: "Was the fasting practiced to demonstrate to God the gravity and solemnity of this occasion? Was it done to indicate humility and inadequacy with respect to the task to which Paul and Barnabas were being sent? One cannot be sure. But clearly Christ taught that fasting should be motivated by a serious felt need (Matt. 9:14–15)." Mitchell goes on to say, "In the Old Testament a fast was a means of demonstrating a humble heart, a repentant spirit . . . . Since fasts in the Old Testament were in response to calamities and were to demonstrate humility and repentance, it would seem that the same purpose and attitudes would hold true for New Testament believers" (Mitchell, "Practice of Fasting," 469).

17. E.g., NASB, NIV, and KJV all use "sent" plus various helping words to translate both ἀπολύω (v. 3) and ἐκπέμπω (v. 4).

18. Moulton and Milligan cite Acts 13:3 as an example of ἀπολύω used to mean "send away on a mission" (Moulton and Milligan, "ἀπολύω," 66). The argument being made here is that, since the other NT occurrences are not translated "send out," then neither should the Acts 13:3 occurrence be so translated.

26:32; 28:18) clearly relate to the release of prisoners. In Acts 19:40, the magistrate dismisses the crowd after the Ephesian riot, and the commander dismisses Paul's nephew in Acts 23:22. Acts 28:25 falls into the same category. ἀπολύω occurs in the middle voice here and could be translated "excused themselves" in reference to Paul's audience in Rome who left after disagreeing with him. Only the Acts 15:30 occurrence seems to demand a translation involving "send." Yet the use of ἀπολύω again in 15:33 shows that "release" is a better translation. In the latter verse, the Antioch congregation released (ἀπελύθησαν) Judas and Silas to return to the ones who had commissioned (τοὺς ἀποστείλαντας) them. Clearly, Judas and Silas had been sent by the so-called Jerusalem council, not by the people who now released (ἀπελύθησαν) them. The juxtaposition of ἀπολύω and ἀποστέλλω in v. 33 suggests that ἀπολύω should not be translated "send" in either v. 30 or v. 33. BDAG offers the following as the third entry for ἀπολύω: "To permit or cause someone to leave a particular location."[19] In light of the preceding discussion, however, it seems preferable to maintain a distinction between "permit someone to leave" and "cause someone to leave." The latter does not seem to be intended in the uses of Acts outside ch. 13, and it is not necessarily present in 13:3. Thus, "permit someone to leave," or "release," seems to be the preferred translation here.

In contrast to the relative frequency of ἀπολύω, ἐκπέμπω occurs only twice in the NT. In Acts 17:10, the brothers from Thessalonica sent (ἐξέπεμψαν) Paul and Silas to Berea for their own protection. It is quite interesting that both ἀπολύω and ἐκπέμπω occur in this context. In v. 9, the authorities released (ἀπέλυσαν) Paul, Silas, and the rest of those who had been detained, and in v. 10 the brothers sent Paul and Silas away (ἐξέπεμψαν). The sense is that the authorities simply let them go, but the brothers sent them for a particular purpose.[20] The same usage is present in Acts 13. Although the prophets and teachers released (ἀπέλυσαν, v. 3) Paul and Barnabas for whatever the Holy Spirit would require, it was the Holy Spirit who sent them out (ἐκπεμφθέντες ὑπὸ τοῦ ἁγίου πνεύματος, v. 4). Thus, the Holy Spirit is the one portrayed as leader in Acts 13. As Johnson eloquently says,

---

19. BDAG, ἀπολύω, 117.

20. BDAG, ἐκπέμπω, 307: "To cause someone to go away (for a purpose), to send out."

The commissioning scene in 13:1–3 therefore serves to give Barnabas and Saul a two-fold validation. First, they are shown to be thoroughly enmeshed in the life of the local Antiochean community. . . . Second, their mission is validated by the direct intervention of the Holy Spirit. Here the reader confronts again the strange doubleness of religious narrative, in which action taking place at the level of human freedom is encompassed by action directed by God's will. The Holy Spirit speaks in the assembly (in its own voice!),[21] directing the setting apart of Barnabas and Saul for 'the work to which I have summoned them' (13:2). And in case we miss the point, Luke repeats that they were sent out 'by the Holy Spirit' (13:4).[22]

Lines of Authority

Despite the fact that the text emphasizes the leadership of the Holy Spirit, the text also yields a number of interesting implications regarding human aspects of leadership in the early church. We have noted how the prophets and teachers were gathered when the Holy Spirit spoke. This gathered group had unmediated communion with the Holy Spirit. There was no need for consultation with priest or apostle in order to hear the voice of the Spirit. While Acts 13 does not imply a doctrine of the priesthood of all believers, it is nonetheless significant that such an important development as the launching of the Pauline mission is initiated without the authorization of any hierarchy related to the Jerusalem στῦλοι (Gal 2:9). The same type of process seems to have occurred already in Acts 8:4, when the scattered believers began to proclaim the Good News quite apart from the impetus of the Jerusalem church. In the case of Acts 13, however, the situation is different in that the gathered leadership of an organized church outside Palestine is involved in

---

21. Johnson correctly points out that the text explicitly says that the Holy Spirit spoke to the gathered prophets and teachers. Other commentators are quick to point out that this speaking was likely through the mediation of one of the prophets (e.g., Bruce, *Acts*, 294; Haenchen, *Acts*, 396; Jervell, *Apostelgeschichte*, 341; Marshall, *Acts*, 216; Witherington, *Acts*, 393). While it may be historically accurate to understand the Holy Spirit as speaking through one of the prophets, so far as Luke is concerned, the important thing is that the Holy Spirit in fact spoke.

22. Johnson, *Acts*, 225-6.

the intentional initiation of a new phase of ministry.[23] Indeed, Jerusalem is not even mentioned in the passage.

Another interesting observation relates to the role of Barnabas in this episode. It will be recalled that in Acts 11:22 the Jerusalem church had commissioned Barnabas to go to Antioch. Yet Barnabas is portrayed in this passage as merely one of the group of leaders in Antioch.[24] If his mandate from the Jerusalem church included authority over the affairs of the Antioch church, we should have expected that Barnabas would have been pictured as presiding over the prophets and teachers. The implication is clear: Barnabas does not seem to have had a special authority above that of the other prophets and teachers in Antioch, and the Antioch church had a high degree of independence from the Jerusalem church.

We have seen that the primary leader in Acts 13 is the Holy Spirit. The Spirit's leadership was exercised within a group of prophets and teachers who submitted to his authority. These prophets and teachers functioned as the human leaders within the Antioch church. They served the church by using their gifts, that is, by prophesying and teaching. Their leadership within the church operated under the unmediated authority of the Holy Spirit. There is no intimation in Acts 13:1-3 to suggest that Jerusalem held authority over the Antioch church. The two churches seem to have been related by deference and a common purpose, rather than by constitutional or juridical formality. As we shall see, this conclusion is further substantiated by examination of the

---

23. Cf. Witherington, *Acts*, 390: "Though there had already been clear contacts with and successes in converting Gentiles prior to the time of the events recounted in Acts 13-14, it is Luke's intent to portray this missionary journey as being the inaugural efforts by a church at planned evangelism of Gentiles as well as Jews, indeed the first planned efforts at overseas missions. Acts 13:1ff., then, must be seen as something of a turning point in the narrative." Cf. also Best, "Acts 13:1-3," 345: "It is the purpose of this note to suggest that the incident represents the first deliberate and professional missionary activity . . . . Wherever Christians went they took the Gospel with them; however, this spread of the Gospel was not a planned activity of the Church; it was the incidental result of outside circumstances and haphazard."

24. Claims such as Best's that Barnabas is pictured as taking the lead in Acts 13 seem to be based on the fact that his name is listed first (Best, "Acts 13:1-3," 345). Luke does not narrate any instances in Acts 13-14 where Barnabas exerts authority over Paul or the other leaders. The most that can be said, therefore, is that Barnabas may be "first among equals." If that is the case, the narrative seems to place the stress on "equal," not "first." Indeed, after 13:9, where Saul is identified as Paul, Paul seems to take precedence over Barnabas.

passages related to inter-ecclesial interaction between Jerusalem and Antioch (see pages 200–216).

Paul's Farewell to the Ephesian Elders (Acts 20:17–38)

Before turning to passages that narrate interactions between diaspora churches and the Jerusalem church, we turn our attention to one more passage that conveys information about ecclesiastical authority outside Palestine. This passage, Acts 20:17–38, describes the interaction between Paul and the leaders of the church at Ephesus. According to Acts 20, Paul summoned the Ephesian elders to Miletus in order to meet with them while he was on his way to Jerusalem.[25] The bulk of the passage consists of Paul's so-called farewell speech to these elders. Because the speech is presented as from one leader to a group of leaders, the passage offers insight into intra-ecclesial authority structures in the diaspora church. Once again, before we turn to a discussion of these insights, it is necessary to explore the historicity of the passage.

---

25. The land around Miletus was originally called Anactoria (Pausanias, *Descr.* 7.2.5) and inhabited by Carians (Pausanias, *Descr.* 7.2.5 and Strabo, *Geogr.* 14.1.3). Strabo lists Miletus with Ephesus as "the best and most famous cities" in the region (Strabo, *Geogr.* 14.1.4 [Jones, LCL]). Herodotus says, "Miletus was then at the height of her fortunes, insomuch that she was the chief ornament of Ionia" (Herodotus, *Hist.* 5.28 [Godley, LCL]). The importance of the city is attested also in poetry (*Homeric Hymns* 3.42). The sources report two invasions of Miletus. The first was by the Cretan, Miletus, who gave the city its name (Pausanias, *Descr.* 7.2.5). Neileus (Neleus in Strabo), who was considered the founder of the city, launched the second invasion from Athens (Pausanias, *Descr.* 7.2.4 and Strabo, *Geogr.* 14.1.3). Strabo mentions an altar on the Poseidium in Miletus, which was erected by Neleus (*Geogr.* 14.1.3). (Apollodorus reports an alternative myth for the foundation of Miletus in *Library* 3.1.2. In this version, Miletus is a son of Apollo, over whom two children of Europa love and quarrel. Because of the resulting war, Miletus fled to Caria, where he founded Miletus.) Little within the preceding accounts suggests a thematic or theological reason for Luke to mention Miletus. There seems to be no explanation other than Luke's own, namely, Paul's haste, as to why Miletus was the chosen location. Cf. Rapske, "Acts, Travel and Shipwreck," 17: "Paul's arrangements to sail by and call the elders to himself at Miletus in such a warm-hearted climate are both logical and consistent, suggesting a dual purpose. The arrangements would avoid the risk of offending the church because in relating to the elders he could be said to be relating to all the Ephesians. At the same time the Miletus locale served as an effective buffer, foreclosing the danger of his plans being held hostage to an affectionate, vigorous and ultimately extended hospitality. Five days in Miletus would hardly seem inconsistent with his travel objective when compared with being obliged in the Ephesian context to accept a hospitality of perhaps several weeks' duration."

Historicity of Paul's Speech

We earlier explored the historicity of Peter's speech in Acts 1:16–22 (see pages 140–43). I argued that the speeches of Acts in general, and Peter's speech in particular, represent the content of actual speeches delivered by the named individuals, though not necessarily their *ipsissima verba*. In the case of Paul's speech to the Ephesian elders, reassessment of its historicity is warranted by the facts that it is Paul's only extended speech to believers in Acts,[26] that it therefore affords direct comparison with Paul's letters,[27] and that it appears to follow the well-known genre of the farewell address.[28]

The high number of verbal parallels between Paul's speech in Acts 20:17–38 and his extant letters creates an interesting question.[29] If, on

---

26. Bruce, *Acts*, 429; Hemer, "Speeches of Acts: Part 1," 77; Watson, "Paul's Speech,"184; Witherington, *Acts*, 610.

27. Cf. Dupont, *Le discours de Milet*, 30: "L'exégèse du discours de Milet doit, en pratique, jouer sur deux tableaux. Il faut éclairer le texte en recourant, d'une part, aux expressions et aux idées similaires qui se rencontrent en d'autres endroits des deux livres de Luc, d'autre part, à ce que Paul écrit dans ses épîtres."

28. Dupont, *Le discours de Milet*, 10–11. According to Dupont, "D'abord le genre littéraire : le discours de Milet est un discours d'adieu : il utilise les principaux thèmes et reflète les préoccupations habituelles aux morceaux de ce genre.... L'Antiquité nous a laissé un grand nombre de discours d'adieu. Il s'agit presque toujours des dernières paroles d'un mourant : recommandations suprêmes, très souvent accompagnées de prédictions ; la croyance en une mystérieuse clairvoyance de ceux qui vont mourir était profondément ancrée dans l'esprit des Anciens." See also Watson, "Paul's Speech," 185. According to Watson, there are eight features of Paul's speech which are common to the ancient farewell addresses: the speaker gathers elders (v. 17); professes blamelessness and exhorts emulation (vv. 18–27, 33–35); predicts approaching death (vv. 22–25, 29, 38); refers to tradition and describes consequences (v. 32); bequeaths tradition to followers (v. 28); offers moral advice (vv. 28, 35); cautions about persecution and false teachers (vv. 29–30); and ends with prayer and tears (v. 37). Watson goes on to analyze the speech by means of rhetorical criticism, concluding that "Luke the rhetor has used *prosopoeia* to create an epideictic encomium and farewell address for Paul as he ends his missionary journey in the East" (Watson, "Paul's Speech," 208). Watson describes *prosopoeia* as "a technique used in historiography in which an historical character is made to speak in the first person with delineation of his or her character and deeds being central" (Watson, "Paul's Speech," 190). Witherington, however, is quite critical of Watson's analysis; he instead classifies the speech as deliberative rhetoric (Witherington, *Acts*, 612–13, 627).

29. Witherington, *Acts*, 610. Witherington lists thirteen parallels from vv. 17–26: "reminder of how he lived when with his converts," "Paul's work called serving the Lord," "on humility (refusing to claim anything for himself)," "on his fears/showing personal concern," "Jewish persecution," "taught from house to house," "helpful/profitable

the one hand, Luke was unaware of Paul's letters, then the presence of the parallels would tend to confirm the speech's historicity.³⁰ If, on the other hand, Luke knew Paul's letters, then the presence of the parallels would tend to suggest literary dependence, not historicity. It seems difficult entirely to avoid circularity of argument in the present case, since there is little concrete evidence aside from the present speech on which to base one's judgment.³¹

As Duane Watson has astutely noted, scholars who maintain the historicity of Paul's speech to the Epheisan elders usually do so according to the following logic: (1) the speech occurs within the "we" section of Acts, implying that the author was an eyewitness to the delivery of the speech, (2) Luke may have used notes, thus assuring an accurate

---

teaching," "preaching to both Jew and Greek," "faith in our Lord Jesus," "Paul's uncertainty about his future," "lack of attempt to preserve his own life," "his job—to preach the gospel of God's grace," "being innocent of his converts' blood." Other parallels may be discerned. For example, ἀπὸ πρώτης ἡμέρας in v. 19 is reminiscent of ἀπὸ τῆς πρώτης ἡμέρας in Phil 1:5, which is part of the introduction to another Pauline communication. Similarly, the phrase ταῖς χρείαις μου καὶ τοῖς οὖσιν μετ' ἐμοῦ ὑπηρέτησαν αἱ χεῖρες αὗται in v. 34 recalls Paul's exhortations to self-sufficiency (1 Cor 4:12, Eph. 4:28, and 1 Thess 4:11) and his boasts of offering the Gospel free of charge and without demanding his rights to physical support (1 Cor 9:1–18 and 2 Cor 11:7–9). Cf. Barrett, *Introduction and Commentary*, 964.

30. According to Edgar Goodspeed, Luke was unaware of the existence of Paul's letters; indeed, it was the publication of Luke-Acts which led one of its readers—whom he identifies as Onesimus, who, as Philemon's run-away slave, had treasured Paul's letter on his behalf—to collect the letters into the Pauline corpus (Goodspeed, *Key to Ephesians*, xi–xiii). Few commentators have attained Goodspeed's degree of confidence on this question. Indeed, according to Wall, "The omission of any direct reference to Paul's letter writing in Acts is much less a problem than it once was in Acts criticism, for two reasons: (1) There are clear allusions to Pauline letters in Acts, and (2) it now seems possible that a collection of Paul's letters was placed in circulation—perhaps even by Paul himself—before the turn of the first century. It is simply inconceivable that Luke would not have known and read these letters, and therefore used them as a secondary source when writing Acts" (Wall, "Acts of the Apostles," 188, n. 461). See also Walker, "Acts and the Pauline Corpus Reconsidered." Walker argues that Luke, as a student of Paul writing in the later part of the first century, could not have been ignorant of Paul's letters. Luke did not mention the letters because the letters were not helpful to his purpose of writing narrative and because he did not wish to draw attention to the conflicts portrayed in the letters. Walker also offers instances where he believes Luke knew and corrected Paul's letters, together with claimed verbal parallels between Acts and the letters.

31. Witherington, *Acts*, 610: "If there is a case to be made that Luke knew Paul's letters, or at least the Pauline message found in those letters, it must be made in the main on the basis of the Miletus speech."

recollection of the specifics of the speech,[32] and (3) the many expressions which parallel the Pauline Epistles are the result of the author of Acts remembering Paul's own speech patterns.[33] Conversely, scholars who reject the historicity of this speech often appeal to the following factors: (1) the parallels with the Pauline Epistles represent an effort on the part of the author of Acts to capture the Pauline ethos, (2) all the speeches in Acts are similar in structure and content, implying a single speech-writer, (3) all the speeches exhibit distinctively Lukan characteristics, suggesting that the single speech-writer is the author of Acts, and (4) the strong similarities of Paul's farewell speech to Jesus' farewell speech in Luke 22 also suggest the same writer created both.[34]

Despite the various arguments just enumerated, whether one accepts or rejects the historicity of Paul's speech depends to a significant extent upon one's assumptions. As Bruce points out, "Much, in fact depends on the way in which one's mind has been conditioned to approach such a subject."[35] To my mind, the historicity of the other speeches in Acts as argued above permits a predisposition toward a presumption of historicity for this speech, as well. With that in mind, I find the following factors to be significant. First, as Hemer has noted, "The simplest [explanation] is that the emotional farewell, the introspective retrospect, and the admonitions for the future were the natural reflection of a real situation . . . that this is a report of Paul speaking on a real and emotional occasion."[36] Second, the fact that farewell speeches were employed for leave-taking as well as for expectations of death[37] further suggests that the speech had a natural setting within the life of Paul.[38]

---

32. The chief proponent of this view is F. F. Bruce. He says, "Shorthand was not an unknown device in the first century A.D., and a man such as the author of Acts reveals himself to have been was just the kind of person to make use of it" (Bruce, "Speeches in Acts," 63).

33. Watson, "Paul's Speech," 186.

34. Ibid., 187.

35. Bruce, "Speeches in Acts," 63.

36. Hemer, "Speeches of Acts I," 79.

37. Gaventa, *Acts*, 283. Cf. Hemer, "Speeches of Acts I," 81, n. 17; Witherington, *Acts*, 613, 618–20.

38. The possibility that Paul's original speech was meant as a farewell of departure does not exclude the possibility that Luke has reframed it as a farewell of anticipated death. As Gaventa notes, "In the context of the repeated references to going to Jerusalem and then Rome (19:21; 21:13; 25:9–12; 28:14) and the parallels to Jesus' own

Finally, we may admit that Luke has placed his own stamp upon this speech without thereby destroying the essence of a genuine speech by Paul with substantially the same content we find recorded in Acts 20. We conclude, therefore, that this speech, like those examined earlier, reproduces the substance of a historical speech without representing Paul's *ipsissima verba*.

The Significance of πρεσβύτεροι and ἐπίσκοποι

Two terms are used in Acts 20:17-38 in reference to the leaders of the Ephesian church: πρεσβύτεροι (v. 17) and ἐπίσκοποι (v. 28). These words, of course, are closely associated with ecclesiastical authority as it developed throughout the history of the church. πρεσβύτεροι, from which we derive the terms presbyter and priest, is usually translated as "elders." ἐπίσκοποι comes into English in the term episcopal and is associated with the word "bishop." Bruce points out that Luke (in the voice of the narrator in v. 17) uses the term πρεσβύτεροι, while Paul addresses the leaders as ἐπίσκοποι.[39] But according to Haenchen, "Verse 28 shows that the individual congregation is led by a presbytery; its members are called ἐπίσκοποι."[40] Haenchen uses this assertion to claim that in Luke's time, "the presbyterian constitution after the Jewish model prevailed."[41] However, the apparent interchangeability between the two terms in this passage suggests instead that neither an episcopal nor a presbyterian system had yet been firmly established.

Still, it would appear from the designation of the elders in v. 17 as τοὺς πρεσβυτέρους τῆς ἐκκλησίας that Luke considered them to be a select body with fixed membership, since Paul was summoning a particular set of people. Yet the remainder of the passage seems to indicate that this group, while fixed, does not yet have official status. When Paul addresses his hearers as ἐπίσκοποι, he says, "προσέχετε ἑαυτοῖς καὶ παντὶ

---

journey to Jerusalem (Luke 9:51; 13:22; 17:11), the speech surely anticipates Paul's death" (Gaventa, *Acts*, 286).

39. Bruce, *Acts*, 429: "It is Luke who calls them πρεσβύτεροι. Paul calls them ἐπίσκοποι (v. 28), but not as though that were a technical term." Cf. Johnson, *Acts*, 360: "The presbyteral structure of the local church from the beginning is assumed by Luke." Johnson cites Acts 11:30; 14:23; 15:2, 4, 6, 22, 23; and 16:4 in support of this assertion.

40. Haenchen, *Acts*, 592. cf. Conzelmann, *Acts*, 173: "Contrary to the historical facts, the institution of elders is assumed for the Pauline congregations."

41. Haenchen, *Acts*, 592.

τῷ ποιμνίῳ, ἐν ᾧ ὑμᾶς τὸ πνεῦμα τὸ ἅγιον ἔθετο ἐπισκόπους ποιμαίνειν τὴν ἐκκλησίαν τοῦ θεοῦ" (v. 28). The language here involves function; neither πρεσβύτερος nor ἐπίσκοπος is a technical term in this passage. Whereas πρεσβύτερος designates a group of individuals, ἐπίσκοπος in this passage relates to the function of the same individuals.

This passage also provides important information regarding the role of leaders in the early diaspora church. In v. 35, Paul exhorts the elders to help the weak (ἀντιλαμβάνεσθαι τῶν ἀσθενούντων). Helping the weak was not an activity usually associated with religious leadership in the first century. Instead, as we have seen, religious leadership was valued as a means of procuring honor for oneself. As Witherington correctly says,

> The Greco-Roman world was honeycombed by social networks grounded in the principle of reciprocity, of "giving and receiving." Paul's exhortation here is to break that cycle and serve and help those who can give nothing in return. This is the practical expression of what being gracious means—freely they had received the good news, and they should freely give with no thought of return.[42]

Therefore, the paradox of leadership in the early church is again demonstrated: through giving of oneself—and thus self-limitation—in favor of others, the leader's own authority is enhanced.

The Referent of τὴν ἐκκλησίαν τοῦ θεοῦ: Local or Universal?

When Paul addresses the elders in v. 28 and describes their ministry as overseers who shepherd τὴν ἐκκλησίαν τοῦ θεοῦ, an interesting question is raised regarding the extent of the elders' flock. Since Paul uses the term ποιμαίνειν to describe their function, it follows that we might ask who are the sheep for whom they serve as shepherds. It is possible

---

42. Witherington, *Acts*, 626. Cf. Walton, *Leadership and Lifestyle*, 136: "The faithfulness of Paul and his Master is particularly seen in their approach to money and work, where Luke portrays both men living and teaching openness, generosity to others and straightforwardness. . . . This represents far more than a collection of vague platitudes; it offers a dynamic, sharply focused model of Christian leadership rooted in Luke's understanding of Jesus, in contrast with other approaches to leadership available in the ancient world (Luke 22:25)." Walton also notes that the view of leadership encouraged in Acts 20 bears affinity with the view expressed by Paul in 1 Thess (Walton, *Leadership and Lifestyle*, 183).

198   THE DIFFUSION OF ECCLESIASTICAL AUTHORITY

to understand ἐκκλησία here as of either local or universal scope. If ἐκκλησία here indicates the universal church, then the Ephesian elders must be understood to have had an unlimited jurisdiction within the church. In such a case, the elders would be understood to have a certain authority over "regular" believers, wherever they may be found, by virtue of their status as elders within the universal church. Their authority would not be unlimited, since they would be subject to the other elders, or to the group of elders as a whole, yet their field of influence would not be limited by geography. On the other hand, if the referent of ἐκκλησία is restricted to the local church or churches in Ephesus, then the jurisdiction of the Ephesian elders is limited, and a different picture of the ecclesiastical authority structures in the early diaspora church emerges. Each group of believers would either be autonomous (with the elders having authority over the local body of believers while not being subject to any other authority) or hierarchical (with the local body of believers at the base, the local elders over the local church, and the elders subordinated to a still higher authority). The possible authority relationships are displayed in Table 6.1.

Table 6.1: Possible Authority Relationships Implied in Acts 20:17–38

	Case 1	Case 2	Case 3	Case 4
Elders' Jurisdiction	Universal ἐκκλησία	Universal ἐκκλησία	Local ἐκκλησία	Local ἐκκλησία
Elders' Accountability	Autonomous	Subordinate	Autonomous	Subordinate
Authority Structure	"Big Man"[43]	Collegial	Independent Cells	Hierarchical

43. Rosman and Rubel, *Tapestry of Culture*, 165–67. According to Rosman and Rubel, "A more complex political organization [than the band organization] is the Big Man structure. There is usually a native term for the Big Man position, and frequently it literally means 'big man.' In comparison with the Yanomamo headman structure, the Big Man structure represents sharper delineation of the leadership position. As leadership becomes more clearly defined, so does the group of followers. This group of followers is usually composed of the members of the Big Man's descent group, though the Big Man may also attract other kinsmen to that group" (165). "The position of the Big Man is dependent on personal qualifications and individual ability. Anthropologists refer to this position as an achieved status, in contrast to an ascribed status, which is a position one inherits. At the prime of his life, a Big Man can carry out all the activities

Authority in the Diaspora Church 199

As we saw in the discussion of Acts 13:1–3, the Antioch church held a high degree of independence from the Jerusalem church. It is reasonable to postulate a similar situation for Ephesus. Yet it is clear from the rest of the Acts narrative that the churches did not consider themselves to be entirely independent, as the so-called Jerusalem council of Acts 15 clearly demonstrates. It seems rather more likely, therefore, that the actual historical situation existed in a state of flux in which the logical ideal types listed in Table 6.1 became juxtaposed in exceptional or even contradictory ways. Some of the conflicts in the early church reflected in Acts and the Epistles were likely the result of different individuals espousing different visions of what the authority structures ought to look like. For example, Paul's struggles against the "super-apostles" might have reflected the difference between Paul's view of a collegial authority structure and the "super-apostles'" view of a hierarchical structure. Paul seems to have viewed himself as having authority independent of the Jerusalem apostles (notice, for example, the tone of Gal 2:5–6: οἷς οὐδὲ πρὸς ὥραν εἴξαμεν τῇ ὑποταγῇ . . . . Ἀπὸ δὲ τῶν δοκούντων εἶναί τι,— ὁποῖοί ποτε ἦσαν οὐδέν μοι διαφέρει· πρόσωπον [ὁ] θεὸς ἀνθρώπου οὐ λαμβάνει), while the "super-apostles" appear to have been trying to bring Paul's congregations under their own authority (2 Cor 10–11).

The question remains, however, whether Acts 20 reflects a universal or local understanding of ἐκκλησία. Several features of the passage suggest a local ἐκκλησία. The natural assumption from the fact that these leaders are explicitly connected with Ephesus (v. 17) is that they had authority only in that city. The qualification of the scope of their flock in v. 28, that they were to keep watch over the ones entrusted to them by the Holy Spirit, tends also to suggest a local jurisdiction. However, the passage even more strongly indicates a universal ἐκκλησία. The first hint comes in v. 18, where Paul refers to his entry into the province of Asia, not just the city of Ephesus. Similarly, in v. 26, Paul declares his innocence of the blood of all, not just the residents of Ephesus. Most importantly, despite the qualification mentioned above,

---

necessary to maintain his influence within his group. However, as he ages, he may no longer be able to do so. In that case, his leadership position may be challenged by other aspiring Big Men. Competition between challengers requires political skills and maneuvering. If the Big Man should die in the prime of life, there is no rule of succession to his position. Though in a patrilineal society the Big Man's son may have an initial advantage, he will not be able to become a Big Man himself if he lacks the necessary abilities" (167).

v. 28 supports a universal perspective. The παντί, because it is singular, is better translated as "whole"; the whole flock is in view, not all the individual members of the flock. Moreover, the flock is connected in the last part of the verse with τὴν ἐκκλησίαν τοῦ θεοῦ, ἣν περιεποιήσατο διὰ τοῦ αἵματος τοῦ ἰδίου. While it is possible that the local church is in view, it seems more likely that the universal church is intended by this phrase.[44] Thus, the qualification ἐν ᾧ ὑμᾶς τὸ πνεῦμα τὸ ἅγιον ἔθετο ἐπισκόπους, sandwiched as it is between two universalizing phrases, is best understood, not as limiting the scope of the elders' authority, but as indicating the source of their authority, namely, the Holy Spirit. We may conclude, therefore, that the passage envisions for the elders a broader scope of authority beyond the church in Ephesus. At the same time, their authority was not unlimited, since each elder's authority would have been tempered by his mutual submission to fellow elders. This authority structure is represented by Case 2 of Table 6.1

Inter-Ecclesial Relations

The passages we have just considered (Acts 13:1–3 and 20:17–38) deal explicitly with situations outside Jerusalem. Indeed, each relates primarily to an ecclesiastical environment restricted to one location. Although it is true that Acts 13:1–3 anticipates the missionary journeys of Paul and his colleagues and Acts 20:17–38 seems to indicate an expanded scope of authority for the Ephesian elders, interactions between leaders from different locations have not been the focus of these passages. We now turn to two passages that do focus on inter-ecclesial interactions. The first, Acts 15, has long been a source for scholarly investigation regarding power structures of the early church. The second, Acts 21:17–26, has not been as extensively mined from this perspective, probably because it relates to individual leaders and not explicitly to authoritative interaction between them. Yet Acts 21:17–26 also yields interesting information related to authority structures in the early church. As we shall see, both Acts 15 and Acts 21 reveal patterns in the early church that differ more from the cultural norms than is often appreciated.

---

44. Cf. Giles, "Luke's Use," 140: "When Acts 20.28 is removed from the discussion because it does not reflect Luke's own theology . . . then we find that there is nothing in Acts to suggest that Luke himself thought of an ἐκκλησία as anything other than a local community of Christians."

The Jerusalem Council (Acts 15:1–35)

Acts 15 has long been a focus for scholarly discussions related to the historicity and the dating of events in Acts. This intricate discussion need not detain us here, for the focus of the present investigation is on the implications Acts 15 holds for the structures of authority in the early church.[45] It has been customary to regard the events of Acts 15 as the primitive church's equivalent of an ecumenical council. Church delegates are thought to have gathered from various prominent ecclesiastical centers to discuss a theological problem facing the whole church. The gathering was held in Jerusalem because the church there held

---

45. The importance of Acts 15 for issues of historicity is readily observable from the fact that this passage provides one of the places in Acts where we may have two independent accounts of the same event. In Gal 2, Paul describes an event which sounds very much like the Jerusalem council in Acts 15. The difficulty arises, however, when scholars attempt to harmonize the two accounts, for they do not agree in every respect. For example, Gal 2 says Paul went up to Jerusalem in response to divine revelation, but Acts 15 says Paul and Barnabas had been sent by the Antioch church. For a discussion of the historicity of Acts 15, see Jefford, "Tradition and Witness," esp. 417-19. See also Barrett, "The Historicity of Acts," esp. 532-34; and Taylor, "Acts and History." One possible solution to the difficulties in reconciling Acts and Galatians is to view Paul's meeting with the Jerusalem "pillars" (Gal 2:1-10) with Acts 11:27-30, not Acts 15 (Bauckham, "James," 468-70; Trobisch, "The Council of Jerusalem," 336-37). In this case, the disagreement with Peter (Gal 2:11-14) coincides with the problems over circumcision reported at the beginning of Acts 15. While this proposal does not remove all difficulties (for example, table-fellowship appears to be the issue over which Paul and Peter disagreed, while Gentile circumcision and law obedience are the issues leading to the council in Acts 15), it does have many advantages. These advantages include explaining the timing of Paul's delivery of the collection (in Acts 11) and precisely placing the composition of Galatians with respect to the narrative of Acts (immediately after the disturbance in Acts 15:1-2 and immediately before the Jerusalem council in Acts 15:4-29). Whatever the solution to the question of the relation between Acts and Galatians, a number of factors support a conclusion of historicity for Acts 15. First, as is commonly acknowledged, Luke usually suppresses evidence of disagreements in the early church. It seems unlikely that Luke would have invented a disagreement that had no historical basis. Second, the last word in the debate belongs to James, even though Peter and the apostles are present. If Luke had invented a council in an effort to lend apostolic imprimatur to his own perspective, he surely would have given Peter the decisive voice. Third, contrary to claims that James could not have delivered the speech attributed to him because it depends on the LXX, James speech has been shown to be plausibly historical (Ådna, "James' Position"; and Bauckham, "James"). Finally, the widespread acceptance of the stipulations of the decree suggests that it was indeed promulgated early by the Jerusalem church. As Bauckham has noted, 'Such wide acknowledgement of the prohibitions in the decree could not have started when Acts became widely known, but must go back to widespread circulation of the terms of the decree from an early period, independently of Acts" (Bauckham, "James," 465).

preeminence. The elders of the Jerusalem church ultimately made the decision and promulgated a binding decree for the universal church.[46] While not challenging this view directly, the present study does call for certain refinements of its expression.[47] As we shall see, the authority structures implied by the narrative of Acts 15 are not as rigid as is sometimes supposed.

The Purpose of the Meeting

The traditional view of the purpose of the Jerusalem meeting is that the Antioch church was seeking clarification from its hierarchical head, that is, the Jerusalem church, regarding theological questions related to Gentile inclusion in the Jesus movement. Supporters of this position take v. 2 as evidence.[48] The phrase περὶ τοῦ ζητήματος τούτου is taken to refer to the theological question raised by the men from Judea. Similarly, many of the arguments raised in the discussion relate to theological questions. The first Jerusalem respondents, for example, insist that the Gentiles be circumcised (v. 5). Even the letter sent by the

---

46. Bauckham, "James," 426: "Against the background of the multifaceted centrality of Jerusalem for 1st-century Jews, Luke's concern to make clear the links between the Jerusalem church and the developing mission both within and beyond Palestine . . . , and his account of the Jerusalem council as the occasion when an authoritative decision was made in Jerusalem which secured and determined the future of the whole Gentile mission (Acts 15), carry much more credibility than those scholars who so readily treat them as tendentious distortions of history have perceived." See also: "The Jerusalem council presupposes the authority of Jerusalem to decide the issue of Gentile Christians' obedience to the Law. Its decision binds not only Antioch and its daughter churches (15:22–31) but also the churches founded by Paul and Barnabas (16:4). When James recalls the decision in 21:25, the effect is to imply that Paul's Gentile mission is still subject to it" (450).

47. Cf. Harnack, *Constitution*, 27–28: "We must guard against exaggeration; for in several passages where we should inevitably expect the mention of the community of Jerusalem, if its influence were so penetrating and expansive, we find that allusion is made quite as a matter of course to the communities of Judaea (see Gal. i. 22; 1 Thess. ii. 14; Acts xi. 1, 29, xv. 1) . . . . On the other hand, to the Palestinian Christians Jerusalem is "the holy city" (Matt. iv. 5, xxvii.53), and it was the natural consequence of the existing circumstances that the community there came to be regarded (even by Paul) as the real centre and starting-point of Christianity."

48. See, for example, Haenchen, *Acts*, 443. He says, "In this situation it is resolved to send Paul, Barnabas and some others to lay the point at issue before the Apostles and the elders (who here appear beside the Apostles as members of the court of reference)." See also Fitzmyer, *Acts*, 539: "Up to this point in Acts Jerusalem has been a focal point, as the mother church and the doctrinal center. To it appeal is again made."

Jerusalem church describes ethical directives the Gentiles are encouraged to follow (v. 29).

Clearly, theological issues loom large in the present passage. However, there seem also to have been underlying sociological concerns, which motivated the theological discussions. At crucial points in the narrative, the emphasis is upon interpersonal relations, not on theological concerns. Returning to v. 2, it should be noted that the verse begins with the participial phrase γενομένης δὲ στάσεως καὶ ζητήσεως οὐκ ὀλίγης τῷ Παύλῳ καὶ τῷ Βαρναβᾷ πρὸς αὐτούς. Thus, the strife and debate in Antioch were a precursor to the Jerusalem council. Put another way, the theological question that formed the content of the debate did not rise to a level requiring a multi-local conference until after it had caused στάσις and ζήτησις.[49] The purpose, then, for sending the delegation to Jerusalem was not merely to answer the theological question, but also to ascertain whether the men from Judea had been commissioned by the Jerusalem church. The delegates were to discover whether the Jerusalem church agreed with the position of the men from Judea and whether there might not be some way to come to agreement.

The delegation to Jerusalem may be compared with the envoy of Philo to Gaius to present the case of the Alexandrian Jews (Philo, *Embassy* 349–73; Josephus, *Ant.* 18.257–60). The non-Jewish citizens of Alexandria had been threatening the Jews of Alexandria, Jewish citizenship rights were being eroded, and there were violent reprisals on both sides. The non-Jews sent a delegation to Rome in order to appeal to Caesar. Under the leadership of Philo, the Jews did the same. Apion, the spokesman for the Greeks, honored Gaius by noting that the Jews alone among the Roman subjects refused to pay divine respect to Gaius (Josephus, *Ant.* 18.257–58). The Jewish delegation honored Gaius more directly, though less lavishly. According to Philo, "When we were brought into his presence the moment we saw him we bowed our heads to the ground with all respect and timidity and saluted him

---

49. The genitive absolute participle in v. 2 is often taken as temporal: when there had been strife and debate (e.g., NASB and KJV; La Sainte Bible[5, rév]: "Après un vif débat et un violente discussion . . . "). Although the genitive absolute is often temporal, according to Blass, Debrunner, and Funk, the genitive absolute in Act is "much freer and more diverse" (BDF 218; cf. Turner, *Syntax*, 153 and 322). With that in mind, it may be possible to employ a causal sense for the participle here: "because of the strife and debate." On this interpretation, the dispute itself was the cause of the decision to send Paul and Barnabas to Jerusalem.

addressing him as Emperor Augustus" (Philo, *Embassy* 352 [Colson, LCL]). Thus, each delegation vied for Gaius's patronage, and both sides paid honor to Gaius in an attempt to win his favor.

The account in Acts 15 also appears to be a case where a group in conflict (the Antioch church) sends a delegation (Paul and Barnabas) to win the favor of powerful patrons (the leaders of the Jerusalem church). It is remarkable, therefore, that so little attention is paid to the relationship between the delegation and the potential patrons. According to Acts 15, Paul and Barnabas do not praise the Jerusalem leadership. Instead, they extol the works of God, voicing their praise both in the cities on their journey (v. 3) and in the presence of the Jerusalem church (v. 12). By drawing attention to the acts of God on behalf of the Antioch church, Paul and Barnabas were attesting to the direct patronage of God. Therefore, despite formal parallels with a patron-client exchange between the two churches, the actual content of the exchange reveals that both churches were clients of the same patron, namely, God himself. For this reason, the account de-emphasizes any power disparity while simultaneously underscoring the dependence of both churches on God.

Underlying sociological concerns are also visible in v. 22. In this verse, the apostles, elders, and entire church select representatives to go to Antioch with Paul and Barnabas. It should be noted that the selection serves to demonstrate the unity between the Jerusalem and Antioch churches.[50] The decision is to send men from the Jerusalem congregation with (σὺν) Paul and Barnabas. The use of this word implies a degree of collegiality between the delegates from Jerusalem and Paul and Barnabas. By sending a delegation comprising members from both cities, a message was being sent that there was solidarity between the two churches. The delegation, therefore, served as a tacit repudiation of the message of the men who had earlier come from Judea. Unity existed between the Jerusalem church (not the men from Judea) and the Antioch church.

---

50. Cf. Wall, "Acts," 204: "The practical purpose of this and other meetings in Jerusalem, then, is an exercise not of religious authority but of corporate solidarity in fulfilling the church's vocation in the world." Cf. also Savelle, "Reexamination," 467, where he argues that the unity of Jewish and Gentile believers was the purpose of the prohibitions of the decree.

A similar emphasis on the importance of unity in the early church is introduced in the formal communication sent by the apostles and elders. From the first sentence of the body, the tone is set regarding the source of the problem and the nature of the solution. The sentence (v. 24) begins with the words ἐπειδὴ ἠκούσαμεν ὅτι. The ἐπειδή indicates that the remainder of the clause gives the purpose for the letter and the decision communicated therein. That clause reads τινὲς ἐξ ἡμῶν [ἐξελθόντες] ἐτάραξαν ὑμᾶς λόγοις ἀνασκευάζοντες τὰς ψυχὰς ὑμῶν οἷς οὐ διεστειλάμεθα. Clearly, the source of the problem was the troubling (ἐτάραξαν—the main verb of the clause) of the believers and the subverting of their souls. It is further noted that these men had not been commanded by the apostles and elders to spread their message of circumcision. Thus, once again the unity of the church is a central issue. The question of Gentile circumcision was surely of great importance, and the trouble it had caused heightened the urgency of resolving the issue.

The Decision

A number of people were involved in the gathering in Jerusalem to discuss the conflict raised in Antioch. In v. 6, we are explicitly told that it was the apostles and elders who met together. Yet v. 12 refers to the whole multitude (πᾶν τὸ πλῆθος), which could hardly mean just the apostles and elders. Similarly, v. 22 asserts that the whole church assented to the final decision (σὺν ὅλῃ τῇ ἐκκλησίᾳ).[51] The wording clearly distinguishes between the apostles and elders, on the one hand, and the church, on the other. Therefore, whereas there existed a subgroup of leaders (the apostles and elders), the leaders did not exercise their authority apart from the presence (and participation?) of the whole group.

Peter, Barnabas, Paul, and James are mentioned by name. The speeches of Peter and James are reported. Peter's speech recalls the earlier episode involving his proclamation of the Gospel to Gentiles.

---

51. It may be too strong to say that the whole church helped make the decision—the σύν could indicate the church merely agreed with the decision. According to Barrett, "It is the apostles and elders who gather for discussion and evidently assume the authority to make a decision; they write the letter in which the decision is promulgated, though the whole church concurs (v. 22)" (Barrett, *Introduction and Commentary*, 709). Nevertheless, the σὺν ὅλῃ τῇ ἐκκλησίᾳ could indicate a greater role throughout the process on the part of the congregation.

The thrust of the speech revolves around the lack of distinction (v. 9) between Jew and Gentile, clearly a theologically charged argument. At the same time, the sameness of Jew and Gentile is surely also a sociologically significant assertion. The theological fact of Jewish and Gentile identity has sociological implications for how believers are to behave. When Peter asks why his hearers are trying to test God, therefore, the question is not based on a theological affront to God alone, but also on the sociological impact of their actions. Peter does not ask why they are testing God by denying a theological precept. Rather, he asks why they are testing God by requiring certain behavior of the Gentiles. Thus, sociology and theology are inseparable here.

James's speech moves in the opposite direction, from theological argumentation to social consequences. In the first part of the speech, he argues from scripture (vv. 15–18).[52] Then he offers a conclusion regarding the ethical precepts the Gentiles should be instructed to follow (vv. 19–21). James probably is given the final word on the matter because he holds the final authority within the Jerusalem church at this time.[53] As already noted, however, the apostles and elders, together with the whole church, assent to the final judgment.

The result of the decision was the letter recorded in vv. 23–29. As noted earlier, v. 28 is often taken to indicate that the Jerusalem church had authority over the Antioch church. Such an interpretation depends upon several key points in the verse. First, it places the emphasis on the dative ἡμῖν over τῷ πνεύματι τῷ ἁγίῳ, which unnecessarily deemphasizes the role of the Holy Spirit as a contributor to the decision.[54] Instead, the phrase should be interpreted as indicating that the decision was formed under the leadership of the Holy Spirit. If, as argued above, God is the patron of both the Jerusalem and Antioch churches, then the reminder of the Holy Spirit's involvement in the decision becomes

---

52. For an incisive analysis of James's use of scripture in this speech, see Bauckham, "James," 452–62.

53. Cf. Bauckham, "James," 450: "James in the period of his supremacy in Jerusalem was no merely local leader, but the personal embodiment of the Jerusalem church's constitutional and eschatological centrality in relation to the whole developing Christian movement, Jewish and Gentile." Cf. also Ådna, "James' Position," 125.

54. Taking ἡμῖν as indicating the Jerusalem church alone also neglects the fact that Paul and Barnabas, part of the original delegation from Antioch, were among the carriers of the letter from Jerusalem. Therefore, taking the ἡμῖν here as indicating a unilateral decision of the Jerusalem hierarchy seems unwarranted.

a strong exhortation from one group of clients to another in order to encourage submission to the dictates of the patron.

An interpretation of the letter as the promulgation of the Jerusalem hierarchy also stresses πλὴν τούτων τῶν ἐπάναγκες over the μηδὲν πλέον ἐπιτίθεσθαι ὑμῖν βάρος. Since the primary theological questions were whether Gentiles were required to be circumcised (v. 1) and to obey the law of Moses (v. 5), the statement seems significant that no greater burden is added to the Gentiles. The wording recalls Peter's speech (vv. 7–11), in which he argues against placing (ἐπιθεῖναι) a yoke on the Gentiles. The thrust of the letter, therefore, is that the Gentiles are not being required to change their behavior.

Finally, the interpretation of the letter as a unilateral dictate of the Jerusalem hierarchy understands the Jerusalem church as the promulgators of τούτων τῶν ἐπάναγκες (v. 28). ἐπάναγκες is a *hapaxlegomenon* in the NT. Liddell and Scott define the word, when used adverbially as it is here, as "on compulsion."[55] Similarly, BDAG gives the meaning, "pertaining to being essential in connection with something, of a necessary nature."[56] The question remains, however, whether it is the apostles and elders of the Jerusalem church who compel obedience to the items listed in v. 29. Given their affinity with the so-called Noachide Commandments, it seems unlikely that they were the invention of the Jerusalem council.[57] Rather, it is more likely that all parties would have agreed already upon the compulsory things listed in v. 29. The πλὴν of v. 28, therefore, introduces a reminder of common ground. As Wall asserts,

> The verdict James renders provides Scripture's validation to what God has already authorized and Paul has already realized (see 15:13–21); James offers nothing really new to the reader of Acts . . . his rhetorical role is to clarify and confirm what the reader already knows, and his decision or the subsequent 'decree' does not change Paul's message or the pattern of his mission. . . . The impression cultivated—especially with the invocation of the

---

55. LSJ, "ἐπανάγκης," 607.
56. BDAG, "ἐπάναγκες," 358.
57. Bockmuehl, "Noachide Commandments," 100. Bockmuehl argues that, even though the Noachide Commandments in their developed form are post-NT, their antecedents belong to the Second Temple period. See also Savelle, "Prohibitions," 457–62. Savelle argues that all three of the usual candidates for the source of the prohibitions (viz., rabbinic teachings, the Noahic precepts, and Lev 17–18) were used.

Spirit's partnership (see 15:28)—is that the publication of the council's agreements functions likes a pastoral exhortation and that they are joyfully embraced by other believers as such (see 15:31).[58]

In light of the preceding discussion, the following modifications to the traditional interpretation of Acts 15 may be enumerated. First, a key purpose of the meeting was to address the conflict in the church, not only to decide an abstract theological dispute. The discussion addressed the theological question, but the unity of the church was also important. That unity ultimately depended upon the very theological point being debated. Second, despite the importance of James and the Jerusalem church, the present episode demonstrates an unusual degree of empowerment granted the delegation from Antioch. Paul and Barnabas are allowed to speak about their work (v. 4), they testify to God's wonders among the Gentiles (v. 12), they appear to have had a part in the final decision, since it affirms their original contention (v. 28), and they are sent with co-delegates from Jerusalem to report the decision back in Antioch (v. 25). We conclude, therefore, that the Jerusalem church extended both honor and authority to the Antioch delegation. Finally, we have seen that the Acts 15 episode may be compared with a plea for the intervention of a patron. The comparison reveals that the delegation from Antioch differs from the usual pattern, in which the clients emphasize the social distance between themselves and their patron by drawing attention to their powerlessness and the patron's power. In Acts 15, in contrast, the supplicants emphasize the great works of God on their behalf, thus identifying God as patron and the Jerusalem congregation as their fellow clients of the same patron.

Paul's Final Visit to Jerusalem (Acts 21:17–26)

According to Acts 21:17–26, Paul and his companions reach Jerusalem and the next day enter the presence of James and the elders, reporting to them the many things that God had been doing through Paul's ministry. Although rejoicing in the good things God had accomplished, James and the elders express concern over the report that Paul had rejected the law and taught others to do the same. In order to dispel

---

58. Wall, "Acts," 204–5.

this false report,[59] the elders recommend that Paul pay the expenses of four men and participate with them in the completion of a vow.[60] The account raises a host of questions, related both to its historicity and to the implied author's vision of ecclesiastical authority. To these questions we now turn.

Historicity of Paul's Final Jerusalem Visit

The conjecture that the historical Paul would not have submitted to instructions to fulfill a vow in order to demonstrate that he himself was a law-abiding Jew (v. 24) raises questions regarding the historicity of Acts 21:17–26. Such passages as Gal 2:21—3:5 and 5:1-12 appear to show that Paul had completely abandoned attempts at law-keeping and that he condemned the so-called Judaizers who insisted that even Gentiles must keep the law. In other words, it appears from Paul's letters that (a) the reports about his teaching people to forsake Moses and circumcision were actually true and (b) Paul would not have acted to disprove such reports.

A full discussion of the issues involved in assessing the arguments for the stance of the historical Paul toward the law goes beyond the scope of the present study. It must suffice here to make two observations that support the historicity of the present passage. First, this passage refers specifically to Paul's message to diaspora Jews (v. 21, τοὺς κατὰ τὰ ἔθνη πάντας Ἰουδαίους). As is well known, a distinction exists between Paul's message to the Gentiles and his message to the Jews.[61] Paul seems to have felt no inconsistency in keeping the law in some situations and eschewing it in others (1 Cor 9:20-21), despite his vehement objection to Peter's similar behavior (Gal 2:11-12). Thus, Paul may have agreed with the statement in Acts 21:24 that he himself kept the law.

---

59. Most commentators agree that Luke portrays the report as false, but see Gaventa, *Acts*, 299: "Although it is often claimed that Acts makes quite clear that the charge is false, the narrative is tantalizingly silent on these points."

60. A great deal of uncertainty surrounds the exact nature of the vows and the purification intended here. Was this a Nazirite vow, a Levitical purification, or some combination of the two? The question need not detain us here. For a succinct presentation of the issues, see Haenchen, *Acts*, 611–12.

61. Bauckham, "James," 472; Bruce, *Acts*, 446; Gaventa, *Acts*, 299; Johnson, *Acts*, 375; Levinskaya, *Book of Acts*, 13; Witherington, *Acts*, 648.

Second, it seems likely that Paul had a more complex attitude toward the law than is sometimes appreciated.[62] For example, although Paul is able to say Ὅσοι γὰρ ἐξ ἔργων νόμου εἰσίν, ὑπὸ κατάραν εἰσίν (Gal 3:10) and κατηργήθητε ἀπὸ Χριστοῦ, οἵτινες ἐν νόμῳ δικαιοῦσθε, τῆς χάριτος ἐξεπέσατε (Gal 5:4), he also says ὥστε ὁ μὲν νόμος ἅγιος καὶ ἡ ἐντολὴ ἁγία καὶ δικαία καὶ ἀγαθή (Rom 7:12) and τοῖς ὑπὸ νόμον ὡς ὑπὸ νόμον, μὴ ὢν αὐτὸς ὑπὸ νόμον, ἵνα τοὺς ὑπὸ νόμον κερδήσω (1 Cor 9:20). It will be observed, of course, that each of these quotations derives from extended discussions about the law. This only serves to further the point: Paul's perspective on the law was complex. He took pains to explain himself, demonstrating that his perspective was nuanced to such an extent that it was not immediately apprehensible to his hearers.

For these reasons, it is not advisable to reject the historicity of Acts 21:17–26 on the basis of supposed inconsistency with the historical Paul. Yet the historicity of this episode is called into question by the apparent logical inconsistency involved in the report in v. 25, which tells Paul, as if for the first time, of a decision to which he was a party in ch. 15. Solutions to the problem include the conjecture that Luke has rearranged his source material, inadvertently retaining this reference to a decree already (mistakenly) inserted into the account in Acts 15.[63] Alternatively, some exegetes view v. 25 as evidence that Paul had not in fact been present at the council described in Acts 15 but indeed learned of the decree for the first time in Acts 21.[64] Still others view the statement as an indication on the part of James and the elders that they were still committed to the earlier agreement and that Paul need not fear their reneging.[65] Another possibility is that the comment is a Lukan construct intended to remind readers that, although Paul was law-observant, Gentile believers were not required to be circumcised or

---

62. Cf. Bauckham, "James," 477: It is notoriously difficult to know what Paul's principle of becoming all things to all people (1 Cor. 9:20–22: '... to those under the law I became as one under the law ... to those outside the law I became as one outside the law ...'; cf. also Gal. 4:12) actually meant with regard to his own observance of the Law in practice."

63. Fitzmyer, *Acts*, 553.

64. Achtemeier, *Quest for Unity*, 14–15.

65. Witherington, *Acts*, 650.

otherwise obey the entirety of the Law.⁶⁶ Whatever the solution may be, it seems ill advised to dismiss the historicity of the entire episode on the basis of this single verse.

Another factor involved in an assessment of the historicity of the present passage is the relationship between the present account and Paul's self-described intention to deliver a collection from the Gentile believers to the Jerusalem church (Rom 15:25–28, 1 Cor 16:1–4, 2 Cor 8:16—9:15).⁶⁷ Acts 24:17 (δι' ἐτῶν δὲ πλειόνων ἐλεημοσύνας ποιήσων εἰς τὸ ἔθνος μου παρεγενόμην καὶ προσφοράς) seems to imply that Paul was carrying funds to be delivered to the Jerusalem church at the time described in the present passage.⁶⁸ Was Luke aware of the collection but intentionally suppressed any mention of it because the Jerusalem church did not accept it?⁶⁹ Or was the collection of which Paul speaks actually delivered earlier (11:29–30)?⁷⁰ Or is it possible that Luke merely omitted reference to the collection because it did not contribute to his narrative purposes? Even if Luke has intentionally omitted historical information pertaining to the present episode, however, we need not for that reason question the reliability of the information that is related.

Nor do there seem to be other grounds for dismissing the historicity of this passage. Rather, the notion that Paul would want to report the results of his mission to the church in Jerusalem seems probable. Moreover, the idea that Paul would desire unity with the Jerusalem believers also seems likely. Therefore, although the following discussion does not rest upon the historicity of Acts 21:17–26, it seems reasonable to accept it, at least on a provisional basis.⁷¹

---

66. Conzelmann, *Acts*, 180–81.

67. According to Barrett, delivery of the collection was the primary purpose of Paul's visit to Jerusalem (Barrett, *Introduction and Commentary*, 1001). It should be noted, however, that Luke never mentions the collection as a possible motivation (see Acts 19:21, 21:10–15).

68. Johnson, *Acts*, 378; Witherington, *Acts*, 644.

69. According to Barrett, "Paul's hope to secure the unity of the church by means of his collection failed; it may be that this is why Luke omitted the collection from his story" (Barrett, *Introduction and Commentary*, 1001).

70. Trobisch, "Council," 336–37.

71. Bauckham offers an even stronger assessment of the historicity of Luke's account of Paul's final trip to Jerusalem, of which the present passage is a part. He says, ". . . it is often overlooked that one of the most important, historically plausible elements in Luke's account of what happened on Paul's last visit to Jerusalem is the information

Paul and James as Colleagues

The account of Paul's visit to Jerusalem could be read as an instance of Paul reporting his missionary endeavors to a superior. The wording of Acts 21:18, where Paul is said to enter (εἰσῄει) into the presence of James, bolsters this impression. Εἴσειμι is an uncommon word in the NT, occurring just four times. Three of the four instances come in the book of Acts, and two of those three are in the passage presently under consideration. On first inspection of the occurrences in the NT, it seems that εἴσειμι is associated with entering a temple. Aside from Acts 21:18, all the NT instances denote entry into a sacred space: in Acts 3:3, Peter and John enter the Jerusalem temple; in Acts 21:26, Paul and the young men who had taken vows enter the Jerusalem temple; and Hebrews 9:6 recounts the entry of priests into the tabernacle. BDAG adds additional instances where the entry is into a sacred space: *Sylloge* 3:982,3; *Urkunden der Ptolemäerzeit* 162 VIII, 19; Ex 28:29; Josephus, *J.W.* 3:325, *Ant.* 3:269; and *Mart. Pol.* 9:1.[72] One might imagine, therefore, that the report in v. 18 that Paul and his companions entered into the presence of James and the elders indicates a sense on the part of Paul that he was entering into the presence of one greater than himself. On this view, it would seem that Paul held a subordinate position to James.

As BDAG also points out, however, there is a secondary usage, in which εἴσειμι is used with the preposition πρός to indicate entry into the presence of another person. Clearly, this is the construction in Acts 21:18. The question remains, however, whether the person into whose presence the subject enters is necessarily considered a superior. Since the present verse is the only one in the NT in which this construction is found, we must go outside the NT to determine whether this is the case. BDAG lists three such occurrences: Sophocles, *Phil.* 953; Xenophon,

---

that he had this reputation [that Paul encouraged Jewish Christians in the Diaspora to neglect the law] among non-Christian Jewish pilgrims from Asia, who mistakenly thought he had taken the uncircumcised Ephesian Trophimus into the inner court of the Temple (Acts 21:28–29) because, in their view, this was logically what the antinomian Paul would have done . . . . There is every reason to believe this account of the circumstances of Paul's arrest" (Bauckham, "James," 476–77).

72. BDAG, "εἴσειμι," 293. The reference in BDAG to *Sylloge* 3:982,3 appears to refer actually to 982,2, which reads εἰσίτωσαν εἰς τὸν τῆς θεο[ῦ ναόν]. Moreover, *J.W.* 3:325 refers to the entry of the Romans into the city Jotapata, not into a temple. *Mart. Pol.* 9:1 is explicitly entry into the stadium, but immediately upon entry a voice is heard from heaven.

Cyr. 2.4.5; and *T. Jos.* 3:6. In the first instance, Philoctetes says, "O cave with double mouth, to thee (πρὸς σέ) I turn (εἴσειμι); Stripped of my arms and lacking means of life" (Sophocles, *Phil.* 953 [Lloyd-Jones, LCL]). Here the speaker turns to a personified object, which is addressed in the second person. The broader context—the betrayal of Philoctetes by Neoptolemus—results in the despair and resignation of Philoctetes, who does not address the cave as of sacred significance.

In Xenophon, Cyrus is reported as presenting (εἰσῄει) himself before his superior, Cyaxares. An ambiguity exists in the text whether Cyrus acts in submission or defiance, for he obeys his superior's command to appear in haste, but he neglects to obey the explicit command to appear in particular attire. Cyaxares questions Cyrus on the matter, but Cyrus replies that it is better to obey in haste with a disciplined army than to obey the exact command with sloth; Cyaxares accepts the explanation. It is clear, therefore, that a certain relationship of authority is implied within the story, but it is unclear whether the subject complies with the requirements of that authority.

The use of εἴσειμι in *T. Jos.* 3:6 again has certain overtones of authority, though here inverted. As in the Biblical account (Gen 39:6–12), according to the passage, the Egyptian woman was making sexual advances toward Joseph, who rebuffed them. 3:6 says that the woman came in to him in the night. Thus, the mistress of the house entered into the presence of the slave. Whereas in the previous example the subordinate entered to the superior, the reverse takes place here.[73]

Thus εἴσειμι often exists in contexts where authority relationships are in question or under attack. Where such relationships are in view, the superior individual may be the one approached or the one who approaches. Yet authority is not always in view. As we saw in the case of Sophocles, the addressee was an inanimate object, and authority structures seem to be excluded. Similarly, the entry for εἴσειμι in Moulton and Milligan points out that the word is often used in notifications about time, which clearly involves a different semantic domain.[74] Therefore, in considering the case in Acts 21, one cannot assume that

---

73. It is interesting to note that earlier in this same passage the mistress had promised Joseph authority over herself and the entire house if he would sleep with her (3:2). Thus, the complexities of the authority relationships are even more convoluted.

74. Moulton and Milligan, "εἴσειμι," 188. By way of example, they offer P. Oxy. X 1278[17], τοῦ ἰσι[ό]ντος κδ (ἔτους), which they translate, "of the coming 24th year."

power and authority issues are involved in Paul's entry to see James. The context of Acts itself must resolve the question.

One question to be answered, then, when looking at Acts 21:17–26 from the perspective of ecclesiastical authority is whether the passage portrays Paul as under the authority of James and the Jerusalem elders. Although Paul agrees to follow the advice of the elders, there are several features of the text that suggest the elders related to Paul as a partner, not as a subordinate. First, the elders address Paul as brother (v. 20). It is possible that this usage of ἀδελφός indicates a formulaic address and not genuine equality. Yet we have already seen how fictive kinship language was used in the early church in a situation where an internal power differential was de-emphasized (Acts 6). There is no reason to suspect disingenuousness on the part of James and the elders here. Second, the question in v. 22 (τί οὖν ἐστιν;) is a stock phrase from deliberative rhetoric, especially diatribe.[75] According to Witherington, "The question means, 'What therefore is to be done?' and should follow the *narratio* once one gets to the point in the deliberative discourse of argument, exhortation, or the stating of what will be beneficial or profitable."[76] Thus, the speech of the elders is intended to persuade Paul to follow the course of action they are recommending, not just to command his obedience. Still, the question of v. 22 is not merely rhetorical, and the concern of the elders for Paul's welfare and for the good name of the church is evident in their explanation of the situation Paul was facing.

If, then, Paul was not coerced to obey the advice of the elders, what motivated him to follow their advice? One aspect of Paul's compliance surely was his commitment to the very issues that motivated the elders' initial advice, namely, the unity of the church and the honor of the group. These concerns are consonant with what we know of Paul from his letters. We see his emphasis on such matters, for example, in Rom 12:18 (εἰ δυνατὸν τὸ ἐξ ὑμῶν, μετὰ πάντων ἀνθρώπων εἰρηνεύοντες), Rom 14:19 (Ἄρα οὖν τὰ τῆς εἰρήνης διώκωμεν καὶ τὰ τῆς οἰκοδομῆς τῆς εἰς ἀλλήλους), 1 Cor 8:9 (βλέπετε δὲ μή πως ἡ ἐξουσία ὑμῶν αὕτη πρόσκομμα γένηται τοῖς ἀσθενέσιν), 1 Cor 9:20 (καὶ ἐγενόμην τοῖς Ἰουδαίοις ὡς Ἰουδαῖος, ἵνα Ἰουδαίους κερδήσω· τοῖς ὑπὸ νόμον ὡς ὑπὸ νόμον, μὴ ὢν αὐτὸς ὑπὸ νόμον, ἵνα τοὺς ὑπὸ νόμον κερδήσω), and

---

75. Johnson, *Acts*, 375; Witherington, *Acts*, 648.
76. Witherington, *Acts*, 648.

Phil 4:2 (Εὐοδίαν παρακαλῶ καὶ Συντύχην παρακαλῶ τὸ αὐτὸ φρονεῖν ἐν κυρίῳ). Therefore, Acts 21:17–26 should be interpreted within the framework of unity, honor, and deference, not of hierarchy, power, or coercion.

Paul and the Four Men as Peers

At first glance, it may seem that a certain sense of hierarchy is retained in the passage when James and the elders exhort Paul to pay for the expenses of the four men who had taken vows. Luke's readers likely would have interpreted the suggestion as indicative of Paul entering into the role of patron of the four (or, perhaps, of broker between the four and the elders).[77] On this interpretation, Paul would have been positioning himself in the eyes of Jerusalem society as an honorable individual, one with means who used his resources on behalf of others. Thus, Paul would have gained honor while simultaneously securing the loyalty of his clients. Yet we have argued above that Acts portrays God as the only patron in the early church. Does the present episode contradict that conclusion?

Two features of the present passage suggest otherwise. First, the direction from James and the elders begins by suggesting that Paul join the four in their purification, not with the suggestion to pay their expenses. It seems unlikely that a potential patron under the normal patronage system would identify himself in this way with his clients. The system depended upon the social distance between patron and client, but Paul's identification with the potential clients suggests social equality. Second, the purpose of Paul joining with the four was to prove his loyalty to the law, not to gain honor for himself. The passage makes it clear that the problem is the perception that Paul teaches other Jews to break the law (v. 21). The solution is aimed at disproving this accusation. According to v. 24, James says, γνώσονται πάντες ὅτι ὧν κατήχηνται περὶ σοῦ οὐδέν ἐστιν ἀλλὰ στοιχεῖς καὶ αὐτὸς φυλάσσων τὸν νόμον. It seems likely that an honor challenge lies at the root of this passage, but the response to the challenge is a denial of the charge. Thus, Paul defended his and the group's honor by demonstrating that he was a law-keeper.

---

77. For a discussion of apostles as brokers, see Moxnes, "Patron-Client Relations," 260–61. See also the discussion of patronage, pages 47–49.

What, then, do we make of the exhortation for Paul to pay for the four men's expenses? I would like to suggest that this entire episode is an instance of the recasting of the dominant cultural scripts by the early church. Not only is Paul received as an equal by the elders, but he himself treats the unnamed four men as equals. In the former case, Jewish sensibility would have expected a hierarchical relationship between Paul, on the one hand, and James and the elders, on the other. We saw earlier that Jerusalem retained an exalted position within Second Temple Judaism, and deference continued to be paid to the Temple priesthood throughout the Second Temple period. It would have seemed a natural extension in the early church, therefore, for the Jerusalem elders to hold an authoritative position. To be sure, there is strong evidence to suggest that the Jerusalem church did enjoy authority in the diaspora church.[78] We do not wish to deny that evidence. The point we are making here is simply that, despite the deference on the part of diaspora Christians to the authority of the Jerusalem church, the evidence further suggests that the Jerusalem elders eschewed the coercive use of that authority in favor of a more collegial approach. As we have just seen, the elders receive Paul as an equal. Similarly, the proposal that Paul pay the expenses of the four men, as we have seen, has overtones of the patronage system. The benefaction component is retained, but the system is here stripped of its social stratification. Thus, Paul recasts the patronage system so that its primary benefits are retained while its drawbacks are minimized.

The Collegiality of Leadership in the Early Church

We have examined four key passages from Acts that relate to the leadership patterns of ecclesiastical authority in the diaspora church. In the first passage, Acts 13:1–3, we observed that the Holy Spirit is the initiator of the action. The apostles and teachers respond to the leadership of the Spirit, and they seem to relate to one another as equals under the Spirit's authority. That authority is unmediated and unbrokered. Even Barnabas, who had earlier been sent by the Jerusalem church to inspect the church at Antioch, is, at most, "first among equals."

The second passage, Acts 20:17–38, incorporates a speech from Paul to the elders of Ephesus. The focus of our attention in this passage was the authority of the πρεσβύτεροι and ἐπίσκοποι and the scope of

---

78. Bauckham, "James," esp. 416–27.

their authority. We argued that the two titles were synonymous and that they did not indicate the presence of established ecclesiastical office in Ephesus. Moreover, we demonstrated that the scope of the Ephesian elders' authority was not limited to the local church. Such a broad scope of authority suggests that the functionaries were officeholders. However, in light of the present study, it seems likely that the quality of personal interactions was the determinative basis for their multi-local authority. To use the language of Max Weber discussed in ch. 2, we conclude that the Ephesian elders possessed charismatic, not only legal authority.

Acts 15:1–35, of course, has often been read in terms of legal authority. Viewed through the lens of developed church history, the account has been reckoned the first ecumenical council of the church, with official delegates from the church's first ecclesiastical centers. The use of the terms, "Apostolic Council" or "Jerusalem Council," to describe the events recorded in Acts 15 reflects such a view. The present study has emphasized the sociological dimensions of Acts 15. In particular, we argued that concern for the unity of the church was an underlying concern of the meeting. Just as importantly, we contrasted the behavior of the Antioch delegation with the usual pattern of embassies seeking favor with a potential patron in order to show that Acts 15 does not support the notion that the Antioch delegation related to the Jerusalem elders as client to patron. Rather, both the Antioch and Jerusalem leaders were equally under the patronage of the same God, who had worked equally for the benefit of both groups.

Insights from a sociological approach also illuminate the final passage, Acts 21:17–26. This passage, in which Paul and his companions appear before James and the Jerusalem elders, could be read as an example of subordinates reporting to their superiors. We argued, however, that Paul relates to James as a colleague. Rather than describing the results of his efforts to fulfill the directives of his superior, Paul relates the work that God had been doing through him to James as to a co-laborer in a common cause. Similarly, although it appears that Paul acts as patron to the four men who had taken vows, a close reading of the text reveals that Paul identifies himself with the four as an equal, not as a patron. The purpose of Paul joining the four in fulfilling the vow was not for Paul to gain clients but to disprove the charge of subversion of the law. Rather than fighting for his personal honor, Paul humbled himself by identifying himself with the four as peers in order to advance the cause of the church.

The common thread that runs throughout all four passages studied in this chapter is the collegiality of leadership in the early church. The prophets and teachers from Antioch were colleagues with Barnabas, the inspector sent from Jerusalem (Acts 11:22);[79] the Ephesian elders enjoyed multi-local authority just like their counterparts elsewhere; the delegation from Antioch were not subordinated to the Jerusalem elders at the council; Paul related to James and the elders as to equals. The basis for this collegiality was the shared acknowledgment of equal dependence upon the patronage of God and upon a shared commitment to the unity of the church and its mission.

---

79. Cf. Wall, "Acts," 175: "When Jerusalem hears of the founding of this new mission [in Antioch], they dispatch one of their own—Barnabas—not to assess or confirm what had taken place but to collaborate with the missionaries already at work."

The Diffusion of Authority in Acts

Summary

The present study set out to discover, so far as possible, the nature of ecclesiastical authority in the early church as described in the NT book of Acts. We were guided initially by the macro-structure of Acts to hypothesize that, even as the gospel was carried from Jerusalem to Rome, so also the authority structures changed and spread. We proposed to follow a sociological approach to the text, first researching the sociology of leadership, then looking at religious authority in the Greco-Roman and Jewish worlds of the first century, and finally examining ecclesiastical authority in Acts as illuminated by the study of the usual practice of religious authority in the ancient world.

Leadership in the First Century

To implement this sociologically informed method, we first developed a number of models to assist in the exploration of leadership in the NT. These models drew from and built upon a variety of research focuses. We began with a broad overview of the dominant theoretical approaches to sociological inquiry. Our interest was held especially by two approaches, structural-functionalism and conflict theory. Structural-functionalism aims to discover universal patterns in order to classify cultures into specific categories that can serve as a basis for comparing cultures as well as for predicting cultural features that have not yet been observed. One theory developed from a structural-functionalist perspective is the grid/group model of Mary Douglas. We noted that the group/grid model is helpful for analyzing first-century cultures because many people would have experienced a strong group/

low grid existence, which differs markedly from the weak group/high grid situation that dominates North American culture. We argued that structural-functionalism offers genuine insights into leadership patterns but is most able to recognize patterns associated with dominant cultures, such as that of the Roman Empire.

Subordinate cultures are more readily appreciated by researchers who approach their subject from the perspective of conflict theory. Conflict theories of sociology were developed in the aftermath of the break-up of the British Empire as scholars began to recognize ways in which cultural features of subjugated societies had been masked by the dominance of the British. We remarked that the British Empire offers an interesting parallel to the first-century Mediterranean region, which was also dominated by a "world" empire. For this reason, we predicted that leadership patterns in the first century would follow both structural-functionalist paradigms (for leaders associated with the Roman Empire) and conflict paradigms (for leaders of subject peoples).

Another model comes from the sociology of religion. This model incorporates a typology of religious systems, including religious leadership. The model draws from Dale Cannon's *Six Ways of Being Religious* and posits a systemic link between a religion's conception of God and the form of leadership preferred within that religion. The most important systems for our present purposes are ritual performance/priests and social action/prophets. In religions where ritual performance is the dominant way of relating to "ultimate reality," priests are necessary in order to assure the proper conduction of the sacred practices. Prophets are the requisite religious leaders for social action because they offer their constituents reminders, on behalf of "ultimate reality," regarding proper actions toward their neighbors.

These theoretical constructs were applied toward the development of models of leadership in the first century. This application was accomplished by means of an examination of five general traits of first-century culture, namely, strong group/weak grid, perception of limited good, valuation of honor/shame, patron/client relations, and dyadic personality. By evaluating the intersection of these five traits with the two general sociological approaches of structural-functionalism and conflict theory, two divergent models of first-century leadership emerged. The two models are represented by the rubrics, "manager-leader" and "innovator-leader." The former is characterized by maintenance of received position, defense of group honor, and incremental change. Leaders of the latter type focus on more rapid change, which is accomplished through such efforts as the re-definition of honor or the subversion of current exchange and interaction systems.

Equipped with these models of leadership, we turned next to an examination of religious leadership in the Greco-Roman world. We examined the civic religions of both the Greek and Roman contexts as well as the mystery religions. Each of these three broad religious systems had its own distinctives. With respect to Greek religion, we observed that the structure of religious authority mirrored that of political authority. In the classical period in Athens, for example, religious authority remained under the control of the people. Even though there were religious functionaries, their authority was not binding upon the *dêmos*. Rather, the individual citizens seem to have had a great deal of autonomy in matters pertaining to religion. With only minimal cultic purity requirements, citizens could often become priests at their own choosing—provided they had the necessary funds to purchase the priesthood. Individual citizens could consult oracles for guidance, sacrifice to particular gods for favor in a given endeavor, or seek healing from the gods. It would appear, therefore, that ancient Greek religion should be categorized predominantly as a way of shamanic mediation and only secondarily as a way of sacred rite. This judgment is consistent with observation that Greek civic religion could be called a religion without priests.[1] The presence of priests and other religious functionaries was necessary to assure the accurate execution of sacrifices, oracles, and healings, but the logic of the religious system centered on the result of these activities, not on their conduct.

With respect to authority in Roman religion, the situation was somewhat different. As a rule, religious authority was more regimented than was the case for Greek religion. The core concern for Roman religion seems to have been maintenance of the *pax deorum*, and the priestly colleges were responsible for various aspects of assessing or preserving the state of the *pax*. Yet during the Republic, authority rested with the Senate, not with the members of the colleges themselves nor with the people more generally. For example, the *quindecimviri* could only consult the Sibylline Books at the behest of the Senate. With the

1. See note 13, page 68.

rise of the Empire, however, even as the Senate's political powers were being scaled back, so also were its religious powers. Moreover, as exemplified especially by Augustus, multiple priesthoods were accumulated by the same individual. Thus, by the middle of the first century, it seems more accurate to describe Roman religious authority as controlled by powerful individuals. These individuals gained authority because they had demonstrated their ability to maintain or restore the *pax deorum* through expert execution of the requisite religious ceremonies. Thus, in contrast to Greek religion, Roman religion was predominantly centered upon sacred rite, and priests were indispensable.

Also prominent in the Greco-Roman world were the mystery religions. We looked at the five best known: the Eleusinian mysteries, the Dionysiac mysteries, the cult of Cybele and Attis, the cult of Isis and Osiris, and Mithraism. In comparison to both Greek and Roman civic religion, the mystery religions exemplified a greater degree of personal connection between the congregant and his or her deity. For this reason, we classified the mystery religions under the deeds of devotion way of being religious. As with the Greek religion, however, the way of the sacred rite comprised a strong secondary classification for the mystery religions. Evidence for this classification can be seen, for example, from the elaborate initiation ceremonies. Because of the popularity of the mystery religions, it is sometimes thought that the civic religions had lost their vitality. Such a conclusion, however, misses the fact that the mystery religions and the civic religions catered to different human needs. The Greek civic religion seems to have appealed both to the need for order, as well as to the need for direction and health in everyday life. The Roman civic religion appealed even more strongly to the need for order. That the mystery religions succeeded in meeting the need for a personal connection to a higher power should not be construed to mean that the civic religions were not successful in meeting the needs they addressed.

As might be expected of religious systems that can be classified as "deeds of devotion," the authority structures of the mystery religions tended to demonstrate a concern for the personal wellbeing and the individual progress of the adherents. This pastoral care can be seen especially in the cult of Isis, but it is also evident, for example, in the familial language of Mithraism. In the case of Mithraism, the fact that the highest grade of initiation is termed, "father," is especially significant. With respect to authority, then, the mystery religions were hierarchical in nature, they incorporated a wide variety of functionaries, but most importantly they exhibited a personal, or pastoral concern.

After examining Greco-Roman religions, we turned next to the leadership structures of Second Temple Judaism. After a brief overview of the history of the period from 538 B.C.E. to 70 C.E., we examined three Second Temple institutions: the *gerousia*, the Sanhedrin, and the synagogue. The *gerousia* was a conservative body comprised of elders from leading Jewish families. It was responsible for the wellbeing of the community and was a predecessor to the Sanhedrin. Contrary to the common conception, the Sanhedrin was not a fixed body of lifetime membership. Indeed, there were multiple sanhedra throughout Palestine, each with authority comparable to that of the earlier *gerousia*. The Jerusalem Sanhedrin is the body normally thought of when the term Sanhedrin is used. Even the Jerusalem Sanhedrin, however, was an ad hoc institution. To be sure, it was comprised of elders with a relatively stable membership, but it did not have a fixed or constitutionally instituted membership.

A third Second Temple institution was the synagogue. The first synagogues seem to have begun as προσευχαί outside Palestine. προσευχαί were then imported to Palestine as synagogues, where they soon became popular. There were two main synagogal functionaries during the Second Temple period, the ἀρχισυνάγωγοι and the ὑπηρέται. The former were responsible for the Sabbath service and order, while the latter oversaw the children and the physical building. The Jewish community leaders, and not synagogal leaders per se, performed other leadership functions. The diversity of synagogal officers apparent from inscriptional evidence post-dates the Second Temple period.

In addition to these Second Temple institutions, there were also a number of well-known religious groups active during the Second Temple period. We looked first at the Pharisees. We argued that the Pharisees were influential during the Second Temple period but did not have exclusive religious authority over the people. Their leadership tended to be advisory and exemplary, rather than official or compulsory.

The Sadducees were similarly placed with respect to both authority and sociological status. Indeed, Pharisees and Sadducees often appear together in the primary literature, which frequently depicts the two groups vying for dominance. In the secondary literature, the Sadducees are more often connected with the Temple priesthood, since it appears that many of the Sadducees were priests and vice versa. We argued, moreover, that a distinction must be maintained between the chief priests and the common priests. The latter functioned in the Temple apart from the direct involvement of priestly supervisors.

A third group, the Essenes, seems to have had a highly developed hierarchical structure. We argued that the Qumran community was Essene. Thus, the distinctive literary remnants of that community may be taken to reflect the form of at least one branch of the Essenes. The Community Rule, in particular, reveals considerable details regarding the internal structure of the Qumran community. According to the Community Rule, each community member was subject to the one ahead of him in the hierarchy. In general, the hierarchy was based upon seniority. Yet an annual review of progress and conduct could result in one moving up or down in the hierarchy. Surprisingly, the community's leaders were elected, which seems to contradict the seniority-based hierarchy. Moreover, there was a priestly aspect to the leadership as described in the Community Rule. It appears that the Qumran community valued priestly rites and maintained readiness to resume responsibilities in the Temple, which they believed God would restore to them.

The Second Temple Jewish religious leadership structures may be compared with those of the Greco-Roman religions. As in the Greco-Roman religions, the Jewish religious leaders tended to be manager-leaders. In general, they seem to have had a conservative outlook. Moreover, both Greco-Roman and Jewish religious leaders tended also to be leaders of their respective communities and vice versa. Despite these similarities, there were also important differences. Unlike in Greek religion, Jewish priesthoods were not for sale. There was also a stronger sense of centralization in Judaism, as exemplified by the importance of Jerusalem and its Temple. To a greater extent, also, Judaism respected the authority of written sources. While it is true that the Sibylline oracles were especially valued in Roman religion, these were only consulted in extreme situations and do not seem to have been considered as repositories of wisdom for the guidance of ordinary individuals.

Ecclesiastical Authority in Acts

On the basis of our sociologically informed examination of Greco-Roman religions and Second Temple Judaism, we turned to several passages in Acts related to the topic of ecclesiastical authority. In particular, we looked first at passages dealing with the church in Jerusalem (1:15–26; 6:1–7; and 12:1–25). In each passage, we noted similarities and differences with respect to culturally expected behavior. In Acts 1, we observed that Peter's speech constituted a normal response to an extreme honor challenge. We argued that Peter, although taking a leadership role in this instance, likely did so under the pressure associated with his role as a leader within a group that looked to him for leadership. As such, despite the actions taken by Peter to restore the honor of his group, his role was that of a manager-leader. He did not undertake the kinds of activities, such as re-defining honor or re-distributing perceived good, which are typical of innovator-leaders.

Acts 6 also describes an honor challenge. In this instance, the discontent regarded the lack of distribution to the Hellenistic widows. Although the charge was directed against the Hebrews as a group, it was the Twelve who responded to the accusation of unfairness. The Twelve wished to solve an internal community problem especially because, as leaders of the group, they were uniquely responsible for safeguarding the group's honor. The Twelve met the challenge in a number of different ways, some of which followed the usual cultural scripts and some of which were innovative. In the latter category we observed that the Twelve employed fictive kinship language. By thus reframing the conflict as an internal family affair, the Twelve voided the situation of its agonistic intensity. Moreover, the Twelve initiated the selection of the Seven, which resulted in the increase of honor, not only for the Seven, but also for the Twelve and the community as a whole. The congregation was granted rights (namely, selection of leaders and laying on of hands) that later in church history were often restricted to ordained leaders. Similarly, the Seven possessed honorable qualifications and performed honorable tasks more akin to the activities of the Twelve than to the "waiting tables" for which they were initially selected. By thus extending honor to others while retaining their own honor, the Twelve proved that—contrary to cultural expectations—honor is an unlimited good. Their counter-cultural response to an honor challenge demonstrated the Twelve to be innovator-leaders.

From Acts 12, which seems to represent the transferal of power in the Jerusalem church from the apostles to James and the elders, we gleaned several important insights regarding ecclesiastical authority in the Jerusalem church. First, we argued that the non-replacement of James (as compared to the replacement of Judas) was the result of the growing understanding in the church that it was not necessary to fill leadership vacancies in order to increase group honor. Next we argued that Peter's departure to a ἕτερον τόπον (12:17) is to be contrasted with Judas's departure to ὁ τόπος ὁ ἴδιος (1:25). Whereas Judas had removed himself from leadership in the church, Peter's departure entailed carrying the Gospel to new locations and thus extending his leadership into new geographical areas. His departure, however, should not be viewed as an absolute renunciation of his authority in the Jerusalem church. Rather, Peter retained a measure of leadership in Jerusalem while initiating a process of power transfer in which he voluntarily shared his authority as a means of advancing the work of the church.

Finally, we examined four passages: two that described leadership interactions within diaspora churches (13:1–3 and 20:17–38) and two that described interactions between leaders of the diaspora churches and of the Jerusalem church (15:1–35 and 21:17–26). With respect to Acts 13:1–3, we argued that the three verses narrate a single event at which only the church leaders, and not the entire congregation, were present. We further argued that the leaders listed by name, while not necessarily the entirety of the Antioch church leadership, were remembered as key figures for the church. Their leadership consisted primarily of teaching and prophesying, though Luke does not expand on what this meant in practice—unless we understand the voice of the Holy Spirit (v. 2) as having been communicated through the agency of one of the prophets. The activity in which these leaders were engaged when the Holy Spirit spoke is described by Luke as λειτουργούντων δὲ αὐτῶν τῷ κυρίῳ καὶ νηστευόντων. We concurred with those scholars who view this expression as a Septuagintalism meaning "to pray." Thus, these leaders were in an attitude of submission when the Holy Spirit spoke. As this fact suggests, the text portrays the Holy Spirit as the real leader in the Antioch church. Luke further emphasizes this point in v. 4 by explicitly stating that the Holy Spirit sent (ἐκπέμπω) Barnabas and Saul on their journey—this after he had just said that the leaders had released (ἀπολύω) the two for the ministry to which the Holy Spirit had called them. This analysis of the passage yielded several interesting observations regarding the human leadership of the Antioch church. First, we noted that the teachers and prophets in Antioch had unmediated access to the Holy Spirit. Similarly, even though Barnabas had been sent to Antioch by the Jerusalem church, he is portrayed as "first among equals" with respect to the leaders of the Antioch church. We concluded, therefore, that the Antioch church enjoyed a high degree of autonomy with respect to the "mother church" in Jerusalem.

We looked next at Acts 20:17–38, which contains Paul's address to the Ephesian elders at Miletus. After discussing the historicity of the speech, we noted several factors related to the authority of the elders in Ephesus. In particular, we noted that both πρεσβύτεροι and ἐπίσκοποι are used to designate the leaders summoned from Ephesus. Whereas πρεσβύτεροι relates to a group designation and ἐπίσκοποι refers to the function of individuals within that group, we argued that neither word functions as a technical term in this passage. Instead, their apparent interchangeability suggests neither a presbyterial nor an episcopal system had yet become normative in the early church. We further observed that Paul's exhortation to these leaders included a charge to give of themselves on behalf of their "flock," a behavior that would have been counter-cultural for religious leaders in the first century. Finally, we argued that the authority structure for these leaders should be classified as collegial, since their charge was to shepherd the universal church while their authority was limited by the understanding that they remained accountable to their counterparts elsewhere.

Having thus addressed two key passages with respect to the diaspora church, we turned to two passages describing interactions between Jerusalem and the diaspora. The first passage, Acts 15, has long been a contentious one for NT scholars. Much of the debate centers on the relationship between this passage and Paul's account of what appears to be the same event in Gal 2. The stakes are high, not only because of the historical issues involved, but also because Acts 15 is often regarded as the center of Acts. In discussing the purpose of the Jerusalem meeting, we noted that underlying sociological factors played a large role. We argued that the unity of the Jerusalem and Antioch churches was of vital concern. The strife caused by the men from Judea, which disrupted that unity, raised the urgency for dealing with the theological problem regarding Gentile circumcision and obedience to the Law. We contrasted the Antioch delegation with the embassy of Philo to Gaius, which is an example of clients lavishing honor as a means of appealing to a patron. The delegates from Antioch, instead of heaping praise on the Jerusalem leadership, reserved their words of praise for the things that God had done, thus demonstrating that both churches were clients of the same patron, namely, God. Similarly, the unity of the two churches was underscored by sending churchmen from both Jerusalem and Antioch to carry the written decree and report the results of the meeting. In examining the decision, we noted, first, that the Jerusalem congregation (ἐκκλησίας, v. 4) was present and may have contributed to the decision. Similarly, the delegates from Antioch appear to have played an important role in the decision-making process. The speeches of two leaders, Peter and James, are reported. Both speeches emphasize the practical components of the disagreement, in addition to utilizing theological argumentation. The council's letter affirms the position that Paul and Barnabas had taken, expressing four requirements (τούτων τῶν ἐπάναγκες, v. 28) but not requiring Gentile circumcision or obedience to the whole Mosaic Law. Therefore, the Jerusalem leaders treated the Antioch leaders with greater deference and granted them greater authority than would have been expected of leaders in the first century.

The final passage, Acts 21:17–26, relates the meeting of Paul and his companions with James and the elders. Although certain features of the text seem to suggest that Paul relates to James as his superior, we argued that the passage more strongly pictures the two as colleagues. This judgment was based upon the observations that (1) Paul is addressed—in apparent genuineness—as brother; and (2) the reported speech of the elders is aimed at persuading Paul to take certain action, rather than commanding him. We concluded that deference and honor, instead of power and coercion were the best descriptors of the interactions in this passage. In the same way, we argued that Paul relates as a peer to the four men whose expenses he paid, not as a patron. Thus, Paul redefines what is honorable: no longer is it honorable to use one's financial resources to create social distance between patron and client; now it is honorable to use those resources for the benefit of the other without entering into a patron-client relationship.

Results of the Study

In the preceding section, we summarized the arguments and the specific findings of the study. It remains for us to discuss the results of the study with respect to the general conception of ecclesiastical authority in the book of Acts. I wish to draw attention to two findings that are especially important. First, ecclesiastical leaders in Acts are best classified as innovator-leaders. According to the model developed in ch. 2 above, first century innovator-leaders would re-define ultimate good, re-define honor, and subvert the patronage system. The present study has shown that leaders in Acts behave in these ways. They demonstrate that personal honor is no longer a good for which to strive. Instead, the growth of the church and the spread of God's word are the good to which believers ought to aspire. Since honor is no longer the ultimate good, the various individuals may now gain honor simultaneously by pursuing the mutual goal of advancing the kingdom of God. Thus, by setting the goal as a different "good," the original good (honor) is no longer limited. Yet honor itself is also redefined by the innovator-leaders in Acts. As we have seen, church leaders recast challenge-riposte games in a variety of ways. Not least among these changes, the innovator-leaders in Acts redefined kinship to include the whole "family" of believers. The leaders in Acts also demonstrated that honor may be granted mutually in such a way that both parties honor one another. The Jerusalem church, for example, retained a high degree of honor (and, therefore, authority) in the early church while simultaneously granting honor to believers from the diaspora by greeting them as brothers, by giving them voice in deliberative assembly, and by treating them as colleagues. Thus, the leaders in Acts demonstrated that it is no longer honorable to win at "games" but to give honor to others. These leaders, moreover, subverted the patronage system. This was accomplished through the acknowledgement of the Holy Spirit as the true leader of the church. Thus, God was recognized as the only patron. Would-be human patrons are at best brokers, and that only until they arrange unmediated access to God. There is no contradiction in the granting of (redefined) honor to fellow humans in addition to God, since honor in human interactions is now based on equal status as co-clients of the same patron. Relationships are now based on the mutual grant of honor, not on an agonistic struggle for superiority. In profound ways the leaders in Acts brought countercultural innovations to the early church.

Second, the innovation of the leaders in Acts fostered a diffusion of ecclesiastical authority. By consistently sharing their authority with others, these leaders allowed the diffusion of authority to new individuals rather than the concentration of authority in the hands of the few. Undoubtedly, this selflessness on the part of the church's leaders contributed to the spread of the Gospel throughout the Mediterranean world. By regularly empowering new leaders, the church was able to release its leaders for ministry in new locations without fear of leaving established churches leaderless. Yet one should not suppose that, through such diffusion, ecclesiastical authority became diluted. As we have seen, the leaders in Acts shared their authority without thereby losing it. They were able to do this because their authority was based on deference and mutual honor, not only on legal rights. Thus, the diffusion of ecclesiastical authority resulted in a net increase of authority, which in turn propelled the growth of the church.

Possibilities for Future Study

It has been customary to assume a predictable progression in the development of ecclesiastical authority in the early church. Documents are dated according to the type of leadership they exhibit on an evolutionary scale. It has not been possible to evaluate this procedure on the basis of our study of Acts. However, Luke's lack of explicit statements regarding the forms of ecclesiastical authority strongly suggests that exact leadership structures were not of primary interest to Luke and his community. This lack of interest further implies that little would have been done at this stage of the church to ensure uniformity of structure throughout the church as it spread across the known world. We should expect, then, that the church in different areas would have progressed via different paths and at different rates. It may be possible to test this hypothesis through the study of extra-biblical literature.

It would also be desirable to further examine early Christian literature from the perspective of leadership function. As disinterested as Luke seems to have been in leadership structure, he proves himself to have had a keen interest in the activities of particular leaders. More precisely, he has demonstrated an interest in how early church leaders acted in creative ways in order to advance the kingdom of God. It would be useful to explore the extent to which other portrayals of leadership in the early church demonstrate a similar innovation. To what extent, for example, do other NT works demonstrate a type of leadership in which honor is perceived as an unlimited good? Can it be demonstrated from the NT and other early Christian literature that the first generation produced innovator-leaders while later generations were more satisfied with manager-leaders who transmitted the innovations of their predecessors? Answers to these and similar questions would be valuable, not only in refining our understanding of the dynamics within the early church, but also for further confirming or enhancing the description of authority we have developed in the present study.

Conclusion

There are tantalizing hints embedded in the text of Acts that seem to indicate an outline of the structures of leadership in the early church. It may be the case, as Johnson argued, that Luke assumes a presbyterial structure from the beginning.[2] Yet there are intimations of changing structures in the early church as indicated by the Seven, by the interchange of πρεσβύτεροι and ἐπίσκοποι, and by the reference to teachers and prophets in Antioch but apostles and elders in Jerusalem. Luke, however, is more interested in the actions of leaders, not the structures of leadership. He narrates how the spirit-guided choices made by church leaders led to the spread of the Gospel. In particular, the leaders of the early church voluntarily limited their own authority in order to empower others for the work of the kingdom. By not grasping power, the leaders in Acts not only granted authority to others but also received authority in return. In the words which Luke attributes to Jesus,

> The kings of the Gentiles lord it over them; and those who have authority over them are called "Benefactors." But it is not this way with you, but the one who is the greatest among you must become like the youngest, and the leader like the servant. For who is greater, the one who reclines at the table or the one who serves? Is it not the one who reclines at the table? But I am among you as the one who serves. (Luke 22:25–27, NASB)

According to their portrayal in the book of Acts, the leaders of the early church put this teaching into practice and thereby demonstrated its paradoxical truth.

---

2. See note 39, page 196.

Bibliography

Primary Sources

Literary Sources

The Ante-Nicene Fathers. 10 vols. Edited by Alexander Roberts and James Donaldson. 1885–1887. Reprinted, Grand Rapids: Eerdmans, 1980.

The Apostolic Fathers. 2 vols. Edited and translated by Bart D. Ehrman. LCL. Cambridge: Harvard University Press, 2003.

Apollodorus. *Library.* 2 vols. Translated by James George Frazer. LCL. Cambridge: Harvard University Press, 1946.

Apuleius. *Metamorphoses.* 2 vols. Translated by J. Arthur Hanson. LCL. Cambridge: Harvard University Press, 1989.

Augustine. *De civitate Dei.* 7 vols. Translated by George E. McCracken, William M. Green, David S. Wiesen, et al. LCL. Cambridge: Harvard University Press, 1957–1972.

Augustus. *Res gestae.* Translated by Frederick W. Shipley. LCL. Cambridge: Harvard University Press, 1924.

Aulus Gellius. *Noctes atticae.* 3 vols. Translated by John C. Rolfe. LCL. Cambridge: Harvard University Press, 1946–1952.

Cato. *De agricultura (De re rustica).* Translated by William Davis Hooper, revised by Harrison Boyd Ash. Rev. ed. LCL. Cambridge: Harvard University Press, 1935.

Charlesworth, James H, editor. *The Old Testament Pseudepigrapha.* 2 vols. Garden City, N.Y.: Doubleday, 1983–1985.

Cicero. *Epistulae ad Atticum.* 3 vols. Translated by E. O Winstedt. LCL. Cambridge: Harvard University Press, 1912–1918.

———. *Epistulae ad Brutum.* Translated by M. Cary. Rev. ed. LCL. Cambridge: Harvard University Press, 1954.

———. *De legibus.* Translated by Clinton Walker Keyes. LCL. Cambridge: Harvard University Press, 1928.

———. *De natura deorum.* Translated by H. Rackham. Rev. ed. LCL. Cambridge: Harvard University Press, 1951.

Dio Cassius. *Roman History.* 9 vols. Translated by Earnest Cary. LCL. Cambridge: Harvard University Press, 1914–1927.

Dio Chrysostom. *De dei cognitione (Or. 12).* Translated by J. W. Cohoon. Vol. 2. LCL. Cambridge: Harvard University Press, 1939.

Dionysius of Halicarnassus. *Antiquitates romanae.* 7 vols. Translated by Earnest Cary. LCL. Cambridge: Harvard University Press, 1937–1950.

Euripides. 4 vols. Translated by Arthur S. Way. LCL. Cambridge: Harvard University Press, 1912.

García Martínez, Florentino. *The Dead Sea Scrolls Translated: The Qumran Texts in English.* 2nd ed. Translated by Wilfred G. E. Watson. Leiden: Brill, 1996.

Herodotus. *Historiae.* 4 vols., vol. 1 revised. Translated by A. D. Godley. LCL. Cambridge: Harvard University Press, 1921–1926.

Homer. *Iliad.* 2 vols. Translated by A. T. Murray. Revised by William F. Wyatt. 2nd ed. LCL. Cambridge: Harvard University Press, 1999.

Homeric Hymns. Translated by Martin L. West. LCL. Cambridge: Harvard University Press, 2003.

Horace. *Carmina.* Translated by C. E. Bennett. LCL. Cambridge: Harvard University Press, 1952.

Jerome. *Epistulae.* Translated by F. A. Wright. LCL. Cambridge: Harvard University Press, 1933.

Josephus. 10 vols. Translated by H. St. J. Thackeray et al. LCL. Cambridge: Harvard University Press, 1926–1965.

Livy. *History.* 14 vols. Translated by B. O. Foster, Frank Gardner Moore, Evan T. Sage, and Alfred C. Schlesinger. LCL. Cambridge: Harvard University Press, 1919–1959.

Lucian. *Alexander (Pseudomantis).* Vol. 4 of 8. Translated by A. M. Harmon. LCL. Cambridge: Harvard University Press, 1925.

Ovid. *Metamorphoses.* 2 vols. Translated by Frank Justus Miller. LCL. Cambridge: Harvard University Press, 1916.

Pausanias, *Graeciae description.* 4 vols. Translated by W. H. S. Jones. LCL. Cambridge: Harvard University Press, 1918–1935.

Philo. 12 vols. Translated by F. H. Colson, G. H. Whitaker, and Ralph Marcus. LCL. Cambridge: Harvard University Press, 1929–1962.

Philostratus. *Vita Apollonii.* 2 vols. Translated by F. C. Conybeare. LCL. Cambridge: Harvard University Press, 1912.

Plato, *Respublica.* 2 vols. Translated by Paul Shorey. Rev. Ed. LCL. Cambridge: Harvard University Press, 1937.

Pliny the Elder. *Naturalis historia.* 10 vols. Translated by H. Rackham, W. H. S. Jones, and D. E. Eichholz. Rev. ed. LCL. Cambridge: Harvard University Press, 1949–1962.

Pliny the Younger. *Epistulae.* 2 vols. Translated by William Melmoth, revised by W. M. L. Hutchinson. LCL. Cambridge: Harvard University Press, 1915.

Plutarch. *Lives.* 11 vols. Translated by Bernadotte Perrin. LCL. Cambridge: Harvard University Press, 1914–1926.

Plutarch. *Moralia.* 16 vols. Translated by Frank Cole Babbitt, et al. LCL. Cambridge: Harvard University Press, 1927–1969.

Sophocles. 3 vols. Edited and Translated by Hugh Lloyd-Jones. LCL. Cambridge: Harvard University Press, 1994–1996.

Suetonius. *History.* 2 vols. Translated by J. C. Rolfe. LCL. Cambridge: Harvard University Press, 1914.

Strabo. *Geographica.* 8 vols. Translated by Horace Leonard Jones. LCL. Cambridge: Harvard University Press, 1932.

Varro. *De lingua Latina*. 2 vols. Translated by Roland G. Kent. LCL. Cambridge: Harvard University Press, 1951.
Xenophon. *Anabasis*. Translated by Carleton L. Brownson. LCL. Cambridge: Harvard University Press, 1921.
———. *Cyropaedia*. 2 vols. Translated by Walter Miller. LCL. Cambridge: Harvard University Press, 1953.

Source Books

Beard, Mary, John North, and Simon Price. *Religions of Rome*. Vol. 2: *A Sourcebook*. Cambridge: Cambridge University Press, 1998.
Dittenberger, Wilhelm. *Sylloge Inscriptionum Graecarum*. 4 vols. Hildesheim: Olms, 1960.
Ferguson, John. *Greek and Roman Religion: A Source Book*. Park Ridge, NJ: Noyes, 1980.
Grant, Frederick C. *Hellenistic Religions: The Age of Syncretism*. Library of Religion 2. Edited by Herbert W. Schneider, Herbert G. May, Henry G. Russell, and Francis R. Walton. New York: Liberal Arts, 1953.
———. *Ancient Roman Religion*. Library of Religion 8. Edited by Horace L Friess, Joseph L. Blau, D. H. Daugherty, Erwin Ramsdell Goodenough, Herbert W. Schneider, and Morton Smith. New York: Liberal Arts, 1957.
Kraemer, Ross S. *Maenads, Martyrs, Matrons, Monastics: A Sourcebook on Women's Religions in the Greco-Roman World*. Philadelphia: Fortress, 1988.
Lifshitz, Baruch. *Donateurs et fondateurs dans les synagogues juives: Répertoire des dédicaces grecques relatives à la construction et à la refection des synagogues*. Cahiers de la RB 7. Paris: Babalda. 1967.
Meyer, Marvin W. *The Ancient Mysteries: A Sourcebook: Sacred Texts of the Mystery Religions of the Ancient Mediterranean World*. 1st ed. San Francisco: Harper & Row, 1987.
Rice, David G., and John E. Stambaugh. *Sources for the Study of Greek Religion*. SBSt 14. Edited by Burke O. Long. Missoula, MT: Scholars, 1979.
Warrior, Valerie M. *Roman Religion: A Sourcebook*. Newburyport, MA: Focus/Pullins, 2002.

Secondary Sources

Achtemeier, Paul J. *The Quest for Unity in the New Testament Church: A Study in Paul and Acts*. Philadelphia: Fortress, 1987.
Ådna, Jostein. "James' Position at the Summit Meeting of the Apostles and the Elders in Jerusalem (Acts 15)." In *Mission of the Early Church to Jews and Gentiles*, edited by Jostein Ådna and Hans Kvalbein, 125–61. Tübingen: Mohr Siebeck, 2000.
André, G. "פָּקַד." In *TDOT* (2003) 12:50–63.
Antonakis, John, Anna T. Cianciolo, and Robert J. Sternberg, editors. *The Nature of Leadership*. Thousand Oaks, CA: Sage, 2004.

Ascough, Richard S. "Voluntary Associations and the Formation of Pauline Christian Communities: Overcoming the Objections." In *Vereine, Synagogen und Gemeinden im kaiserzeitlichen Kleinasien*, edited by Andreas Gutsfeld and Dietrich-Alex Koch, 149–83. STAC 25. Tübingen: Mohr Siebeck, 2006.

Ayman, Roya. "Leadership." In *Encyclopedia of Sociology*, edited by Edgar F. Borgatta and Rhonda J. V. Montgomery, 3:1563–75. 5 vols. New York: Macmillan, 2000.

Ayman, Roya, and Martin M. Chemers. "Relationship of Supervisory Behavior to Work Group Effectiveness and Subordinate Satisfaction Among Iranian Manager." *Journal of Applied Psychology* 68 (1983) 338–41.

Barrett, C. K. "The Historicity of Acts." *JTS* 50 (1999) 515–34.

———. *Introduction and Commentary on Acts XV–XXVIII*. Vol. 2 of *A Critical and Exegetical Commentary on the Acts of the Apostles*. ICC 44. Edinburgh: T. & T. Clark, 1998.

———. *Preliminary Introduction and Commentary on Acts I–XIV*. Vol. 1 of *A Critical and Exegetical Commentary on the Acts of the Apostles*. ICC 44. Edinburgh: T. & T. Clark, 1994.

Bartchy, S. Scott. "Cultural and Religious Environment of Early Christianity." Classroom lectures presented at Fuller Theological Seminary, Pasadena, CA, February 16, 2006.

———. "Divine Power, Community Formation, and Leadership in the Acts of the Apostles." In *Community Formation in the Early Church and in the Church Today*, edited by Richard N. Longenecker, 89–104. Peabody, MA: Hendrickson, 2002.

———. "Who Should be Called Father? Paul of Tarsus Between the Jesus Tradition and Patria Potestas." *BTB* 33 (2003) 135–47.

Bass, Bernard M. "Some Observations about a General Theory of Leadership and Interpersonal Behavior." In *Leadership and Interpersonal Behavior*, edited by Luigi Petrullo and Bernard M. Bass, 3–9. New York: Holt, Rinehart and Winston, 1961.

Bass, Bernard M., and Ralph M. Stogdill. *Bass & Stogdill's Handbook of Leadership: Theory, Research, and Managerial Applications*. 3rd ed. New York: Free Press, 1990.

Bauckham, Richard. "James and the Jerusalem Church." In *The Book of Acts in Its Palestinian Setting*, edited by Richard Bauckham, 415–80. Vol. 4 of *The Book of Acts in Its First Century Setting*. Grand Rapids: Eerdmans, 1995.

Bauer, Walter, Frederick W. Danker, William Arndt, and F. Wilbur Gingrich. *Greek-English Lexicon of the New Testament and Other Early Christian Literature*. 3rd ed. Chicago: University of Chicago Press, 2000.

Baur, Ferdinand Christian. "Die Christuspartei in der korinthischen Gemeinde, der Gegensatz des petrinischen und paulinischen Christenthums in der ältesten Kirche, der Apostel Petrus in Rom." *TZT* 4 (1831) 61–206.

———. *Paul, the Apostle of Jesus Christ: His Life and Work, His Epistles and Teachings*. Edited by Eduard Zeller. 2 vols. Translated by Allan Menzies. 2nd ed. London: Williams and Norgate, 1876.

Beard, Mary. "Priesthood in the Roman Republic." In *Pagan Priests: Religion and Power in the Ancient World*, edited by Mary Beard and John North, 17–48. Ithaca, NY: Cornell University Press, 1990.

Beck, Roger. "The Mysteries of Mithras." In *Voluntary Associations in the Graeco-Roman World*, edited by John S. Kloppenborg and Stephen G. Wilson, 176-85. London: Routledge, 1996.
Bede. *The Venerable Bede: Commentary on the Acts of the Apostles*. Translated by Lawrence T. Martin. Kalamazoo, MI: Cistercian, 1989.
Best, Ernest. "Acts 13:1-3." *JTS* 11 (1960) 344-48.
Blass, Friedrich, and Albert Debrunner. *A Greek Grammar of the New Testament and Other Early Christian Literature*. Translated by Robert Walter Funk. Trans. and rev. of the 9th-10th German ed. Chicago: University of Chicago Press, 1961.
Blue, Bradley. "Acts and the House Church." In *The Book of Acts in Its Graeco-Roman Setting*, edited by David W. J. Gill and Conrad Gempf, 119-222. Vol. 1 of *The Book of Acts in Its First Century Setting*. Grand Rapids: Eerdmans, 1994.
Bockmuehl, M. "The Noachide Commandments and the New Testament Ethics with Special Reference to Acts 15 and Pauline Halakhah." *RB* 102 (1995) 72-101.
Botterweck, G. Johannes, Helmer Ringgren, and Heinz-Josef Fabry, editors. *Theological Dictionary of the Old Testament*. 14 vols. Translated by J. T. Willis, G. W. Bromiley, and D. E. Green. Grand Rapids: Eerdmans, 1974-2004.
Brehm, H. Alan. "The Significance of the Summaries for Interpreting Acts." *SwJT* 33 (1990) 29-40.
Brent, Allen. *The Imperial Cult and the Development of Church Order: Concepts and Images of Authority in Paganism and Early Christianity Before the Age of Cyprian*. VCSup 45. Leiden: Brill, 1999.
Brooten, Bernadette J. *Women Leaders in the Ancient Synagogue: Inscriptional Evidence and Background Issues*. BJS 36. Chico, CA: Scholars, 1982.
Brown, Raymond E., and John P. Meier. *Antioch and Rome: New Testament Cradles of Catholic Christianity*. New York: Paulist, 1983.
Bruce, F. F. *The Acts of the Apostles: The Greek Text with Introduction and Commentary*. 3rd ed. Grand Rapids: Eerdmans, 1990.
———. *The Letter of Paul to the Romans: An Introduction and Commentary*. 2nd ed. TNTC 6. Leicester, England: InterVarsity, 1985.
———. "The Speeches in Acts—Thirty Years After." In *Reconciliation and Hope: New Testament Essays on Atonement and Eschatology*, edited by Robert Banks, 53-68. Grand Rapids: Eerdmans, 1974.
Buber, Martin. *I and Thou*. Translated by Ronald Gregor Smith. Edinburgh: T. & T. Clark, 1937.
Burkert, Walter. *Ancient Mystery Cults*. Cambridge: Harvard University Press, 1987.
———. *Greek Religion*. Translated by John Raffan. Cambridge: Harvard University Press, 1985.
Burtchaell, James Tunstead. *From Synagogue to Church: Public Services and Offices in the Earliest Christian Communities*. Cambridge: Cambridge University Press, 1992.
Byatt, Anthony. "Josephus and Population Numbers in First Century Palestine." *PEQ* 105 (1973) 51-60.
Calhoun, Craig J., editor. *Dictionary of Social Sciences*. Oxford: Oxford University Press, 2002.
Campbell, R. Alastair. *The Elders: Seniority within Earliest Christianity*. Edinburgh: T. & T. Clark, 1994.

Campenhausen, Hans von. *Ecclesiastical Authority and Spiritual Power in the Church of the First Three Centuries*. Translated by J. A. Baker. 1969. Reprinted, Peabody, MA: Hendrickson, 1997.

Cannon, Dale. *Six Ways of Being Religious: A Framework for Comparative Studies of Religion*. Belmont, CA: Wadsworth, 1996.

Capper, Brian. "The Palestinian Cultural Context of Earliest Christian Community of Goods." In *The Book of Acts in Its Palestinian Setting*, edited by Richard Bauckham, 323–56. Vol. 4 of *The Book of Acts in Its First Century Setting*. Grand Rapids: Eerdmans, 1995.

Chilton, Bruce. *The Temple of Jesus: His Sacrificial Program within a Cultural History of Sacrifice*. University Park, PA: Pennsylvania State University Press, 1992.

Claussen, Carsten. "Meeting, Community, Synagogue—Different Frameworks of Ancient Jewish Congregations in the Diaspora." In *The Ancient Synagogue from Its Origins until 200 C.E.: Papers Presented at an International Conference at Lund University, October 14–17, 2001*, edited by Birger Olsson and Magnus Zetterholm, 144–67. ConBNT 39. Stockholm: Almqvist & Wiksell, 2003.

Collins, Randall. "Conflict Theory." In *Encyclopedia of Sociology*, edited by Edgar F. Borgatta and Rhonda J. V. Montgomery, 1:414–17. 5 vols. 2nd ed. New York: Macmillan, 2000.

Conzelmann, Hans. *Acts of the Apostles: A Commentary on the Acts of the Apostles*. Translated by James Limburg, A. Thomas Kraabel, and Donald H. Juel. Hermeneia. Philadelphia: Fortress, 1987.

Coppens, Joseph. "L'imposition des mains dans les Actes des Apôtres." In *Actes des Apôtres: Traditions, rédaction, théologie*, edited by Jacob Kremer, 405–38. BETL 48. Gembloux, Belgium: Duculot, 1979.

———. Review of Eldon Jay Epp, *The Theological Tendency of Codex Bezae Cantabrigiensis in Acts*. *ETL* 43 (1967) 274.

Deissmann, Gustav Adolf. *Light from the Ancient East: The New Testament Illustrated by Recently Discovered Texts of the Graeco-Roman World*. Translated by Lionel Richard Mortimer Strachan. Rev. ed. New York: Doran, 1927.

Dollar, Harold E. "A Biblical-Missiological Exploration of the Cross-Cultural Dimensions in Luke-Acts." Ph.D. dissertation, Fuller Theological Seminary, 1990.

Douglas, Mary. *Natural Symbols: Explorations in Cosmology*. London: Barrie & Rockliff, 1970. Reprinted, New York: Vintage, 1973.

———. *Natural Symbols: Explorations in Cosmology*. 2nd ed. London: Routledge, 1996.

Dowd, Sharyn. "'Ordination' in Acts and the Pastoral Epistles." *PRSt* 29 (2002) 205–17.

Dunn, James D. G. *The Partings of the Ways: Between Christianity and Judaism and Their Significance for the Character of Christianity*. London: SCM, 1991.

Dupont, Jacques. *Le discours de Milet: Testament pastoral de Saint Paul (Actes 20, 18–36)*. LD 32. Paris: Cerf, 1962.

Elliott, John H. *What is Social-Scientific Criticism?* Minneapolis: Fortress, 1993.

Epp, Eldon Jay. *The Theological Tendency of Codex Bezae Cantabrigiensis in Acts*. Cambridge: Cambridge University Press, 1966.

Esler, Philip Francis. *Community and Gospel in Luke-Acts: The Social and Political Motivations of Lucan Theology*. SNTSMS 57. Cambridge: Cambridge University Press, 1987.

Estrada, Nelson P. *From Followers to Leaders: The Apostles in the Ritual of Status Transformation in Acts 1-2*. JSNTSup 255. London: T. & T. Clark, 2004.

Evans, Craig A. *Noncanonical Writings and New Testament Interpretation*. Peabody, MA: Hendrickson, 1992.

Ferguson, Everett. "Laying on of Hands: Its Significance in Ordination." *JTS* 26 (1975) 1-12.

Ferguson, John. *The Religions of the Roman Empire*. Aspects of Greek and Roman Life. London: Thames & Hudson, 1970.

Festugière, A. J. *Personal Religion Among the Greeks*. Sather Classical Lectures 26. Berkeley: University of California Press, 1954.

Fitzmyer, Joseph A. *Romans: A New Translation with Introduction and Commentary*. AB 33. New York: Doubleday, 1993.

———. *The Acts of the Apostles: A New Translation with Introduction and Commentary*. AB 31. New York: Doubleday, 1998.

Foster, Matthew R. "Saying What We Mean: Methodological Reflections on Dale Cannon's *Six Ways of Being Religious*." *JES* 37 (2000) 354-80.

García Martínez, Florentino. Introduction to *The Dead Sea Scrolls Translated: The Qumran Texts in English*. Translated by Wilfred G. E. Watson. 2nd ed. Leiden: Brill, 1996.

Garland, Robert. "Priests and Power in Classical Athens." In *Pagan Priests: Religion and Power in the Ancient World*, edited by Mary Beard and John North, 73-91. Ithaca, NY: Cornell University Press, 1990.

Garrett, Susan R. "Exodus from Bondage: Luke 9:31 and Acts 12:1-24." *CBQ* 52 (1990) 656-80.

Gaventa, Beverly Roberts. *The Acts of the Apostles*. Abingdon New Testament Commentaries. Nashville: Abingdon, 2003.

Giles, Kevin N. "Luke's Use of the Term ΕΚΚΛΗΣΙΑ with Special Reference to Acts 20:28 and 9:31." *NTS* 31 (1985) 135-42.

Goldingay, John. "Leadership Theologically Considered." Paper presented at Fuller Theological Seminary, Pasadena, CA, March 1, 2006.

González, Justo L. "Reading from My Bicultural Place: Acts 6:1-7." In *Social Location and Biblical Interpretation in the United States*, edited by Fernando F. Segovia and Mary Ann Tolbert, 139-47. Vol. 1 of *Reading from This Place*. Minneapolis: Fortress, 1995.

Goodspeed, Edgar Johnson. *The Key to Ephesians*. Chicago: University of Chicago Press, 1956.

Gutmann, Joseph. "Synagogue Origins: Theories and Facts." In *Ancient Synagogues: The State of Research*, edited by Joseph Gutmann, 1-6. Chico, CA: Scholars, 1981.

Haenchen, Ernst. *The Acts of the Apostles: A Commentary*. Translated by B. Noble, G. Shinn, H. Anderson, and R. McL. Wilson. Oxford: Blackwell, 1971.

Harnack, Adolf von. *The Constitution and Law of the Church in the First Two Centuries*. Edited by H. D. A. Major. Translated by Frank Lubecki Pogson. Crown Theological Library 31. New York: Williams & Norgate, 1910.

Bibliography

Harrill, J. Albert. "The Dramatic Function of the Running Slave Rhoda (Acts 12.13–16): A Piece of Greco-Roman Comedy." *NTS* 46 (2000) 150–57.

Harris, R. Laird, Gleason Leonard Archer, and Bruce K. Waltke, editors. *Theological Wordbook of the Old Testament*. 2 vols. Chicago: Moody, 1980.

Heifetz, Ronald A. *Leadership Without Easy Answers*. Cambridge, MA: Belknap, 1994.

Heimerdinger, Jenny. "The Seven Steps of Codex Bezae: A Prophetic Interpretation of Acts 12." In *Codex Bezae: Studies from the Lunel Colloquium, June 1994*, edited by David C. Parker and Christian B. Amphoux, 303–10. NTTS 22. Leiden: Brill, 1996.

Hemer, Colin J. "The Speeches of Acts: Part 1: The Ephesian Elders at Miletus." *TynBul* 40 (1989) 77–85.

Hengel, Martin, and Roland Deines. "E P Sanders' 'Common Judaism,' Jesus, and the Pharisees." *JTS* 46 (1995) 1–70.

Hill, Craig C. *Hellenists and Hebrews: Reappraising Division within the Earliest Church*. Minneapolis: Fortress, 1992.

Hunt, James G. "What is Leadership?" In *The Nature of Leadership*, edited by John Antonakis, Anna T. Cianciolo and Robert J. Sternberg, 19–47. Thousand Oaks, CA: Sage, 2004.

Jefford, Clayton N. "Tradition and Witness in Antioch: Acts 15 and Didache 6." *PRSt* 19 (1992) 409–19.

Jervell, Jacob. *Die Apostelgeschichte*. KEK 3. Göttingen: Vandenhoeck & Ruprecht, 1998.

Johnson, Allan G. *The Blackwell Dictionary of Sociology: A User's Guide to Sociological Language*. Edited by G. Johnson Allan. 2nd ed. Malden, MA: Blackwell, 2000.

Johnson, Luke Timothy. *The Acts of the Apostles*. SP 5. Collegeville, MN: Liturgical, 1992.

Käsemann, Ernst. *Commentary on Romans*. Translated by Geoffrey W. Bromiley. Grand Rapids: Eerdmans, 1980.

Keener, Craig S. *The IVP Bible Background Commentary: New Testament*. Downers Grove, IL: InterVarsity, 1993.

Kilmartin, Edward J. "Ministry and Ordination in Early Christianity against a Jewish Background." *Studia liturgica* 13 (1979) 42–69.

Kittel, Gerhard, and Gerhard Friedrich, editors. *Theological Dictionary of the New Testament*. 10 vols. Translated by Geoffrey W. Bromiley. Grand Rapids: Eerdmans, 1964–1976.

Klauck, Hans-Josef. *The Religious Context of Early Christianity: A Guide to Graeco-Roman Religions*. Translated by Brian McNeil. Studies of the New Testament and Its World. Edinburgh: T. & T. Clark, 2000.

Kloppenborg, John S. "Edwin Hatch, Church, and *Collegia*." In *Origins and Method: Towards a New Understanding of Judaism and Christianity*, edited by Bradley H. McLean, 212–38. JSNTSup 86. Sheffield: Sheffield Academic, 1993.

Latourette, Kenneth Scott. *The Thousand Years of Uncertainty*. Vol. 2 of *A History of the Expansion of Christianity*. New York: Harper & Brothers, 1938.

Layton, Robert. *An Introduction to Theory in Anthropology*. Cambridge: Cambridge University Press, 1997.

Levine, Lee I. "The First Century C.E. Synagogue in Historical Perspective." In *The Ancient Synagogue from Its Origins until 200 C.E.: Paper Presented at an International Conference at Lund University, October 14-17, 2001*, edited by Birger Olsson and Magnus Zetterholm, 1-24. ConBNT 39. Stockholm: Almqvist & Wiksell, 2003.

———. "The Revolutionary Effects of Archaeology on the Study of Jewish History: The Case of the Ancient Synagogue." In *The Archaeology of Israel: Constructing the Past, Interpreting the Present*, edited by Neil Asher Silberman and David Small, 166-89. JSOTSup 237. Sheffield: Sheffield Academic, 1997.

Levinskaya, Irina. *The Book of Acts in Its Diaspora Setting*. Vol. 5 of *The Book of Acts in Its First Century Setting*. Grand Rapids: Eerdmans, 1996.

Lewellen, Ted C. *Political Anthropology: An Introduction*. 2nd ed. Westport, CT: Bergin & Garvey, 1992.

Liddell, H. G., R. Scott, H. S. Jones. *A Greek-English Lexicon*. 9th ed. with revised supplement. Oxford: Oxford University Press, 1996.

Lightfoot, Joseph Barber. *The Christian Ministry*. New York: Macmillan, 1901.

Locke, Edwin A., Shelley Kirkpatrick, Jill K. Wheeler, Jodi Schneider, Kathryn Niles, Harold Goldstein, Kurt Welsh, and Dong-Ok Chah. *The Essence of Leadership: The Four Keys to Leading Successfully*. New York: Lexington, 1991.

MacDonald, Dennis R. "Luke's Emulation of Homer: Acts 12:1-17 and Illiad 24." *Forum* 3 (2000) 197-205.

———. *Does the New Testament Imitate Homer? Four Cases from the Acts of the Apostles*. New Haven, CT: Yale University Press, 2003.

Malina, Bruce J. *Christian Origins and Cultural Anthropology: Practical Models for Biblical Interpretation*. Atlanta: John Knox, 1986.

———. *The New Testament World: Insights from Cultural Anthropology*. 3rd ed. Louisville: Westminster John Knox, 2001.

Malina, Bruce J., and Jerome H. Neyrey. "First-Century Personality: Dyadic, Not Individualistic." In *The Social World of Luke-Acts: Models for Interpretation*, edited by Jerome H. Neyrey, 67-96. Peabody, MA: Hendrickson, 1991.

Marshall, I. Howard. *The Acts of the Apostles: An Introduction and Commentary*. TNTC 5. Leicester, England: InterVarsity, 1980.

Martin, Luther H. *Hellenistic Religions: An Introduction*. New York: Oxford University Press, 1987.

Martini, Carlo Maria Cardinal. "La tradition textuelle des Actes des Apôtres et les tendances de l'Église ancienne." In *Actes des Apôtres: Traditions, rédaction, théologie*, edited by Jacob Kremer, 21-35. BETL 48. Gembloux, Belgium: Duculot, 1979.

Mason, Steve. "Chief Priests, Sadducees, Pharisees and Sanhedrin in Acts." In *The Book of Acts in Its Palestinian Setting*, edited by Richard Bauckham, 115-77. Vol. 4 of *The Book of Acts in its First Century Setting*. Grand Rapids, MI: Eerdmans, 1995.

Mea, William J., and Shawn M. Carraher. "Leaders Speak: Success and Failure in Their Own Words." In *Leadership: Succeeding in the Private, Public, and Not-for-profit Sectors*, edited by Ronald R. Sims and Scott A. Quatro, 297-317. Armonk, NY: Sharpe, 2005.

Merkelbach, Reinhold. *Mithras*. Königstein/Ts.: Hain, 1984.

Metzger, Bruce M. *A Textual Commentary on the Greek New Testament*. 2nd ed. Stuttgart: United Bible Societies, 1994.

Milavec, Aaron. *The Didache: Faith, Hope, and Life of the Earliest Christian Communities, 50–70 C.E.* New York: Newman, 2003.

Misumi, Jåuji. *The Behavioral Science of Leadership: An Interdisciplinary Japanese Research Program*. Edited by Mark F. Peterson. Ann Arbor: University of Michigan Press, 1985.

Mitchell, Curtis C. "The Practice of Fasting in the New Testament." *BSac* 147 (1990) 455–69.

Morris, Leon. *The Epistle to the Romans*. Grand Rapids: Eerdmans, 1988.

Morton, Russell. "Acts 12:1–19." *Interpretation* 55 (2001) 67–69.

Moulton, James Hope, and George Milligan. *The Vocabulary of the Greek Testament: Illustrated from the Papyri and Other Non-literary Sources*. London: Hodder and Stoughton, 1952.

Moxnes, Halvor. "Patron-Client Relations and the New Community in Luke-Acts." In *The Social World of Luke-Acts: Models for Interpretation*, edited by Jerome H. Neyrey, 241–68. Peabody, MA: Hendrickson, 1991.

Murray, John. *The Epistle to the Romans: The English Text with Introduction, Exposition and Notes*. 2 vols. NICNT 45. Grand Rapids: Eerdmans, 1959.

Nagel, Norman. "The Twelve and the Seven in Acts 6 and the Needy." *Concordia Journal* 31 (2005) 113–26.

Neusner, Jacob. *Formative Judaism: Religious, Historical, and Literary Studies*. BJS 37. Chico, CA: Scholars, 1982.

———. "Mr Sanders' Pharisees and Mine: A Response to E P Sanders, Jewish Law from Jesus to the Mishnah." *SJT* 44 (1991) 73–95.

Oakman, Douglas E. "The Countryside in Luke-Acts." In *The Social World of Luke-Acts: Models for Interpretation*, edited by Jerome H. Neyrey, 151–79. Peabody, MA: Hendrickson, 1991.

Öhler, Markus. "Die Jerusalemer Urgemeinde im Spiegel des antiken Vereinswesens." *NTS* 51 (2005) 393–415.

Oppenheimer, Aharon. *The 'Am Ha-Aretz: A Study in the Social History of the Jewish People in the Hellenistic-Roman Period*. Translated by I. H. Levine. Arbeiten zur Literatur und Geschichte des Hellenistischen Judentums 8. Leiden: Brill, 1977.

Pervo, Richard I. "Meet Right—and Our Bounden Duty: Community Meetings in Acts." *Forum* 4 (2001) 45–62.

Pilch, John J. "Sickness and Healing in Luke-Acts." In *The Social World of Luke-Acts: Models for Interpretation*, edited by Jerome H. Neyrey, 181–209. Peabody, MA: Hendrickson, 1991.

Potter, David. *Prophets and Emperors: Human and Divine Authority from Augustus to Theodosius*. Cambridge: Harvard University Press, 1994.

Praeder, Susan M. "Luke-Acts and the Ancient Novel." In *SBLSP, 1981*, 269–92. SBLSP 20. Chico, CA: Scholars, 1981.

Price, S. R. F. *Religions of the Ancient Greeks*. Cambridge: Cambridge University Press, 1999.

———. *Rituals and Power: The Roman Imperial Cult in Asia Minor*. Cambridge: Cambridge University Press, 1984.

Rapske, Brian M. "Acts, Travel and Shipwreck." In *The Book of Acts in Its Graeco-Roman Setting*, edited by David W. J. Gill and Conrad Gempf, 1–47. Vol. 1 of *The Book of Acts in Its First Century Setting*. Grand Rapids: Eerdmans, 1994.

Rengstorf, Karl Heinrich, editor. *A Complete Concordance to Flavius Josephus*. Leiden: Brill, 1973.

Riesner, Rainer. "Synagogues in Jerusalem." In *The Book of Acts in Its Palestinian Setting*, edited by Richard Bauckham, 179–211. Vol. 4 of *The Book of Acts in Its First Century Setting*. Grand Rapids, MI: Eerdmans, 1995.

Ropes, James Hardy, editor. *The Text of Acts*. Vol. 3 of *The Beginnings of Christianity, Part 1: The Acts of the Apostles*. Edited by F. J. Foakes-Jackson and Kirsopp Lake. London: Macmillan, 1926.

Rosman, Abraham, and Paula G. Rubel. *The Tapestry of Culture: An Introduction to Cultural Anthropology*. 5th ed. New York: McGraw-Hill, 1995.

Rowe, C. Kavin. "Authority and Community: Lukan *Dominium* in Acts." In *Acts and Ethics*, edited by Thomas E. Phillips, 96–108. NTM 9. Sheffield: Sheffield Phoenix, 2005.

Safrai, S. "Jewish Self-government." In *The Jewish People in the First Century: Historical Geography, Political History, Social, Cultural and Religious Life and Institutions*, edited by S. Safrai, M. Stern, D. Flusser and W. C. van Unnik, 377–419. CRINT 1. Philadelphia: Fortress, 1974.

Saldarini, Anthony J. *Pharisees, Scribes and Sadducees in Palestinian Society: A Sociological Approach*. Wilmington, DE: Michael Glazier, 1988.

Sanders, E. P. *Jewish Law from Jesus to the Mishnah: Five Studies*. London: SCM, 1990.

———. *Judaism: Practice and Belief, 63 BCE–66 CE*. London: SCM, 1992.

Savelle, Charles H. "A Reexamination of the Prohibitions in Acts 15." BSac 161 (2004) 449–68.

Schiffman, Lawrence H. *From Text to Tradition: A History of Second Temple and Rabbinic Judaism*. Hoboken, NJ: Ktav, 1991.

Schweizer, Eduard. *Church Order in the New Testament*. Translated by Frank Clark. SBT 32. London: SCM, 1961.

Scott, James M. "Luke's Geographical Horizon." In *The Book of Acts in Its Graeco-Roman Setting*, edited by David W. J. Gill and Conrad Gempf, 483–544. Vol. 1 of *The Book of Acts in Its First Century Setting*. Grand Rapids: Eerdmans, 1994.

Scott, John, and Gordon Marshall, editors. *A Dictionary of Sociology*. 3rd ed. Oxford: Oxford University Press, 2005.

———. "Conflict Theory." In *A Dictionary of Sociology*, 103–4. 3rd ed. Oxford: Oxford University Press, 2005.

Slee, Michelle. *The Church in Antioch in the First Century CE: Communion and Conflict*. JSNTSup 244. London: Sheffield Academic, 2003.

Spencer, F. Scott. *Journeying through Acts: A Literary-Cultural Reading*. Peabody, MA: Hendrickson, 2004.

———. "Out of Mind, Out of Voice: Slave-Girls and Prophetic Daughters in Luke-Acts." BibInt 7 (1999) 133–55.

Stark, Rodney. *The Rise of Christianity: A Sociologist Reconsiders History*. Princeton: Princeton University Press, 1996.

Stepp, Perry L. *Leadership Succession in the World of the Pauline Circle*. NTM 5. Sheffield: Phoenix, 2005.

Stogdill, Ralph M. *Handbook of Leadership: A Survey of Theory and Research*. New York: Free Press, 1974.
Stogdill, Ralph Melvin, and Bernard M. Bass. *Stogdill's Handbook of Leadership: A Survey of Theory and Research*. Rev. and exp. ed. New York: Free Press, 1981.
Strathmann, H. "λειτουργέω, λειτουργία, λειτρουγός, λειτουργικός." In *TDNT* 4 (1967) 215–31.
Streeter, B. H. "Codices 157, 1071 and the Caesarean Text." In *Quantulacumque, Studies Presented to Kirsopp Lake by Pupils, Colleagues and Friends*, edited by Robert P. Casey, Silva Lake, and Agnes K. Lake. London: Christophers, 1937.
Swartz, Michael D. "Sage, Priest, and Poet: Typologies of Religious Leadership in the Ancient Synagogue." In *Jews, Christians, and Polytheists in the Ancient Synagogue*, edited by Steven Fine, 101–17. New York: Routledge, 1999.
Taylor, Justin. "Acts and History." *Colloq* 26 (1994) 105–15.
Tead, Ordway. *The Art of Leadership*. New York: Whittlesey House, McGraw-Hill, 1935.
Theissen, Gerd. "Evangelienschreibung und Gemeindeleitung: Pragmatische Motive bei der Abfassung des Markusevangeliums." In *Antikes Judentum und frühes Christentum: Festschrift für Hartmut Stegemann zum 65. Geburtstag*, edited by Bernd Kollmann, Wolfgang Reinbold and Annette Steudel, 389–414. BZNW 97. Berlin: Walter de Gruyter, 1999.
Tripolitis, Antonía. *Religions of the Hellenistic-Roman Age*. Grand Rapids: Eerdmans, 2002.
Trobisch, David. "The Council of Jerusalem in Acts 15 and Paul's Letter to the Galatians." In *Theological Exegesis: Essays in Honor of Brevard S. Childs*, edited by Christopher R. Seitz and Kathryn Greene-McCreight, 331–38. Grand Rapids: Eerdmans, 1999.
Turcan, Robert. *The Cults of the Roman Empire*. Edited by T. J. Cornell. Translated by Antonia Nevill. The Ancient World. Oxford: Blackwell, 1996.
Turner, N. *Syntax*. Vol. 3 of *A Grammar of New Testament Greek*. Edinburgh: T. & T. Clark, 1963.
VanderKam, James C. *An Introduction to Early Judaism*. Grand Rapids: Eerdmans, 2001.
Vogliano, Achille. "La grande iscrizione bacchica del Metropolitan Museum." *American Journal of Archeology* 37 (1933) 215–31.
Walker, William O. "Acts and the Pauline Corpus Reconsidered." *JSNT* (1985) 3–23.
Wall, Robert W. "Successors to 'the Twelve' according to Acts 12:1–17." *CBQ* 53 (1991) 628–43.
———. "The Acts of the Apostles: Introduction, Commentary, and Reflections." In *NIB* 10. Nashville: Abingdon, 2002.
Walton, Steve. *Leadership and Lifestyle: The Portrait of Paul in the Miletus Speech and 1 Thessalonians*. SNTSMS 108. Cambridge: Cambridge University Press, 2000.
Watson, Duane F. "Paul's Speech to the Ephesian Elders (Acts 20.17–38) Epideictic Rhetoric of Farewell." In *Persuasive Artistry: Studies in New Testament Rhetoric in Honor of George A. Kennedy*, edited by Duane F. Watson, 184–208. Sheffield, England: JSOT, 1991.

Webber, Randall Clark. "An Analysis of Power in the Jerusalem Church in Acts." PhD diss., Southern Baptist Theological Seminary; University Microfilm International, 1989.

Weber, Max. *Max Weber: The Theory of Social and Economic Organization*. Edited by Talcott Parsons. Translated by A. M. Henderson and Talcott Parsons. New York: Free Press, 1947.

———. *Wirtschaft und Gesellschaft; Grundriss der verstehenden Soziologie*. Edited by Johannes Winckelmann. Köln: Kiepenheuer & Witsch, 1964.

Wilcken, Ulrich, ed. *Papyri aus Oberägypten*. Vol. 2 of *Urkunden der Ptolemäerzeit (Ältere Funde)*. Berlin: Walter de Gruyter, 1935.

Wilson, Stephen G. "Voluntary Associations: An Overview." In *Voluntary Associations in the Graeco-Roman World*, edited by John S. Kloppenborg and Stephen G. Wilson, 1–15. London: Routledge, 1996.

Wissowa, Georg. *Religion und Kultus der Römer*. München: Beck, 1902; 2nd ed., 1912.

Witherington, Ben. *The Acts of the Apostles: A Socio-Rhetorical Commentary*. Grand Rapids: Eerdmans, 1998.

Zetterholm, Magnus. *The Formation of Christianity in Antioch: A Social-Scientific Approach to the Separation between Judaism and Christianity*. London: Routledge, 2003.

Zwiep, Arie W. *Judas and the Choice of Matthias: A Study on Context and Concern of Acts 1:15–26*. WUNT. Zweite Reihe 187. Tübingen: Mohr Siebeck, 2004.

www.ingramcontent.com/pod-product-compliance
Lightning Source LLC
Chambersburg PA
CBHW050851230426
43667CB00012B/2248